COPPER JACK

COPPER JACK

Jack Webster
with **Rosemary Aubert**

Toronto and Oxford
Dundurn Press
1991

Editing: Doris Cowan
Cover Design: Green Graphics
Text Design and Production: JAQ
Printing and Binding: Gagné Printing Ltd., Louiseville, Quebec, Canada

The writing of this manuscript and the publication of this book were made possible by support from several sources. The publisher wishes to acknowledge the generous assistance and ongoing support of **The Canada Council, The Book Publishing Industry Development Programme** of the **Department of Communications,** and **The Ontario Arts Council.**

Care has been taken to trace the ownership of copyright material used in the text (including the illustrations). Credit for each quotation is given at the end of the selection. The author and publisher welcome any information enabling them to rectify any reference or credit in subsequent editions.

J. Kirk Howard, Publisher

Illustration Credits
Cover photographs were provided by the Metropolitan Toronto Police Force, with the exception of the picture of Jack Webster escorting Arthur Lucas, which was supplied courtesy of the *Globe and Mail*. Police photos within the book were provided by the Metropolitan Toronto Police Force. Jack Webster provided personal photographs.

Canadian Cataloguing in Publication Data

Webster, Jack (John D.)
    Copper Jack

ISBN 1-55002-148-6

1. Webster, Jack (John D.). 2. Metropolitan Toronto (Ont.).
Police Force – Biography. 3. Police – Ontario – Toronto
Metropolitan Area – Biography. I. Aubert, Rosemary.
II. Title.

HV7911.W43A3 1991   363.2'092   C91-095558-1

Dundurn Press Limited
2181 Queen Street East,
Suite 301
Toronto, Canada
M4E 1E5

Dundurn Distribution Limited
73 Lime Walk
Headington, Oxford
England
OX3 7AD

This book is for my wife, Marion,
who has been my partner for forty-four years —
without a badge.

CONTENTS

Metropolitan Toronto Police

Address all correspondence to:

Wm. J. McCORMACK
Chief of Police

40 College Street, Toronto, Ontario, Canada. M5G 2J3
(416) 324-2222   FAX 324-6345

Please reply attention of

File No. ....

When Staff Superintendent Jack Webster retired from the Metropolitan Toronto Police in 1988, he left behind an unmatched record of service.

In addition to having received more meritorious service awards than any other member of the Force, he has a personality that has made him one of the most popular and respected officers ever to have served.

As he so capably describes in this book, he has walked the lonely beat, done motorcycle patrol duty, risen through the ranks in the criminal investigation branch, becoming Chief of the Homicide Squad and Chief of Detectives.

Only Jack Webster, with over forty years of police service to back him up, can tell the stories and experiences that he has lived through with the vividness they deserve.

I am proud to have served as a young detective on the Homicide Squad when Jack Webster was the commander.

I am proud to have a person like him serve under me, as the Chief of Police of this metropolis.

I am proud to call Jack Webster a comrade and a friend.

Chief of Police.

During the course of his career with the Metropolitan Toronto Police Force, Jack Webster served in a number of senior posts. These are two of the badges he wore.

CHAPTER ONE
Boyhood

COPS ARE BORN, NOT MADE. *John D. "Jack" Webster performed his first official police duty in the winter of 1932, when he was nine years old.*

He and his friends lived within a few blocks of a park called Willowvale, better known even then by its now official name, Christie Pits. The Pits was the boys' stomping ground. There were hockey games in winter, baseball in summer and fall, and the opportunity to meet girls of the neighbourhood all year round. There was always a feeling of excitement and danger in the Pits. It was set off from the neat rows of houses on the surrounding streets by a steep embankment and by paths that wound down to the bottom, lending a subterranean feel to the place – especially at night.

But what really made this place exciting was the haunting presence of the notorious Pit Gang. This was a close collection of neighbourhood toughs – young men in their teens and early twenties whose off-handed, cocky swagger was pretty appealing to a tame ten-year-old. The gang was perfectly exempt from everything little Jack Webster already knew was required of decent people. They didn't work. They didn't refrain from obscenity. They obeyed no rules but their own. The gang possessed a combination of traits that Jack was going to see a lot of in years to come. But they seemed quite exotic to him then!

Most of the gang members were white Anglo-Saxons, but the best fighters in the group were rumoured to be a family of black brothers. Everybody steered clear of them. Strangers to the neighbourhood – including visiting hockey and baseball players – were always considered fair game to the Pit Gang. There was hardly a night in the week when little Jack didn't get to see one hell of a fight. The best part was that, being only nine and ten, Jack and his buddies weren't taken seriously by the gang – in fact, they were hardly noticed at all. So they had ring-side seats for every Pit Gang escapade they cared to witness.

The number one top enemy of the Pit Gang was the police. Often, a pair of mounted officers would patrol the park. It would have been foolish to send a constable alone, or on foot, into such hostile territory. That was proved in the winter of 1932, when a single officer who tried it was disarmed by a gang member right in front of Jack and his pals. The boys knew the cop well. His nickname was "Spoofer," and the only thing stronger than the Pit Gang's contempt for him was his hatred of them.

As Jack watched in shock, the gang leader wrested the gun away from Spoofer. The leader himself was immediately grabbed by his own brother who shouted, "Don't shoot the cop!" At the very idea of seeing a policeman gunned down in front of his eyes, Jack started to feel faint.

But he was brought back to alertness by a quick series of events. The gang leader declared arrogantly, "I wouldn't waste a bullet on the son of a bitch." He lifted his arm and flung the gun across the park's pleasure-skating rink, where it slid in a graceful curve all the way across the smooth stretch of ice. Before it had reached the other side of the rink, the gang had taken off. Spoofer turned to Webster and asked him if he thought he could guard the gun until police reinforcements could be called in. Agreeing without hesitation, Jack Webster stood over the gun and stayed there until more police arrived. Dutifully, he indicated the weapon's position to the officers. Job well done.

In the summer of 1933, Jack witnessed more official police action in the Pits, and this time it was no job for an amateur. It was his first experience of the frightening power of a mob out of control.

One day that August, Webster and his young friends were playing at the Pits when they became aware that something was brewing. There was an extraordinarily high level of excitement in the Pits. Before the day was out, it had become general knowledge that the Pit Gang was getting set for a particularly important fight – a fight such as the Pits had not seen in some time. The exact details weren't clear, but Webster and the other ten- and eleven-year-olds rushed supper and headed for the Pits as soon as they could get away from the table in order not to miss the first blows.

From the moment they could see into the Pits, they knew something was up. Baseball attracted quite a nice little crowd in the Pits then. It still does today. But what Jack Webster saw that evening was a bigger crowd than he had ever seen in the park. Before the evening was out, it would swell to ten thousand. Even the fact that two exceptionally excellent playground teams,

Harbord and St. Peter's, were playing did not account for the crowd.

Webster knew, as did his pals, that Harbord was a Jewish team and St. Peter's was mostly Catholic. Being just children, they may not have known (though the adults in the crowd surely did) that only a week before there had been an ugly skirmish between Jews and non-Jews on the eastern beaches of the city. It had been part of continuing hostilities between an organization called the Balmy Beach Swastika Club and Jews who used the beach for recreation. By the summer of 1933, Hitler's vow to eliminate the Jewish people was causing worldwide concern. The swastika was known throughout Toronto as a symbol of Hitler and his message of hate.

All Jack knew was that these two teams had played each other time and again without any hint of trouble. But this time was different. Sitting on the east side of the park, on the Christie Street hill, he watched as someone in the crowd – in the middle of the game – flashed a swastika flag. The reaction of the spectators was immediate and violent. At first, Jack and his friends thought they were merely watching an especially good version of the usual nightly brawl. But when he turned to see a large contingent of mounted police charging full speed down the Christie Street hill and into the Pits, he decided it might be worthwhile to venture closer to the action.

It was no scene for a child – even a brave, curious, tough one like Jack. The Pit Gang and others from the neighbourhood, he soon saw, were armed with baseball bats and lead pipes. The Jews were fighting hard, too. The recent events had spurred the formation of Jewish defence groups, and when news of the fight in the Pits got out onto the surrounding streets, it spread fast. It wasn't only the cops who were sending in reinforcements. Both sides of the fight were growing right before Jack's eyes. Stunned, but remaining at the centre of the action, he gaped at the destruction around him. People he knew, as well as total strangers, were staggering under blows from pipes, bats, and fists. There was a lot of blood, mostly from face wounds and lacerated scalps.

The fighting went on for six hours. More police continued to arrive on foot, but Jack stuck close to the mounted men at the very centre of the park. He and his friends thought the fighting was never going to stop. It grew dark in the Pits. The noise and confusion was terrifying in itself, but more terrifying was the stubborn resistance of the fighters, who simply would not keep their fists – and their weapons – away from each other, even when it was nearly impossible to see who was hitting whom with what. Order was only gradually restored, partly by mounted officers herding the crowd out of the park with their riding crops. Jack saw a mounted policeman strike one of the Pit Gang members. The member shouted, "How come you don't hit the Jews?"

"Don't you tell me who to hit! Get out of this park, or I'll beat you to a pulp!" yelled the cop.

Jack thought this was an interesting exchange and was waiting for the rest of the repartee when the officer unexpectedly turned on the boy and his friends. "You young bastards, get on home or I'll give you a taste of this, too." He brandished his crop and leaned forward on his huge horse.

Really scared for the first time that night, the boys turned and ran as fast as they could toward the western edge of the Pits, up the Crawford Street hill and all the way home.

For days afterward, Jack and his pals told lies to their friends at Essex School about how they had played a major role in the quelling of the riot, embellishing with fine detail the story of all the heroic things they had done. The famous Christie Pits riot was the first time that history and the life of Jack Webster intersected in a dramatic and personal way. It was the second time he had a story to tell about his involvement in police heroics. But it was far from the last. As his life unfolded, the stories ceased to be lies, and the hero of the story became himself.

Iɴ 1910, ᴛʜᴇ ʏᴇᴀʀ ᴍʏ parents met, Glasgow was a city of unemployed. The Clydeside shipyards were almost idle, and thousands of Glaswegians were living in abject poverty. The mean tenement streets were rife with gangs of razor-carrying, out-of-work toughs of all ages, whose main occupation was to obtain by fair means or foul the few pennies necessary to buy a litre or two of the curse known to the Glasgow poor as "red biddy." This harsh, cheap wine was known to make a wild man wilder and was the greatest contributing factor to the continual violence on the streets and in the homes of Glasgow's tenement areas.

James Webster, my father, was a fresh-complexioned young railway worker, twenty-two years old. At five feet ten inches, he was noticeably taller than most of the young Glasgow men who resided in the Gorbals area of the city, where he lived in a third-floor tenement with his parents, two brothers and three sisters. They were not originally Glasgow people, but had moved from the Highlands of Scotland around the turn of the century, because of a zero employment situation and crop failures that had made even subsistence farming impossible. Their Highland speech and appearance, as well as their willingness to take any kind of work, caused the Websters problems with their neighbours at first, but before long they were accepted and respected for their hard work, honesty, and the simple virtues of poor Highland folk: to help one another and to thank the Lord continually for all the blessings He had bestowed upon them. Their example was their legacy to me and I have tried my best to live by it, both as a soldier and a police officer.

One day in the spring of 1910, a fellow railway worker, Peter Shields from the tough Gallowgate tenements of Glasgow, introduced my father to his seventeen-year-old sister when she brought her brother's lunch to him at Central Station. The brown-haired, blue-eyed Sarah Shields immediately stole Jim Webster's heart, and she was to remain his one and only girl until his death in 1967.

Young Jim Webster, now engaged to be married, could not see much of a future in Scotland, and when he read a notice that the Grand Trunk Railway urgently needed experienced railroad firemen, with successful applicants to receive free passage to Canada and an excellent starting salary, he applied and was accepted. He told Sarah of his decision, promising to save enough money to send for her in two years. Tearfully, Sarah agreed to the long separation, and Jim Webster sailed for Canada in September of 1910.

The Atlantic crossing was long and rough, and then there was an uncomfortable train ride to Toronto, where lodgings were provided for him and the other immigrants at the Railway YMCA, then situated at Front Street and Spadina Avenue. Life in the new country was comfortless and cheerless for him at the beginning, but my father worked hard to fulfil his contract with the Grand Trunk Railway, and two years later, true to his word, he sent for my mother, who arrived in Toronto on November 6, 1912. Wedding arrangements had been made before her arrival, and they were married that same day.

By the time I was born, on August 12, 1923, my parents had already had two other children, my brother Andrew, who did not survive infancy, and my brother Jim. My sister, Gladys, was born in 1926.

After my father had fulfilled his contract with the Grand Trunk, he left the railways and became a teamster, working for one of the many cartage companies that had been formed by earlier Scottish immigrants. With a growing family to maintain, he was always on the alert for ways to earn extra money. It wasn't always easy for an immigrant with a heavy accent and little formal education. But Jim Webster was a strong man, with more than average determination. He worked twelve- and sometimes fourteen-hour days, six days a week and part of Sundays, and by 1928 my parents had squirrelled away enough nickels and dimes to pay for a second-hand truck.

From that time on, my father was in business for himself, as the J. Webster Cartage Company.

Our house on Henderson Avenue was in the centre of Toronto's Little Italy, and it was a happy neighbourhood to grow up in. As a small boy, I loved the spicy smells of garlic and olive oil that wafted from the hundreds of small houses on those streets, especially at supper time. Even the constant aroma of horse manure (from the many horse-drawn milk, bread, and peddlers' wagons) was a pleasant and familiar part of city life.

During the 1920s and '30s, the streets of Little Italy – Clinton, Manning, Belwoods, Henderson, Mansfield, Claremont – were reputed to have more bootleggers per household than any other area of Toronto, including the part of Little Italy commonly known as the "Ward." The people in our area did not look upon selling a little wine or beer to friends and neighbours as a crime. After all, no one was victimized. The only loser was the government, which did not receive the full tax on these products – and that failed to trouble the conscience of the hardworking Italian labourers and their unusually large families. Bootlegging was seen as a way of survival in a foreign country.

The few Irish and Scottish neighbours of these fine people soon adapted to this slightly illegal lifestyle and were often the first to give the warning if they saw any sign that a police raid was imminent. In a neighbourhood where all the men wore rough working clothes, with peaked cloth caps, it was not too difficult to spot unwelcome strangers wearing three-piece suits and Panama hats.

When a police booze raid was in progress at one of the houses, which happened frequently, we kids would sneak over and let the air out of the tires of the unguarded police cars. Then we'd watch from a distance as the usually fat plainclothes officers exerted themselves at the hand pump. If the householder and found-ins had been arrested, they would have to stand on the sidewalk in the centre of a circle of evidence, usually a few gallons of wine or cases of beer, while the officers pumped away at the flats, all the while being treated to a continual chorus of jeers from neighbours on adjoining verandas and lawns.

Many years later, when I was a police officer myself and had to leave my car to make an arrest, I would sometimes come back to find the tires slashed – it reminded me of my own youthful participation in such vandalism. That didn't make me like it any better than the men I had tormented must have liked it! Many of the police of that era were also customers of the booze cans, the only difference being that they were not paying customers. In fact, the bootleggers complained that the cops were going to drink them out of business. It was the laugh of the street when a popular Scottish policeman spent a little too long in a local grocery store, and upon leaving, fell off his bicycle. A dozen people ran from their front stoops to help him up, and some of the kids wheeled his bike and gently guided this friendly cop to the Claremont Station.

ONE SUNDAY MORNING, SHORTLY AFTER my father had bought his truck, I looked out through our frilly parlour curtains and saw two Italian neighbours coming up the walk. They asked my dad if they could rent his truck for two hours to do a small moving job. "We'll pay five dollars," they said, "and we have our own driver." Although my mother was doubtful, my father agreed.

Not long after that a policeman on a bicycle appeared at our house and ordered my father to present himself at Number 3 Police Station, on Claremont Street. The first thing he saw there was his truck in the yard, loaded with cases of bootleg beer from a nearby brewery.

It was only after the plainclothesman consulted with the divisional inspector that they let my father have his truck back, once he had helped unload the beer into the police station. My father often mentioned that the plainclothes police officer who successfully argued for giving him back his truck was an Irishman named John O'Driscoll. (His son, Frank O'Driscoll, was to be a comrade and partner of mine on the hold-up squad in the 1950s.) I was deeply impressed by this act of kindness toward my father by a rough, tough plainclothes police officer. Inspired by men like John O'Driscoll, I tried throughout my many years of police service always to be as compassionate as circumstances would permit.

The neighbours who had borrowed the truck were released on bail and immediately came to our house to offer their profuse apologies. They were accompanied by a third man, also Italian though not a neighbour, who was unknown to my father and mother. He was introduced to my parents as "Rocco" and he gave them each a ten-dollar bill to compensate them for the trouble they had been put to. Years later, my dad told me that Rocco was in fact Rocco Pirri, later known as the King of the Bootleggers, who disappeared in the 1940s and was never seen again.

MY FATHER HAD A SECOND brush with the law, in the late twenties. He parked his truck on Clinton Street one noon hour and went home for lunch. When he returned, the truck was gone, and with it $10,000 worth of cloth that was being shipped in eighty-yard bolts to various garment manufacturers on Spadina Avenue. Today, this would represent a value of about $400,000.

My father had only a small fraction of that amount in theft insurance, so it was entirely possible that we would be ruined. I watched in fear as my parents sank into the depths of despair over this incident. Their distress wasn't helped by the severe and critical questioning my father was subjected to by detectives in Number 3 Police Station, on Claremont Street.

At the supper table that evening, when he was telling my mother about this grilling, he said the questioning stopped when Harry Hughes, for whose firm my father was hauling the cloth, arrived at the police station. According to my father, Mr. Hughes informed the police in no uncertain terms that he would trust Jim Webster with his life, and instead of abusing an innocent man, they should be out looking for the thieves.

As young as I was at this time, I understood what was happening and I hated the police for abusing my father, whom I dearly loved. I never forgot that inside view of what intense interrogation could do to a private citizen, even when it was my job to do the interrogating myself.

The truck was recovered later that day, minus the load of cloth, and a few weeks after the theft the station master at Parkdale Railway Station became suspicious of some packing cases, labelled "farm implements," that were being shipped to Winnipeg. He notified the police, who opened the cases and recovered the stolen cloth.

The subsequent investigation resulted in the arrest of a man who, after a brief court appearance, was sentenced to a penitentiary term. During the trial, the accused man made threats against my father, which so terrified my poor mother that she wanted the family to return to Scotland. My father refused to be intimidated and decided to remain in Toronto. A short time after the truck thief was released from the penitentiary, he murdered his brother-in-law during a business dispute, and was subsequently convicted and hanged – much to the relief of my mother.

THERE WERE SEVERAL MORE MOVES for the Webster family: to rented houses on Manning Avenue, north of Queen Street; Mechanics Avenue, in Parkdale; Yarmouth Road, in the Christie and Dupont area; and finally, to a house at 1061 Shaw, just south of Dupont.

I was ten years old when we moved to Shaw Street, and my life revolved around my days at Essex Street Public School. My free time was spent at meetings of the Boy Scouts at St. Paul's Presbyterian Church, as well as among the loosely bound members of our neighbourhood gang.

I enjoyed my school days. It was a big, central Toronto school, with approximately twelve hundred pupils. I visited it in 1988 and found a student body about evenly divided among Caribbean, Portuguese and Italian children, as well as a considerable number of East Indians, Vietnamese, Chinese and Koreans. But in my time, Toronto was predominantly a WASP society. Just about everyone's father was either an Orangeman or a Mason or both, and this was reflected in the population of the Essex Street School of old, in which 98 percent of the pupils were of Anglo origin.

I was a bright student and school work came easily to me. My report cards were filled with As, and in the eight years at public school I never stood lower than third in my class. Several times I stood first, and was named Honour Student of the school. Of course this made my immigrant parents very proud, but if my studies were not a source of concern there were a few other matters that did worry them.

On one occasion, when I was about twelve years old, I got into a fight at school. With only a few minutes of recess left, we were playing volleyball and, according to the game rules, it was my turn to play, but suddenly the school bully stepped in front of me. He was three years older than I, and had an advantage of four inches in height and twenty pounds in weight.

"You have to go to the back of the line," I said.

"Who's going to make me?" he taunted.

Suddenly there was absolute silence in the schoolyard. I had to decide very quickly whether to back down or fight. If I backed off, I would be called a coward, not only in the school, but throughout the neighbourhood. I would have brought dishonour on my entire family. Without further thought for the consequences I threw one punch that hit the surprised tough guy in the nose. Blood flew in every direction. He started to cry and ran home.

Immediately after recess, the school principal arrived at my classroom and demanded to see John Webster. The teacher pointed me out, and the principal said, "Come along, boy." Together, the principal and my teacher marched me straight home to see my parents. It must have been wash day, because when they knocked, my mother came to the door with a load of washing in her arms.

"What's the matter?" she asked anxiously, in her deep Glasgow accent. The principal introduced himself and his colleague, and my mother readily ushered them into the parlour, which was always the best-furnished room in the house, reserved for special company.

Without mincing words, the principal informed my mother that I had brutally assaulted another boy, who was entirely innocent and had done nothing to provoke the attack. He went on and on about my terrible crime. Finally, in conclusion, he prophesied, "Mrs. Webster, if you and your husband do not take this boy in hand, he will wind up on the gallows."

"The gallows? What's that?" my mother asked, in all innocence.

"The boy," the principal declared, "is going to hang."

At this dire prediction my mother burst into tears, but somehow managed to collect herself and show them out. I was sent upstairs to await my father's return from work. That evening, as my tired, hard-working dad was washing his hands and face at the kitchen sink, my mother, who was trying to introduce the subject calmly, suddenly could not contain herself any longer and cried out, "Dad, they're going to hang Jackie!"

Continuing to dry his hands, my imperturbable father asked, "What the hell has he done now?" My older brother, Jim, was home by this time and he was able to recount what had actually happened. When he had heard the story, my father said he would like to go to the school in the morning and administer the same punch to the principal – for frightening my mother.

And so for a short time I was a hero in my house, and the boys in the neighbourhood called me "Slug" – until my mother heard of it and put a stop to it. The incident was closed, but it has been a belief of mine over the years that it taught me a valuable lesson: to think of all the possible consequences of what I was about to do, before taking action. In that situation, I had only thought of how I would hate to be known as a coward. I was lucky in striking first and becoming somewhat of a local hero, but the end result would have been far different, for my challenger and for me, if one of us had been knocked down and struck his head on the pavement, suffering serious permanent injury. We would both have had to live with that for the rest of our lives.

Despite the ever-present necessity in my work as a soldier and a police officer to think and act fast, I have always tried to put a little extra thought into what I was about to embark on, and I firmly believe this has saved me, on more than one occasion, from anguish, serious injury, or even death.

IT WAS THE MID-THIRTIES, AND the Depression was at its peak. With so many able-bodied people out of work, crime was rampant. My father's truck was the open-stake type, covered only by a tarpaulin, and his cargo was usually bolts of cloth of all sizes. Consequently, his vehicle was a prime target for the thieves who prowled the garment district of Spadina Avenue and Adelaide Street – especially on winter afternoons, when the darkness set in early. After school, my brother Jim and I would take the streetcar down to the corner of Spadina and Adelaide, where my father met us, and we would sit on the back of the truck, to guard against thieves. It was a cold two or three hours, but on the road home, with the three of us sitting in the truck cab, Jim and I were happy because we knew we were really helping my dad and, in turn, the whole family. Later in life as a police officer, I had similar feelings when I was able to arrest dangerous criminals, and thereby remove them from circulation. I was glad to know my actions had benefited the public at large, and made the quality of life that much better for the community.

ONE VERY WARM JULY DAY in 1935, I was at work as the one and only bellhop in a small, seedy, central Toronto hotel. I was twelve years old, and thrilled to have captured this summer job in competition with eight or nine other boys seeking to earn three dollars a week plus tips – this was in the middle of the Depression, and employment was hard to come by.

However, after a few days on the job, I'd discovered the work was difficult and the tips few. The many prostitutes who engaged rooms for short periods of time were the most generous with tips. It was very seldom that these girls, with their heavily rouged faces and bizarre choice of clothes, would fail to flip a quarter in my direction, even though they had no trunks or suitcases for me to carry.

About eight o'clock on this particular evening, the manager, who also served as the desk clerk, gave me the pass key to a room on the third floor. "The guy's behind in his rent and hasn't been seen for several days," he said. "Run up there, boy. Let yourself in. Look around. Whatever luggage the man has, you bring down here to the front desk. Got that?"

I nodded. It was no surprise to me that an occupant might be behind in his rent. I knew some of them stayed on a weekly basis, some even for months. There was no elevator, so I headed for the stairs and sprinted up them as fast as my legs would carry me. As soon as I got to the third floor, I could smell it. It was an odour so foul that my throat seemed to close at the stench. It was something I knew I'd never smelled before. And I didn't like it a bit.

Nevertheless, I knocked over and over. When I received no reply, I inserted the pass key and opened the door. I was immediately overwhelmed by the odour. It was stronger and far more sickening here than in the hall. I stifled a tremendous urge to vomit. The room was in terrible disarray, with what appeared to my young eyes to be countless empty wine bottles. They were everywhere, all over the floor and perched on the room's few chairs.

With my hand covering my mouth, I carefully picked my way through the bottles toward the bathroom. The door to this room was partially open, but when I tried to push it, I could feel that it was blocked by something on the floor. Even though the stench was making me feel weak at the knees, I had to see what was behind that door. I stuck my head through the open space. Looking down, I saw the badly decomposed body of a naked man.

I couldn't control myself for another second. As I ran out of the room and down the stairs, I left a steady trail of vomit behind me.

Screeching to a stop in front of the stunned desk clerk, I breathlessly reported what I'd just seen. Without even going upstairs himself, he phoned the police. "Come have a seat in the lobby, boy," he said, guiding me to one of the deep, much-used armchairs.

As I sank gratefully into it, I suddenly remembered that in my mad rush down the stairs I had somehow lost my pillbox hat. Should I run back up and retrieve it? Would I have to pay for it if it somehow got lost or crushed in the moments that were surely coming – the moments in which they carried that awful thing back down the hotel steps?

It seemed years before the huge, uniformed officer arrived and the clerk-manager informed him of what I had seen. The officer told me to remain where I was. In company with the desk clerk, he puffed up the stairs to the third-floor room. Within minutes they were down again. As they entered the lobby, the ashen-faced manager held a handkerchief over his mouth, while the policeman phoned for assistance. As he did so, he noticed me sitting desolately in the lobby, and when he put down the phone he commanded, "Don't touch anything. The headquarters detectives are on the way."

After issuing this order, he seemed to notice how terrified I was, and came over, kindly and stout in his uniform, and did his best to comfort me, while the manager brought me a cold bottle of Orange Crush. Little did any of us know that that naked human body, in the final stages of putrefication, was only the first (though the most unforgettable) of many hundreds that I would eventually have to deal with in my forty-three years as a police officer.

THE NEXT FEW YEARS PASSED uneventfully, until September of 1939, when the clouds of hostility finally burst and the second Great War was upon us. The day war was declared, I was selling the *Toronto Evening Telegram* (for three cents a copy) at the corner of Dupont and Christie streets. Although I had never been a newspaper boy, a local newsagent had approached my friends and me that day, in front of Johnny's Cigar Store at Dupont and Shaw. When he offered us one cent for each newspaper sold, we all jumped at the opportunity and were soon hawking the latest news at various intersections. The papers sold quickly, and as I recall we spent our profits in the local bowling alley, called the Christie Recreation Club, in what is now the Planter's Peanut building, at the northwest corner of Christie and Dupont.

It wasn't very long before dozens of local boys volunteered for the armed forces, and soon they were to be seen in the neighbourhood wearing the uniforms of the navy, army and air force. My pals and I, who were between fifteen and seventeen years of age, prayed desperately that the war would not be over before we were old enough to enlist.

The tragedy of the war may have been remote and uncomprehended by me then, but in May 1940 a personal tragedy befell our family. The eight-year-old son of a local storekeeper fell off his bicycle and was run over by the rear wheels of my father's truck. This happened in the laneway behind our house, and was particularly devastating to my father because as the young boy was passing my father's truck, he had waved at my dad and my dad had smiled and waved back. An instant after the youngster passed the front of the truck, my father felt a slight bump; the child, who was well known to us, died almost immediately.

My father never fully recovered. Even after a coroner's inquest completely absolved him, I can truthfully say that he was never the same happy person again, and the accident had its effect on the immediate neighbourhood as well. However, many friends and neighbours visited my father to console him, and even the parents of the dead boy came to our house and in tears told my dad he was not to blame, and that it was God's wish that their son should be taken at that time. There is no doubt this tremendous demonstration of local goodwill assisted my father in regaining his composure, although the terrible accident never really left him and marked him forever.

This sad incident, along with the trouble overseas, ended my boyhood. I was sixteen, and I suppose that, had I given it any thought, I might have seen clues that pointed toward my someday becoming a cop, like the ones who had been so much a part of the day-to-day life of my youth. But it would be a while before that way became clear. A different duty called first.

John "Jack" Webster, aged sixteen, just before leaving for overseas duty, 1940. He served with the Royal Canadian Engineers.

CHAPTER TWO

Soldier

IT WAS 1940, AND THE war was going badly for the British and French forces. Even at the age of sixteen, I knew that these were dark times for civilization and the freedom we enjoyed in Canada. Regardless of the Allied defeats, though, the backbone of the Canadian people seemed to stiffen, and enlistment in the armed forces soared to new heights.

I made several futile attempts to join the army. Although it was very warm in June and July of 1940, I pedalled my bicycle to all the armouries and recruiting offices and presented myself as a prospective soldier for the 48th Highlanders, the Royal Regiment of Canada and the Toronto Scottish. My sixteen-year-old body with its almost skinny frame gave me away every time, and I was gently turned down. On one occasion, however, the recruiting sergeant, a gruff old First World War veteran, was not so kind and told me to get the hell out and stop wasting his time.

That evening, I read in the newspaper that the Royal Canadian Engineers were recruiting for a unit called the Eighth Field Company. The recruiting office was on Atlantic Avenue, near King and Dufferin in Parkdale. I duly presented myself at the office, bright and early the next morning, only to find a long line of men waiting to be interviewed. I parked my bicycle and joined the line. At last it was my turn to be interviewed by the recruiting officer, who sat at a desk with a pile of attestation papers in front of him. My heart sank as the sergeant who had ushered me in said, "This kid looks kind of young to me, sir."

The officer looked at me, studying me carefully. "Yes, he does, sergeant," he replied, "but he's a good-looking boy, clean and neat as a pin, and the army will make a man of him. Take his application. The best of luck to you, son," he added.

I was so happy I wanted to shout "I'm a soldier, a real soldier!" I could hardly wait to get a uniform and be sent overseas to fight the war. When I informed my parents at the supper table that night, my mother wept, and my father became very quiet. "Well, Jackie," he finally said in a strained voice, holding back, I am sure, strong emotion, "you have made your bed. Now you will have to lie in it."

My brothers and sister seemed to think it was all a joke. How could their brother Jackie be a real, live soldier? Many years later, my mother told me that my father, comforting her in private that evening, had advised her not to worry. The army, he said, would discover my true age and toss me out.

That thought had also occurred to me, so when I arrived at Camp Borden two days after my enlistment, and an officer of our unit asked for twenty-one soldiers to go overseas immediately, I volunteered at once. We were to be reinforcements for an infantry regiment believed to be the Toronto Scottish. We were sent by train to Halifax to board a troopship, the *Georgic*.

For the most part, the three-week Atlantic crossing was uneventful – except for what I learned about gamblers and cheaters. Each soldier on the ship had been issued a pay advance of twenty-five dollars. This was a considerable sum of money for many hundreds of soldiers to have in their hands at one time. Many of them still suffered from the invisible wounds left by the Depression thirties and the bitter memories of relief camps and food handouts. These were a hard, tough group of men, and in my particular company, they were mostly hard rock miners from northern Ontario.

The poker and dice games got under way as soon as our convoy of about thirty ships had sailed out of Bedford Basin and into the Atlantic Ocean. This was a brand-new experience for me, and I sat spellbound for hours watching the exchange of vast sums of money. After three days of twenty-four-hour poker games, most of the players had lost their twenty-five-dollar pay advances to a few lucky and jubilant winners.

In one of the games that I had been observing with intense interest, the final winner was a forty-five-year-old miner from Sudbury, Ontario. He had relieved his fellow card players of several thousand dollars in four or five days. When they had nothing left, the smiling winner got up from the table, thanked the now downcast losers and went off to the ship's canteen for a beer. The losers discussed his incredible luck. One group of three or four, suspecting that more than luck was at work, decided to go to the winner's bunk and search his belongings. He had readily provided fresh decks of playing cards before each game, and now, in his kit bag, they found several brand-new decks of cards, which close examination revealed to have been "clock-marked" with a daisy-like pattern, with missing petals indicating the value of each card to the skilled observer.

The searchers took possession of this damning evidence, and word spread rapidly among the many losers. Shouting obscenities, a raging crowd gathered and rushed to the ship's canteen, where they seized the cheater. Four men held him, while others searched his pockets and took his cash. The furious soldiers then dragged him, through a gauntlet of punching, kicking fellow losers, out onto the windswept deck, where two of them lifted the hysterical and screaming man and were about to throw him into the Atlantic. A military policeman who had been on duty in the canteen only managed to stop them by pulling his revolver and declaring, "Put that man down, or I'll shoot you both dead." They dropped him to the deck and gave him one parting kick in the face. Then the grumbling and still hostile mob dispersed.

The cheat spent the remainder of the voyage confined in the officers' area of the ship for his own safety. When we landed in Scotland he was escorted off the ship by two military policemen. He never rejoined the unit.

The whole episode was terrifying to a young boy like myself. For the rest of the voyage, I only left my sleeping quarters when I couldn't avoid it. (Remarkably, I was to see the man again many years later. My partner, Sergeant of Detectives Hodgson, and I were driving north on Ossington Avenue one day in 1955 when I spotted the card cheat of 1940 standing in front of a store. I stopped the car, walked back to the man and said "Hello, Fred, do you remember me, from the war and our trip on the *Georgic*?" His face paled and he replied, "I wasn't in the war." Then he quickly turned and walked away.)

The city of Glasgow was experiencing one of its first heavy bombing raids of the war: the German Luftwaffe were intent on putting the important Clydeside shipbuilding yards out of commission. Some of the German bombers would drop their leftover bombs at random as they headed home. The harbour at Gourock, where the *Georgic* had anchored, received its share of destruction the evening of our arrival, when the enemy observed the vast troopship convoy just off-shore. We were transported to land in small boats called "tenders." Hearing the bomb bursts and deafening anti-aircraft fire was terrifying. I thought of my siblings, safe with my parents, and a wave of homesickness nearly overpowered me. I fought it off. It was only the first of countless times in a life of danger that I had to push aside thoughts of home.

Our battalion was transported by troop train to Aldershot, in Hampshire, England. We marched to our barracks with full pack and rifle as what looked like thousands of soldiers, Canadian and British, lined the route of our march, shouting, "Suckers! You'll be sorry . . . " and other such words of encouragement. After drawing a blanket, we were assigned to our barrack room, which contained about forty iron beds. The mattress was made up of three square cushions, which the troops called "biscuits." When I finally crawled, cold and tired, into these crude sleeping arrangements, with a barrack-box underneath the bed containing what was now the sum total of my possessions, thousands of miles from home, I started to cry, and I'm sure I wasn't the only rookie soldier who cried himself to sleep that night.

A month passed. One night in September 1940, we were awakened at 2:00 a.m. by our NCOs (non-commissioned officers) and ordered to get dressed in full battle order as quickly as possible. In those days, full battle order was helmet, respirator, small pack, webbing equipment, water bottle, gaiters, and a Lee Enfield .303 calibre rifle.

The night air was chilly. In the distance, ripping flashes of bomb blasts from the London area were quite visible. The city was obviously taking a real pasting from the Luftwaffe bombers. The dull thunder of anti-aircraft fire could be heard periodically. We were issued five rounds of ammunition each, ordered not to smoke, and boarded onto one of sixty hundred-weight army trucks. Only then were we told by our officers that the Germans had invaded the south coast of England, and that we were being transported there to fight the tough German paratroopers and army assault troops – even though we were as green as grass, with no training and only five rounds of ammunition each! But after two hours of sitting in the army trucks, without moving, we were told the invasion was a false alarm, and ordered to turn in our ammunition and return to barracks.

During the terrible months of the "London Blitz," September, October and November 1940, our unit was in London along with many other military formations, helping to clear rubble and search the bombed houses and other buildings for survivors, and taking away the dead to temporary mortuaries nearby. The landscape was one of utter devastation, permeated by the ever-present odour of pulverized plaster and brick and the lingering smell of high explosives. The people of London were suffering through hideous attacks, but they accepted injury and family dislocation without complaint. My admiration for them grows rather than diminishes with the opportunities for reflection the ensuing years have brought.

For the balance of 1940, through 1941, right up to the spring of 1944, our training was intense. Still, there were plenty of chances to travel during leaves. On my first leave, I was delighted to have the opportunity to

Left: *Jack as a seventeen-year-old soldier in London, England, September 1940.*
Right: *The Webster brothers in Glasgow, Scotland, 1942.*

visit Glasgow and to meet my grandparents for the first time. Seeing them made the stories my mother and father had told me come alive; the Glaswegians of my "ancient" past were suddenly flesh-and-blood people, and my connection with the United Kingdom suddenly personal.

Two or three incidents out of countless army experiences still stand out crystal clear in my memory. One small misadventure proved to me that impeccable military grooming is its own reward – though in this particular case I had been hoping for something more! Still, the care I learned stood me in good stead later, in times when I had to look my very best, as for instance, when I was called upon to serve in the presence of royalty.

What happened was this: When I was stationed at Guillemont Barracks at Cove, just outside Camberley, I would periodically be assigned to guard duty. This was a ritual that had to be performed constantly. Army veterans will recall that most guards had one more soldier assigned than was needed. This was to provide an incentive for the members of the guard to be splendidly turned out, because after inspection of the new guard on the parade square, one man would be identified as the best-dressed soldier and would be designated "stickman." He would be ordered to take one pace forward, then would be marched off the square by the sergeant major. His reward was twenty-four hours off – to do as he pleased. It was army tradition that if a soldier was named stickman on three occasions, he would automatically be promoted to lance corporal, the first step up from the ranks.

I had had the honour of being named stickman on two successive guard details, and as the new day's detail approached, the excitement in my platoon was tremendous. Remember, all of the men were considerably older than I was and wanted to see "young Jackie" win this coveted prize. The whole unit participated in shining my boots, pressing my uniform and cleaning my rifle in hopes of ensuring that the unheard-of third stickman appointment would be mine. My comrades even carried me to the edge of the square, to prevent my boots from getting even slightly dusty!

As the guard formed up, every window in the barracks seemed to have a face at it, and during the slow, meticulous scrutiny by the officer in charge of the guard, I felt as if my breathing had stopped. I waited, with a dry mouth and my heart pounding so hard I could hear it, for the all-important decision.

The officer called out, "Number six man, stickman, fall out." That was me. I thought I was going to faint. As I stepped forward, I could hear cheers from all over the barracks. But then, to my confusion, the sergeant major stepped up to the officer, saluted and said something in a low voice. After their brief, whispered conference, I was ordered to return to my position in the guard detail! The officer then shouted, "Number nine man, stickman, fall out." In disbelief, I looked on as the sloppiest person in our unit, who always looked like an unmade bed, stepped forward in my place. My throat closed with fury as I watched him being marched off the square. The only explanation I could arrive at, after much thought, was that the sergeant major could not stand the thought of having this poor excuse for a soldier mounting the main gate guard, so he had suggested to the officer that the untidy one should be named stickman in order to get rid of him.

I was completely devastated by this turn of events. The other members of my regiment felt that the sergeant major had been so unfair that they should send a delegation to our colonel to complain, but even at my young age, I could foresee the possible ramifications of that, and persuaded them to forget it. (The sergeant major's name was Gzowski, and he was a member of the renowned Canadian military family. He was a very fine man, and a soldier from the top of his head to the toes of his boots. His son is Peter Gzowski, the famous author and radio personality. I met Peter for the first time a few years ago, at the Winnipeg airport. I told him this and a few other stories about his father, which he listened to with interest.)

In August 1942, the Dieppe raid brought the reality of the war and its dangers suddenly home to us, with great impact. It was my good fortune not to be sent to take part in that disastrous expedition, but to my great sorrow, I lost friends from school and the neighbourhood, some of them killed and others captured on the fireswept beaches.

After Dieppe, the Canadian army was inactive for many months – until the invasion of Sicily in 1943. Hard-fought battles raged there, and then moved onto the mainland of Italy; Allied casualties began to mount. While the First Canadian Infantry Division and the Fifth Canadian Armoured Division were actively engaged in Italy, the Second and Third Infantry Divisions and the Fourth Canadian Armoured Division were still training in England, along with many thousands of other troops. In the early spring of 1944, a general feeling of anticipation began to grow in southern England; military activity was intense, with thousands of tanks and artillery on the move, clogging the narrow lanes of Surrey and Hampshire. No one knew when or where our commanders planned to strike, but there was no doubt in any mind that an invasion of mainland Europe was imminent.

There were several alerts that turned out to be false or were aborted, and then the world awakened on the morning of June 6, 1944, to the news that massive Allied forces had invaded the Normandy coastline of France.

I cannot claim the honour of being a D-Day hero. Fortunately or unfortunately, my unit did not land in Normandy until June 22, and by that time we were able to go ashore without even getting our feet wet. New troops were arriving in almost unbelievable force – in hundreds of thousands. The Allied forces were on mainland Europe to stay.

Our unit journeyed a few miles inland, to Fontaine Henri, a small Norman town, where we raised tents and began our stint as part of First Army Troop Headquarters. Bitter, hand-to-hand, house-to-house fighting by the front-line infantry units was raging a mile or so to the north of us, and the sounds of gunfire and explosives filled the air twenty-four hours a day. It is surprising how accustomed we became to this, and as for myself I have no doubt that my years in England during the bombing raids had made me, a frightened boy soldier in 1940, into a mature man.

The deadly battle in the north was for the city of Caen, we learned. This was a main German stronghold, and its defence was being mounted by stubborn young paratroopers of a Hitler Youth Division. Their commander was one of the youngest major generals in the German army – Kurt Meyer, aged thirty-three. It was Meyer who upon his capture after the war was tried in a military court for ordering his fanatical paratroopers to take no prisoners: they obeyed, and shot defenceless soldiers of the Third Canadian Infantry Division. Meyer was convicted and sentenced to hang, a sentence that was commuted by the commanding Canadian general to life imprisonment. After serving a few years in Dorchester Penitentiary in New Brunswick, he was released and returned to Germany, where he died in 1961 at the age of fifty-one.

One sad day in July 1944, I drove the senior Protestant padre of Army Troop Headquarters to Beny-sur-Mer military cemetery, near the landing beaches of Normandy, for the burial of the twenty-odd young soldiers who had been shot after capture by the Hitler Youth soldiers. The service at the cemetery, which was heavily attended by senior officers of the fighting units, forcefully brought home to me just how heavy a cost in fatalities the war was exacting. I observed the constant arrival of army ambulances and jeeps, each one carrying two dead soldiers on stretchers, covered by groundsheets or blankets.

We were sitting beside the road shortly after our arrival at the small town of Fontaine Henri, eating lunch from our mess tins, when a large convoy of tanks passed us, going north toward the battle area. It was the Polish Armoured Division, which had just landed, and every tank turret had a jubilant Polish soldier smiling and waving to us. "We're going home, we're going home," they shouted to us in English and Polish.

Later that same evening a massive bombing attack by British and American planes was launched with the intention of softening up the entrenched and stubborn German forces in Caen and the surrounding area. As we listened to the thunder of the exploding bombs and watched the brilliant colours of the fiery bursts that welled up from the ground toward the sky, we commented on what a pasting the enemy was getting. But we were wrong. Next morning we were awakened, hauled out of our foxholes and herded into jeeps to be taken to the battle zone. Some of our bombers, we were informed, had dropped their loads short, accidentally destroying the very Polish division we had seen pass a few short hours before. It was up to us now to help in the evacuation of the dead and wounded.

I will never forget the burning tanks and trucks – the brilliant colour of flame no longer triumphant, but deeply tragic. The screams of the wounded seemed to hurt my ears, and their moans cut into my heart. Despite all my years of war, it was the first time I had ever seen the real aftermath of battle; the memory and the dreadful irony haunt me still though I know that errors and mistakes in war are unavoidable – as unavoidable as they are in law enforcement.

With the fortunes of war appearing to shift in favour of the Allies, the Canadian government decreed that the military could now start to return long-serving personnel to Canada for a period of home leave. The order of priority was to be decided on the basis of points: so many for being married, so many for each month of service, etc. My long service overseas, four and a half years by this time, earned me enough points for a trip home – even though I was unmarried and had just turned twenty-one.

Jack Webster, shortly after his arrival home in 1945, no longer the boy he was when he first enlisted.

The troopship *Mauretania* carried about five thousand happy and singing soldiers – me among them – when it docked in Halifax just before Christmas 1944. When our troop train arrived in Toronto at the Pure Food Building in the Canadian National Exhibition grounds, we were met by thousands of family and friends. For me the greeting party was my parents and my sister, Gladys. It was a gloriously happy group that journeyed by taxi to our house on Shaw Street, where my mother, with the help of our old family friend Annie Airth, had prepared a feast of cold roast beef, pickled onions, crusty bread and real butter.

My thirty-day leave passed very quickly, and almost at once, it seemed, I had to report back to the Exhibition grounds, to Military Headquarters of Number Two District, located in the Horse Palace. A neighbour of ours on Shaw Street, Mr. Leef, had a limousine that he rented out for weddings and funerals, and my mother decided to hire it to take me and another Toronto soldier, whom I had met on the boat coming home, back to the barracks. When we arrived at Exhibition Barracks, Mr. Leef drove right up to the front doors of the Horse Palace, and as we got out of the car our driver saluted us and we walked into the building ignoring the wide-open mouths of staring fellow soldiers. I guess I have always had a taste for the little luxuries of life!

We fully expected to be returned overseas, and in some perverse way were actually looking forward to getting back into the war. But we were not immediately sent back. From January to April of 1945, we were kept reasonably busy at the Exhibition Barracks, providing prisoner escort duties.

As a corporal, I was sent all over Ontario with a party of eight to ten soldiers, to escort army deserters, from various military detachments, back to Number Two Military District Headquarters in Toronto for court-martial. These deserters were all conscripts who had refused to volunteer for overseas services. When the need for infantry became desperate in northwest Europe, the government of the day, with much anguish, ordered a sizeable number of these conscripts to be sent overseas. In December 1944 and January 1945, they deserted in thousands, some even destroying their equipment. The military police simply did not have the resources to locate, detain and escort so many offenders to their place of trial – so ordinary troops, rather than military police, were pressed into service to do the escorting.

We returned them to Toronto by train, and although my men and I were all overseas veterans we could not help feeling some sympathy for a lot of those deserters after listening to their stories during the long train rides. I don't think I can recall one soldier, of the hundreds I escorted, who could be classed as cowardly for not willingly serving overseas. Many of them were from families that had already sent two or three sons overseas, where they had been killed or wounded, and their parents had begged their remaining sons not to go. Others described their farm homes on the Prairies, where parents were old or ill and hired hands could not be obtained even to feed the cattle. I found the French-speaking Canadians to be very sincere. These tough young soldiers did not mince words: they said they would fight and die for Canada, but would not die in a foreign land for a country other than their own.

This was not a pleasant assignment for me and my men, but I was about to get another, even less pleasant one, which turned out to be my last, and saddest, task of the war.

T ODAY, CHORLEY PARK IS ONE of the quietest corners of the peaceful, el-
egant neighbourhood of Rosedale. Overlooking the Don Valley, it is little
more than a stretch of smooth lawn, interrupted by stately trees and a drive
that winds out toward the street, suggesting that something else must once
have occupied this site. Indeed, many things have, including the home of
five lieutenant-governors of Ontario. What the site gives no hint of is the
veritable city it had become at the end of the Second World War. As a military hospital, Chorley Park retained little of its air of restrained elegance.
It was a bustling place where the tough work of dealing with the aftermath
of overseas casualties was a separate battle all its own.

It was here that as a twenty-one-year-old veteran of five years of overseas service, Jack Webster found himself in command of a ten-man guard
unit whose assignment it was to watch over one single man. This soldier
had recently arrived from England under an overwhelming burden of guilt
and shame. He had been in an artillery unit fighting in Italy. One day, he,
like thousands of other soldiers before and since, drank too freely of the
plentiful local wine. When he finally managed to stumble back to his unit,
he found all of his comrades gone. The unit had been ordered to mount a
barrage while he, missing from his position on a gun, had been off on his
drunk.

Unable to ignore his intoxication and its effect on his sense of duty, the
battery sergeant major and other senior officers immediately did what their
own sense of duty demanded and reminded him that he had failed himself,
his fellow soldiers and his country. They no doubt let him know that no self-
respecting man lets others down as he just had. They ordered him to withdraw to his tent and to sit there until the barrage was over and he could be
given the punishment he so clearly deserved.

The soldier obeyed, withdrew. Not for long. Soon he was back, but this
time he had his Sten gun with him, and it was as loaded as he was. He
walked straight to where senior officers were directing the barrage. Without a word, he opened fire on the officers, shooting two dead and wounding
several others.

Then he turned the Sten on himself and fired at his own head. Unfortunately, he only almost missed. He shot away one whole side of his face.

After months of hospital treatment and countless operations, he was finally deemed fit to stand trial. At his court-martial, he was sentenced to

death, but the sentence was commuted to life at Kingston Penitentiary. This tortured individual was incarcerated at Chorley Park, not a prison but a hospital, in order to undergo more operations and skin grafts before he could be declared healthy enough to do his time in the pen. As the officer in charge of the guard, Webster himself spent plenty of time with his prisoner. The man's ability to speak had been reduced to a nearly incomprehensible growl, but Webster was able to figure out that the prisoner was a soft-spoken, mild person whose thoughts turned often to his children and his wife.

A very remarkable thing about those who kill is how often they will tell you that they can't remember a single thing about committing their crime. Like accident victims, they will recall vividly the last few seconds before anything went wrong, then nothing. Commonly a killer will say, "I looked down and saw the victim lying there bleeding from a bullet wound, and there was a gun on the floor beside him. I don't know how it – or he – got there." Sometimes they are lying. Sometimes they were so drunk, stoned or furious during the crime that reason was blotted out. And sometimes, the horror of what they have done is so great that their mind exercises its prerogative of mercy and wipes the murder from memory forever.

Webster's prisoner had no recollection of any of the events leading up to or during the tragedy that wrecked his life.

When Webster had been on this duty for a week, the head nurse took him aside. With compassion, and some apprehension, she explained that arrangements had been made for the prisoner to have a visit from his wife and children the following morning. She didn't have to point out what a risk this would present for all concerned. There would certainly be security risks if the man became difficult to handle from excitement or grief. But more frightening was the emotional risk. When the man had left home three years before, he was handsome, whole and a hero about to serve his country, and his children were babies.

When he had a chance to think about the visit, the prisoner realized what a terrible shock it would be for his family to see what he had become. Webster and his men, guarding the man twenty-four hours a day, could not help but witness the tragic soul-searching that went on. Finally, love and loneliness won. The prisoner decided he wanted a brief reunion with his wife in his room. Hospital officials agreed. But everyone felt it would be best for the children to remain outside.

At the moment of reunion, Webster stood silently as husband and wife tearfully embraced. Though he had to stay in the room he tried not to overhear the personal words that passed between the two. Then he had to walk with the woman along the echoing corridor of the hospital, down the stairs, and outside, where a nursing sister – trying hard to hide her own feelings – played with the couple's children.

Webster reached down and picked up one of the small, laughing tots. "Look," he said softly, "there's your daddy up there. See?"

Looking up, everyone near the busy site glimpsed the tragic figure on the second-floor balcony. The horrible disfigurement of the patient's face was hidden by bandages, but nothing could hide his sense of loss as he leaned down to wave at the little figures below.

"Wave to your father," their mother instructed, and dutifully, they did.

Nurses, doctors, guards – including Webster – held tight to the composure expected at a military establishment like Chorley Park.

But the next day, Webster requested reassignment of duty. His request was not refused.

CHAPTER THREE

Police Recruit

J ACK WEBSTER'S STRONG SENSE OF *humour and hunger for adventure served him well when he was a young policeman. Like all cops, he ran into things ordinary people seldom even know about, let alone experience. The fact that he could see the humour in some of what he encountered kept him from dwelling on the grimness.*

On West Lodge Avenue in Parkdale, there was a detention centre operated by nuns for the government. In effect at this time was a nasty piece of legislation called the Female Refuges Act. Under this law, a woman between fifteen and thirty-five could be held for as long as two years without the nicety of a trial. A girl could simply be declared incorrigible – for example, by parents who found their daughter to be disobedient. The Home of the Good Shepherd was not a jail in that the girls held there hadn't necessarily been convicted of any criminal offence. Nonetheless, they were held under strict supervision, so strict, in fact, that one girl met her death during an escape attempt involving tied bedsheets dangling from a window.

Some of the girls of Good Shepherd, though not criminals, were no saints. One late summer afternoon, a panicky call put in to Number 6 Police Station reported that a "disturbance" was in progress at the refuge. Webster was in the station enjoying his supper when the call came – a supper packed by his honourable, decent, law-abiding mother and sister. The women he was about to meet made the women of his family seem like a separate species.

Number 6 was almost across the street from West Lodge, so he and the other available officers were on the scene almost at once. As they pulled up to the home, a fluster of nuns ran out to them, breathlessly explaining how the girls had rebelled – throwing and breaking things, swearing, threatening – in short, rioting. The nuns told the police that they had managed to corral the worst of the lot – the seven ringleaders – and were holding them under lock and key in the basement. The nuns were no slouches. They'd already phoned ahead to the Mercer, which most definitely was a jail, and had made sure that the prison was ready to receive seven tough girls. What the nuns mostly needed, they said, was someone to transfer the wild young girls to Mercer.

As Webster and his colleagues thought that over, two veteran detectives pulled up, followed by the paddy wagon. The detectives immediately took charge over the uniformed cops, including Webster, and led the expedition into the nether reaches of the basement of the Good Shepherd home.

The men followed carefully as one of the nuns wound along the narrow passages of the cellar. The only sound was their feet scraping on the rough floor. Then, far off, Webster could hear the faint sound of female screaming. As they drew nearer to where the nun was leading, the sound became more distinct, more intense. But when the nun turned her key in the door at the end of their path, it was not sound that hit Webster first. It was sight – the sight of seven yelling, jumping, stark-naked girls.

He never did figure out who was most aggressive in rounding them up – the detectives, the uniformed constables or the nuns. But after a battle that a veteran soldier like himself had to admire, the girls were finally brought back up to ground level and into the reception hall. However, their dress left quite a bit to be desired, for no matter how hard the nuns tried to get some clothes on the girls, they couldn't manage it. Eventually they just gave up, and one by one the police carried the nude struggling girls into the open doors of the wagon.

As soon as the young women caught sight of Webster – who at twenty-one was handsome, slim, tall, and obviously very strong – they really let loose. They gestured and called out to him. The obscenity of their motions and the lewdness of their taunts shocked Webster. With flirtatious abandon, they spelled out exactly what they would like to do with the young cop if they could get him alone.

Their suggestive teasing and astonishing boldness – especially in the presence of nuns and his superiors – made Webster burn with embarrassment.

"Up you go then, son. In with them . . . " One of the detectives signalled toward the wagon indicating that he was ordering Webster to ride inside with the girls to guard them during the ride to the Mercer.

For the first time in his career, Webster knew the difficulty of choosing between insubordination and resignation – because there was no way he was going to obey. But when he raised his red face to look at the detective, he saw that he and all the other cops were laughing at his distress. He breathed a long sigh of relief that the order was only a joke.

As the last girl was herded into the wagon, she took a wide, playful swipe at one of the officers and scooped off his cap just at the moment the door of the wagon slammed shut. Without further incident, the big wagon pulled out followed by the two cars full of detectives and constables. The procession made its way along King Street West to the Andrew Mercer Reformatory.

Opened in the late nineteenth century, the Mercer was the only prison for provincially sentenced women in Ontario until it was closed in 1969 and replaced by the Vanier Institute. Like other prisons for women, both before and after, the Mercer was a grim, forbidding fortress both inside and out. As Webster and the others arrived, they were met by the keepers of the place, a stalwart platoon of sturdy matrons.

Carefully, one of the detectives took pains to explain to the matrons how tough and hard the girls he had brought were. He warned the women to stand back and stay on their guard, because the minute the wagon door opened, trouble was sure to erupt.

The head matron, whom Webster would always remember as somebody who looked like an old buzzard, just laughed. "Obviously your men have no idea how to handle female prisoners," she declared. "Just watch."

She stationed herself outside the door. The instant it was opened, the stolen cap, now full of urine, came flying out and hit the matron full in the face.

As if getting a faceful of urine was the most natural thing in the world, the tough old blister didn't even flinch. She and her sisters simply took the girls by their arms and marched them off into the grim caverns of the Mercer from which Webster was never to see them emerge. The ride in the wagon, the matron's powerful bearing, the very atmosphere of the Mercer itself, served to subdue the girls quite effectively.

Detective Sergeant Pringle, who had been the officer in charge then, would ask Jack Webster for years to come if he had heard from any of his girlfriends from the Good Shepherd home.

By MAY 1945 IT WAS obvious that we were not going to be sent back overseas. Our unit officers began to prepare us for our return to civilian life; we were given lectures and presentations and encouraged to learn about the possible future occupations available to us. I was advised by a placement officer to return to school and obtain my matriculation, for university entrance. Because of my long service overseas, he told me, I had accumulated enough educational points not only to have all my tuition fees paid for, but to receive a weekly subsistence allowance as well. It was a chance that would never come again. I was impressed with that young captain for taking so much time to counsel me – he almost begged me, in fact, to return to school. With the special exemptions that were in place for returning service people, I could have become a lawyer in a mere four years. But after being subjected to rigorous military discipline for so long, the last thing I wanted was to subject myself yet again to the strict regimentation that school would undoubtedly bring (which is pretty ironic, considering what I ended up doing).

I have sometimes regretted that I declined this educational opportunity, but when a uniformed police inspector, Edward Dunn, came to talk to a group of veterans about the Toronto Police Force, I was ready to listen. He told us that to qualify one had to be a Canadian of British descent, at least five foot ten, minimum weight 165 pounds, and between the ages of twenty-one and twenty-nine. (These very stringent requirements with regard to heritage were relaxed in 1947. As it was, a few Italians were the exception before that year.) The salary was $25 a week to start, with a pension of $25 per month after twenty-five years of service.

I had always been interested in the police force, and when one of my chums, Frank Thompson, joined the force as a seventeen-year-old cadet in the spring of 1939, I had presented myself at police headquarters, on College Street, to apply for cadet employment, but of course, at sixteen, I was too young. Now, as Inspector Dunn spoke to our group of soldiers, my interest was rekindled. Ten of us, who felt we had the necessary qualifications, decided to apply and were taken by army bus to police headquarters.

This was a foreboding, fortress-like building, six storeys high, at 149 College Street. It had originally been a school, but as a police headquarters it had acquired a grim atmosphere that encouraged pedestrians to quicken their steps as they passed. (What a contrast with the modern, multi-storey, new headquarters building at 40 College Street! This very costly structure has almost an art-gallery appearance, which invites pedestrians to enter and explore.)

After being escorted to the recruiting office on the fifth floor, my group of prospective recruits spent about an hour taking preliminary tests, which included height and weight measurements and a short, written test of our general knowledge about the city of Toronto. At the conclusion of these tests, six of our group of ten were accepted by the Toronto City Police Force on the spot.

What a vast difference there is between that procedure of recruitment and what is in place today! It now takes anywhere from six months to nine months from the time a prospective recruit applies until his (or her) final acceptance. The very searching background scrutiny, the extensive educational and physical examinations, the elaborate and sophisticated psychological testing would certainly make a farce of the procedure we underwent. That is not to say that today's police recruit will turn out to be a better law enforcement officer than those of my day; in fact, some people believe these modern young men and women will have to strive just to be as good as we were! In any event, the percentage of successful applicants in 1945 was about 50 percent of those applying. In 1989, only 10 percent of all applicants were accepted.

The five of us who were sworn in together spanned the accepted age limits: I was the youngest at twenty-one and the others were between twenty-seven and twenty-nine. (Now, of course, there is no upper age limit, because of the Human Rights Act and the employment equity programs. I don't think the sponsors and supporters of this type of legislation have a clue about the rigours of street police work.)

Because we had been accepted for civilian employment, we received our honourable discharges from the army, and on June 12, 1945, we took the oath of office. We were sworn in as police constables by Brigadier General D.C. Draper, a crusty old ex-cavalry officer from the First World War, who was then the chief of police. The ceremony took place in the chief's office, a large high-ceilinged room on the ground floor of headquarters. It was a solemn occasion for us five veteran warriors, four of us from the army and one from the air force. We stood at attention, wearing our respective military uniforms, and even after some forty-four years, I can still remember the thread-bare rug we were standing on, and the swords and muskets displayed on the walls.

After administering the oath of office, the chief of police said to us, as we still stood at attention, "Remember this, young men; there are two things that have ruined more young police officers than anything else, and those two things are booze and women and," he added, "not necessarily in that order of importance." His final advice to us was to lead a clean, moral and sober life. He then sent us to talk to our training instructor, who explained that when a sufficient number of new police constables had been recruited – about thirty – we would be recalled to headquarters to undergo six weeks of instruction, as a group, in the duties of a police officer. But we were to start work at once, the next morning.

After we had drawn our (used) uniforms from the stores unit – including the old Bobby-style helmet – we were issued a revolver and a baton. It was assumed that because we were veterans, we would be experienced in the use of firearms. We were assigned to a numbered police station. At the time, the policy was not to assign a recruit to the police division in the area of the city where he resided, and so I was posted to Number 6 Division, in the Parkdale area, farther to the west than Number 7, which was in the Ossington and Bloor area where I lived with my parents.

The training instructor then sent us to telephone our designated police station, to find out what shift, or "relief," in police parlance, we would be working the first day on the job. I was told over the phone that I had been assigned the 4:00 p.m.-to-midnight relief, and would be required to parade for duty at 3:45 p.m. I was also told to be in the police station at least half an hour before parade time, to record stolen and wanted automobiles in my issued memo book. After that, we were dismissed. All five of us, keeping in mind the chief's warning about leading a clean and sober life, promptly went to the nearest beverage room and drank several beers.

WITH IMAGES OF STOLEN VEHICLES and crooks on the lam racing through my dreams, I found it hard to sleep that night and could hardly wait to report for duty. Daylight finally arrived, and at about 1:00 p.m. my mother made me a lunch and put it in my new black lunch pail. I got dressed in my uniform, put on my Bobby hat, and with my belt and revolver properly in place, I stood in my parents' kitchen, ready to be inspected by my mother, my sister, Gladys, and my mother's friend Annie Airth. They checked me over from the toes of my shining new boots – which I had had to pay for myself – to the top of my head. With the chinstrap of my helmet resting just below my lower lip, I let them view me from all angles, and was not at all surprised when they unanimously declared that I looked beautiful.

I wanted to get to the police station early, so I left our house about 1:30 p.m. and walked to the streetcar stop at Hallam and Ossington, very conscious of the stares and comments of admiring neighbours, who had not seen a fresh-faced, young policeman for a long time. Recruiting of constables had been suspended during the war, and most of the officers who had joined just before the war, in 1938, had still not returned from military service. It would be quite correct to say that, at that time, I was a novelty.

It would also be correct to say that I was lost. Although born and raised in Toronto, I had left it as a very young soldier, and when I was a boy one didn't stray too far from one's own neighbourhood. As a result, there were many areas of the city that I was unfamiliar with – and that included the west end. There were twelve police stations in Toronto in those days (there are now eighteen). Number 6 was situated at the corner of Queen Street and Cowan Avenue. I had no trouble getting to Queen, but didn't have the foggiest notion of where Cowan was. Dressed in my uniform and carrying my lunch pail, I got off the streetcar at Queen and Ossington and stopped a passing citizen to ask directions to the station house on Cowan. He stared, burst out laughing, slapped me on the back, and said I had a real sense of humour. Then he went on his way. Fortunately a kindly TTC motorman noticed my plight and told me to get on a westbound streetcar and get off two stops past the Dufferin Street underpass. I arrived at work without further embarrassment.

At the police station, I approached the front desk and was greeted with almost open hostility by the grumpy old constable who was working behind the counter. My spirits sank but quickly rose again when the desk sergeant got up and walked toward me with an outstretched hand of welcome.

I have never forgotten that desk sergeant, now long departed; his name was Murray Hamilton and he was then about forty-five years of age. He personally escorted me the short distance to the guard room, showed me where to put my lunch pail, how to read the teletype messages, and where to record stolen and wanted cars in my memo book. He was a fine man, a First World War veteran who, after showing me around the station, promptly signed me up as a member of the Toronto Police War Veterans' Association. I have been a member ever since.

Around three o'clock, the other uniformed police constables who would be working my shift started to arrive at the guard room. They seemed old to me, some obviously overweight, most with lined and unhappy faces. It was clear to me at once that newcomers were not enthusiastically welcomed. In fact, most of the older officers were brutally rude and offensive to the new, young, and slim constables. I asked one of them a simple question about whether I should list the stolen cars ahead of the wanted cars or vice versa. He got up, broke wind, said to me in a loud voice, "Find out the way I had to," and moved to the other end of the table.

Members of the Toronto Police Force in 1945 worked six days a week, with a half-hour for lunch in the summer and a full hour in the fall, winter and spring. There was no payment for overtime, and court appearances were on your own time, unless they happened to coincide with your shift. The Toronto Police Association was in those days largely ineffectual in fighting for the rights of its members, though it was later to become a very powerful and militant police association. I believe one of the main reasons for this vast increase in power is that the elected officials of the organization, all members of the force, are now granted leave of absence from normal duties so that they are free to devote themselves full time to the welfare of over seven thousand members. Their salaries and benefits are reimbursed by the association to the force. One should not be confused by the name "association" – no matter how you cut it, it's still a union in every sense of the word.

In the thirties, forties and fifties, any member of the force holding elected office in this organization was a marked man. The senior brass considered any complaint about working conditions as next door to Communist-inspired. It is a fact that not more than thirty-five years ago, spies were sent out from headquarters to observe who attended association meetings, especially if there was some contentious issue to be discussed. Well, those days are gone, and it goes without saying that the present-day salary levels and other more than acceptable working conditions are entirely due to the efforts of the hard-working and dedicated elected people in the Metropolitan Toronto Police Association. However, as a retired veteran command officer, I have to say that my personal view is that on occasion the executive members of the association have allied themselves to causes that have not been in the best interests of the police at large.

In 1945 a police division had an average personnel strength of about sixty-five men. This would include the commander (who held the rank of inspector), three sergeants, four patrol sergeants, one detective sergeant, and two detectives; the remainder were constables. In contrast, some of today's police divisions have a personnel strength of from 200, all ranks, up to 450, all ranks. The police division in Metropolitan Toronto today is almost a police unit itself. Some of the larger divisions are commanded by superintendents. Each of these people has a vast support staff of inspectors and senior non-commissioned officers to assist him.

When I was a young constable, the commander of a police division had tremendous power over the day-to-day working conditions of the men under him. For example, if you displeased your immediate supervisor in any way, by some real or imagined breach of discipline or regulations, he would notify the inspector, who would promptly assign you to a long period of nights – the midnight-to-eight-a.m. shift. So, instead of working two weeks of days, two weeks of afternoons, and two weeks of nights, it was quite possible, and it happened, that a constable would be assigned to three months of night duty. If the officer had the foolish notion to complain, he would be peremptorily told that if he didn't like it he could quit; thousands of others, he would be informed, were just waiting to take his job. That might have been true during the dark days of the Depression, but not, in my opinion, at any time from 1945 right up to the present day. I do not believe there have been "thousands" of people desperately trying to become police officers. Recruitment of police constables – that is, the recruitment of the right type of constables for the very arduous and often dangerous duties of the job – has always been difficult, certainly during my period of service, and especially in a city as large, complex and dynamic as Toronto.

Despite the threat of harsh treatment by some (though certainly not all) supervisors, there were many reasons for a Toronto police officer to stay on the job. There was the matter of pensions, for example. One of the main reasons for staying a number of years was that if an officer left prior to the completion of his twenty-five years his contributions were seized and not returned. I felt then, and I still do, that this was out-and-out theft by the Toronto Police Benefit Fund. Thankfully, that section of the police fund regulations was rescinded in 1946, and since then any member leaving the force prior to pension time has had all of his contributions returned, with accumulated interest.

But the tragedy of pension difficulties, as well as the power of those in charge, was brought home to me in my earliest days on the force. While I was attending the police school in July and August of 1945, an ex-detective who had left the force after twelve years of service was picketing headquarters, complete with a sandwich board that declared, front and back, the unfairness of this pension money grab, and demanded the return of his contributions. Although the amount as I recall was only $1,500, it was a lot of money in 1945. Sadly, even after the embarrassing publicity he brought upon himself and his family by taking such a radical step – out of financial necessity – he was unsuccessful and never did receive a refund. All he received were the uncomplimentary names assigned to him by headquarters brass – the milder among them "troublemaker" and "Commie" – and we recruits were warned in class, on pain of dismissal, not to talk to him during our smoke breaks in front of the headquarters building.

No, these were certainly not the "good old days" we sometimes refer to. Yet, if I had any doubts or misgivings about my new profession, they were completely dispelled by an experience I had about three weeks into my on-the-job training as a police officer. I had reported on the early day relief, at 7:45 a.m., and at parade was detailed by the sergeant to attend at a funeral home on Eglinton Avenue West at 1:00 p.m. sharp. A forty-five-year-old detective had died of cancer, and, at the request of the family, there was to be a formal, uniformed police funeral. This was the first of many such ceremonies that I would attend in the years to come. Upon arriving at the funeral home, I joined a crowd of 250 other policemen in uniform who had gathered on Eglinton and spilled into the surrounding side streets, some, but not all, managing to get inside the home.

At one-thirty, the service inside the chapel concluded and the men began to leave. I looked up to see a police inspector heading purposefully toward me. I stood still to receive instructions. "I see from your age and bearing," he began, "that you must have been a military man . . . "

"Yes, sir."

"Recently discharged?"

"Yes, sir," I replied, adding that I had been five years in the army.

"Very well, constable. I'd like you to take charge of this assembly. Form them up in columns of three behind the pipes and drums." He advised me that he would give the command to march off and that I was to stay at his side to act as a sort of sergeant major.

Stunned at this turn of events, I hastened to comply, but I must admit that when I shouted in my loudest voice for the assembled policemen to line up quickly in columns of three, I was amazed at the speed with which they obeyed my order. It seemed to matter not at all that they were experienced officers, for the most part in their forties and fifties, and I was a raw recruit just into my twenties.

When the men had obeyed my command, the inspector gave the order to move off. The pipes and drums of the 48th Highlanders began to play as we slowly proceeded east on Eglinton toward Mount Pleasant Cemetery.

Behind me I could sense the steady movement of this long procession of my sombre-faced, blue-uniformed colleagues, wearing their Bobby helmets, marching with firm steps to the mournful music of the pipe band. The sense of oneness that I felt not only with them, but with the departed brother we had gathered to honour, made such an impression on me that at that moment I knew, once and for all, that I had made the right choice. I wanted to remain a part of this group of wonderful men forever.

I ENJOYED WALKING THE BEAT, although at the start I could barely make it home because of my burning feet. My mother would always fetch a basin of hot water, spiked with a good handful of Epsom salts. What a relief it was to soak my poor feet, while my ever-devoted mother served me breakfast or supper!

Patrolling on foot was a tremendous way to meet people, and the streets of Parkdale, like most areas of a large city, had their share of characters. Although regulations stipulated that we were not supposed to talk to anyone very long, under threat of a discipline charge of "gossiping," it was still possible to pass more than just the time of day with citizens and storekeepers of all types. They were, by and large, friendly to a young, new police constable and appeared always to be happy to see you.

In September of 1945, I developed a serious gum infection which my dentist diagnosed as "trench mouth." This was a very common, painful condition that if not quickly and properly treated could affect one's teeth, as the gums receded. In the armed forces, whole units had come down with it as a result, it was thought, of washing eating utensils in the same water used by hundreds of others. I had escaped the disease in the army, but now, in civilian life, it had struck me with a vengeance. I visited a dentist on a daily basis for about a week, and on each occasion he would paint my gums with a blue liquid, which was both unsightly and downright torturous. Eating was almost impossible, and even a drink of coffee or tea brought on acute discomfort.

While walking the beat one night I dropped in to the Gladstone Hotel at the corner of Dufferin and Queen (where it is to this day). I was in the habit of stopping by for a short conversation with the night desk clerk, to pass a few minutes of the long night hours.

It was about two o'clock in the morning, and my mouth was killing me. I explained my gum problem to the sympathetic clerk, and as I prepared to leave the hotel lobby, he suggested, "Why don't you ask Doc O'Leary if he can do something for you?"

"Who is Doc O'Leary?" I asked. My friend pointed to a small man in his late sixties, who was sleeping soundly in one of the ancient overstuffed armchairs in the less than elaborate hotel lobby. Dr. O'Leary, the clerk said, had been one of the finest doctors in Toronto, on staff at one of the largest hospitals, when he became an alcoholic and was struck from the medical register. He had lost his family and was now without a home or possessions. He spent his days drinking with the wine hounds of the neighbourhood, but because he still had the refinements of a professional man the hotel staff allowed him to sleep in the lobby every night.

I awakened this elderly man and, opening his eyes, he said in a very soft voice, "Good morning, officer, I was just leaving."

"No, no," I said, "I'm not moving you, I just wanted to know if you could help me with a gum problem . . . "

If you can visualize a fully uniformed police constable down on one knee in a fourth-rate hotel lobby, while a short, shabbily dressed wine hound peered into his mouth, saying over and over again, "I see. Aha, I see," you may be thinking that I needed a psychiatrist and not a medical doctor, but if you knew the pain I was suffering you would understand.

Doc O'Leary said, "I can give you a prescription that will clear that infection up in twenty-four hours, but you must not have it filled anywhere in this area." With that, he took a crumpled, stained prescription pad from his pocket, and wrote a short medical prescription, signed it O'Leary M.D., and handed it to me, with instructions to apply the medication to my gums three times a day.

I thanked the courteous little man and offered him a two-dollar bill. He very politely declined. "No," he said, smiling. "They won't catch me practising without a licence. Let me know how you make out."

I could hardly wait for the drugstore at Dupont and Christie to open to get my prescription filled. I told my mother that I had something new to try, but I did not tell her about the doctor or the circumstances. After five or six applications of this powerful but unknown medication, my gums became normal and the pain disappeared. I was cured, as the former doctor had said I would be, in twenty-four hours. I saw "Doc O'Leary" on many occasions after that, but he would never accept any money from me, saying he was glad to help.

One of the sadder conversations I used to have on the beat was with a very fine man who operated a fruit store on Queen. This elderly Italian gentleman had had a son on the Toronto Police Force who was killed riding a police motorcycle on New Year's Eve fifteen years before, when he was still in his early twenties. The father never recovered from this tragedy, and whenever he observed me walking by his store, he would run out and give me a large orange or an apple. He said I reminded him of his long-dead son, and he would talk endlessly about him. The conversation would only end when he would be overcome with tears and have to retreat back inside the store. His son, Joseph DeFarrari, was one of the first Canadian boys of Italian descent to join the Toronto Police Force and it is no wonder that his father mourned him so intensely. I have spoken to many old-timers who knew and worked with young Joe, and everyone of them has said that he was a first-class young man, and one of the finest athletes Toronto has ever produced.

How delightful it was to be walking your beat and have ladies out doing their shopping, merchants, and obviously retired gentlemen stop you and engage in friendly conversation! They would tell you about their families, about illnesses, births, marriages and deaths. I always believed that these citizens felt a bond with the policeman on the beat and were grateful that you were there, standing tall and strong as a symbol of safety and protection for them. As these reminiscences show, there used to be a high level of regard and public respect for the police, but it seemed to deteriorate once patrol cars became the accepted way of policing a neighbourhood. Officers became nameless and faceless to the public in general, with little chance of forming the bonds of familiarity and trust that the public had had with the walking cop. Happily, the trend has reversed today, with more and more foot patrols being established in police divisions under the fancy name of "community-based policing." Call it what you like, but it is still a return to the old cop-on-the-beat system, and once again, our officers are becoming human beings in the eyes of the public they serve. I know from personal experience as a command officer that the foot-patrolling police officer has regained the respect and co-operation of citizens and businesspeople throughout Metropolitan Toronto. When I had an established foot patrol in a certain neighbourhood, and some exigency of the service required them to be reassigned temporarily to some other area, my phone used to ring off the hook with calls from citizens and businesspeople wanting to know why "Bill and Al" were not out, or why "Helen and Peter" had not been seen in the malls for a few days. Were their police friends sick, they would inquire, or worse, had the foot patrols been cancelled? Over and over I would explain to these anxious callers that, no, the officers were not ill, and no, the foot patrols had not been suspended, and as soon as the emergency demand for their services elsewhere had subsided, they would be back. There would be many sighs of relief and many thank-yous.

Today, the average police division in Metropolitan Toronto has about forty motor vehicles at its command. In 1945, Number 6 Division had only three: one unmarked car for the detectives and two unmarked cars for scout car patrol. As a matter of fact, all police vehicles at that time were unmarked, with the exception of patrol wagons and some trucks. They were, however, always readily identifiable by the very long radio aerial on the back of the car. This radio system enabled the car crews to receive calls, but they were unable to respond over the radio to the dispatcher. In other words, it was a one-way communication system, and you had to rely on stopping at one of the police call boxes that dotted the main corners of the division.

The drill was that you attended the assigned detail, and on completion you used the call box to say that the detail was concluded and your unit was again available for calls. It was quite a primitive system compared with today's very elaborate and sophisticated methods of communication, but call boxes were very effective in communicating with an officer on each beat. Each box had a loud bell, and a red light mounted on top of the box pole. The inside officer at the police station, commonly referred to as "the station duty man," had a large switchboard at his desk, and if he wanted to contact an officer on a certain post or beat, he could flash the light on at a particular box, and have the bell ring intermittently; he could also, of course, alert all beats at the same time if a general message had to be transmitted. Because the bell seemed even louder at night there was a standing order that it was not to be used after midnight, so as not to disturb sleeping citizens. Many times, walking the beat after midnight, I would be alerted by streetcar motormen or taxi drivers that my light was on at a corner not yet in my sight. The key for the call box was a large brass object, and on countless occasions it was the foot-patrolling officer's best friend. I still have my key, although the only call box left is on display in the police museum.

I disliked scout car duty. The permanent car crews were all long-serving constables, so young officers would only be assigned when one of the old-timers was off sick, or on annual leave. That suited me fine, because I liked walking my beat alone, summer and winter, rather than being assigned to ride in a patrol car with a man over twice my age, who was usually cranky and very often less than energetic.

My first afternoon beat extended west along Queen Street from Dovercourt, the boundary on the east, to Roncesvalles Avenue, and back again. On any given day, I probably covered ten miles in the course of the seven hours I was on the beat. I would be on the look-out for illegally parked motor vehicles, disorderly or suspicious persons, and any other trouble; I would direct traffic from time to time; and on the night shift I would try the front-door handles of business premises, to check that they were secure. It is surprising how many shopkeepers would close their businesses for the day and forget to lock the front door. If we found unlocked doors we were not allowed to enter the premises alone, but had to summon the roving patrol sergeant to the scene to enter with us.

This procedure was partly for protection in case you surprised burglars at work inside, but chiefly it was because of an episode in the mid-thirties, when a whole group of policemen working out of a downtown station were arrested for stealing from stores and other businesses, after claiming they had found the premises insecure. Many times, this unscrupulous gang would do the break-in themselves, take whatever merchandise they wanted, and hide it in a laneway, to be picked up later when they reported off duty. Once their theft was complete, they would summon the patrol sergeant.

The daily papers dubbed this group of dishonest uniformed Toronto policemen the "Hundred Percent Gang" because, when the suspicion became public that most of the thefts plaguing the downtown merchants were caused by policemen on the beat, the unsuspecting inspector in command of this particular police station held a press conference and stated that it was a false rumour and that all of his men were "a hundred percent."

Shortly after this, headquarters detectives made a swoop and arrested a dozen or so of his hundred-percent constables. After a much publicized trial, some of them went to jail, and one man who was charged committed suicide. It was the worst scandal ever to strike the Toronto City Police Force. The shame and disgrace lasted for many years; even in 1945, in fact, when I joined, the odd drunk or ticketed motorist would still ask you where you stole your shoes from.

Temptation, however, is always the policeman's lot. On the north side of Queen Street, near Lansdowne Avenue, there was a cigar store operated by a very friendly man. He was especially friendly to the police officers of nearby Number 6 Police Station. One December night, when I was setting out for my tour of duty on the midnight-to-8:00 a.m. shift, one of the veteran constables drew me aside and whispered in my ear that if I was assigned the Queen Street beat, I was to look between the doors of a particular cigar store, where I would find a small bottle with about three ounces of Scotch whisky in it. This, I was told, was always left by the store owner during the cold winter months for the policeman walking the beat. I was further informed that it was especially good after you had your lunch, in the middle of the night.

Around three o'clock in the morning, I took a peek between the doors of the store. There it was: a small jar containing an amber liquid. I had no intention of drinking it, since I was afraid of being charged with drinking on duty, and losing my job, but for about three nights I checked the doors, and sure enough, the little jar of whisky would be there every night.

On the morning of the fourth day, I was leaving the station after reporting off duty when I was accosted by two veteran constables who were on the day shift. They inquired if I was aware of the little bottle of whisky left by the cigar-store owner. I replied that, yes, I was aware of it, but I did not want to drink it, because I was on duty. At this, they became very abusive. In no uncertain terms they told me to throw it out if I didn't want it, but not to leave it untouched. Apparently the store owner was beginning to think that his goodwill gesture was not wanted any more, and he had told my veteran associates that he was going to discontinue the practice. Whereupon they decided that I had to be spoken to.

For the rest of the winter, when I was on the night shift on Queen Street, I would quietly remove the bottle, pour the contents on the road and replace the empty bottle between the doors – though sometimes, on those cold, snowy nights, I would smell the lovely aroma of the Scotch whisky before pouring it out, and I was sorely tempted.

IN MY YOUNG DAYS, A police division was simply divided into a series of numbered beats. For example, Queen Street from Dovercourt to Roncesvalles Avenue was one, two and three post, and Roncesvalles from Queen Street to Bloor was four, five and six post. The two scout cars would be detailed to the east and west sides, with the division being a main north-and-south artery. Today the divisions in Metropolitan Toronto are so large, with so many additional responsibilities for the personnel to deal with, that they are divided into zones, patrol areas, and of course the recently rein-carnated beats.

The patrolling police constables no longer work a day or afternoon shift, or even a night shift. They now work as a "platoon," with as many as five platoons in a division, and at certain times they overlap one another. The same sergeants and constables can remain on the one platoon for years, and as a senior officer I did not think this arrangement was good for the force, or for some of the individual officers. I am not alone in this belief – it is a view shared by the majority of district and divisional commanders. The non-commissioned officers become too friendly with their troops, and dis-cipline can be a problem. The platoon itself becomes so tightly knit and protective of its members that it runs the risk of becoming a clique.

Traffic control, too, has greatly changed over the years. Today it is al-most a police profession in itself, but in 1945 a beat cop could expect to be called upon to assist in traffic matters at any time. This was strikingly brought home to me in my first few days on the force. When I was paraded, the sergeant directed me to pay particular attention to the traffic at Roncesvalles and Queen from 5:00 p.m. on. This junction was a busy one at any time of the day, even in 1945. There was no Gardiner Expressway for east-west traffic, and during the evening rush hour motor vehicles con-verged on this intersection from every possible direction. At the designated time I stood, as instructed, on the northwest corner of the intersection, feel-ing resplendent in my uniform.

I watched with interest as a Toronto Transit Commission inspector, in the centre of the busy traffic hub, waved his arms with great skill, guiding the huge streetcars and other vehicles to move almost gracefully into the proper traffic channels. When I had enjoyed several minutes of his compli-cated manoeuvres, he suddenly stopped all the traffic, strode over to me, and shouted in a voice made even more commanding by his imperious Eng-lish accent, "You're not here to look pretty, constable, get in here and get to work!" I quickly joined him in the middle of the nightmare of cars, trucks, streetcars, bicycles and pedestrians, and with vehicles coming at me from all sides, I received blow-by-blow instructions in the art of traffic manipulation from this highly knowledgeable and experienced civilian (who was to be a friend of mine for many years to come).

One sunny Saturday in July of 1945, I was again walking Queen Street. I had been instructed by the parading sergeant to keep the sidewalk clear in front of a notorious pool hall on the north side of Queen, near Elm Grove Avenue. Queen Street, then as now, was packed with afternoon shoppers on Saturday, and as I approached the area of the pool hall I could see that a group of wine hounds and other hooligans was blocking the sidewalk and forcing the pedestrians to detour onto the street in order to pass. As I approached the drunken group I took note of their obscene language – such language being far less in evidence on the street then than it is in these days!

In the most officious voice I could muster, I said, "All right, let's move along now." When I'd repeated this twice, the gang finally started to move slowly away, with the exception of one well-built, red-headed tough, who refused to budge and challenged me to make him. By this time the shoppers had stopped strolling, and in no time at all there was a crowd of about four deep surrounding me and my pugnacious challenger. They could smell a fight, and wanted to see how this young, somewhat skinny cop would handle the situation. I knew I could not back down. If I had, I might just as well have walked to my nearby station and resigned.

In a naïve display of bravado, I removed my police helmet, took off my belt and revolver and then my uniform jacket. One of the onlookers, a less than respectable-looking alcoholic, volunteered to hold my clothing and gun while the fight was on. So, there I was, a majestic member of the Toronto Police Force, standing on a very busy street on a sunny Saturday afternoon, wearing only my boots and police trousers with suspenders over a short-sleeved vest. With my heart pumping, I put up my dukes.

The minute the red-headed tough saw that I really was ready to fight, he took a step back, put up his hands and declared, "Okay, copper, you win." He turned and disappeared up a laneway at the side of the pool hall, with his rowdy buddies following. Which was fine with me. I retrieved the rest of my uniform from the helpful citizen minding it and went about my business.

But about ten minutes after this confrontation a scout car pulled up beside me at Queen and Lansdowne, with a patrol sergeant as the escort. "In the back, Webster," the sergeant ordered, then off we drove back to the station. I was directed to the inspector's office, and there the desk sergeant and the patrol sergeant proceeded to tear strips off me. I was told that I was a disgrace for removing my uniform to fight in the street like a common ruffian. In future, they admonished, if I encountered a similar situation, as no doubt I would, I was simply to draw my baton at once and hit my antagonist anywhere I could, preferably not on his head. With this advice, I was summarily dispatched back to my beat, a wiser and more subdued rookie police constable. To my discomfort, my would-be assailant approached me the very next morning as I was walking my beat near the Gladstone Hotel, at Queen and Dufferin. He was alone and I was alone, and I thought, "Here we go again . . . "

But no, he held out his hand for me to shake and apologized profusely for any embarrassment he had caused me the previous afternoon. I accepted his apology, and this red-haired, slightly-older-than-me tough guy became my friend and stayed so for many years after. In fact, when I was a detective sergeant on the homicide squad, he telephoned me and provided critical information that resulted in the arrest of a murder suspect.

About the middle of July 1945, just before I was recalled to headquarters for commencement of my formal police training, I was standing at the corner of Roncesvalles and Queen when an out-of-breath citizen ran up and told me there had been a stabbing in an apartment along Queen Street, near St. Joseph's Hospital. I immediately used the call box located on the corner. When the station answered, I passed on to the operator all the information I had just received, gave the location of the apartment building as identified by the citizen, and requested help. I then ran along Queen Street with my informant, who directed me to an apartment kitchen where amongst the confusion of screaming people, I observed the body of a young man, who had obviously been stabbed to death. The deceased (I later learned) was a member of a prominent Canadian musical family, and his death was the culmination of a dispute over a woman.

Detective and uniform cars began to arrive, and I was abruptly relieved of any further duties at the scene. This was the first of many hundreds of scenes of murder and violent death that I was to attend over the next forty-two years. Being summarily dismissed from the scene by the gruff detectives caused me a considerable amount of hurt. This "Okay, officer, get back to your beat" philosophy was quite common in those days, but in today's enlightened and sophisticated methods of criminal investigation, the "first officer at the crime scene" is an important integral witness in the subsequent court proceedings, and he remains at the scene to assist the investigators in any way he can. There is no doubt in my mind that this first exposure to a murder scene, with its hustle and bustle and the quiet but determined movements of the cream-of-the-crop detectives, left an indelible impression on me. I wanted to be a "murder detective."

IN THE THIRD WEEK OF July 1945, I at last reported to the police school. Here on an upper floor of the old headquarters building, I met again the friends I had joined with. Together with some more-recent arrivals, we made up a class of thirty-two young men. The dozen or so of us "old-timers," who had been on the street doing what we thought was big-time police work for almost five weeks, felt infinitely superior to these rookies, though of course we were really almost as green as the newcomers. Inexperienced we may have been, but what a fine group of young men I found myself among! Every one of us was an overseas veteran, and we had our share of decorated heroes from the navy, army and air force, with all ranks represented, from corporal to air force squadron leader. Because we shared that common background, our whole class got along famously. Six weeks of instruction passed quickly, and we were returned to our respective police stations to begin our duties as highly trained police constables.

This brief period of formal training is in stark contrast to the almost year-long period of in-school instruction that the police recruits of today must undergo, but there is no doubt that, short as our training course was, it made us much more confident of the law of the land and knowledgeable about how we could participate in the administration of it. This newfound confidence was due in part to the lectures we received with regard to our powers of arrest – what, in fact, we could do and not do.

My first shift assignment, when I got back to the station, was as driver to the patrol sergeant. A patrol sergeant is referred to as the "first line supervisor," and holds the rank immediately above that of constable. I didn't care much for this assignment, because even after my short and limited service, I had identified this particular sergeant as an ass-kisser who would sacrifice anyone to further his career. In police circles, as in other professions, people of this persuasion are not uncommon, but some are more readily identifiable than others. These are the ones who, because of their rank and their contempt for those who stand below them in the hierarchy, believe they can openly display their discreditable actions to those who are junior in rank without any fear of retaliation or condemnation.

My personal evaluation of this sergeant proved to be accurate. Later that afternoon we received information over the radio that a soldier who had been drinking in the Gladstone Hotel was armed with an automatic firearm and had threatened some of the waiters. The soldier was reported to have left the hotel and to be walking west on Queen Street. We were instructed to use extreme caution. I was driving east on Queen, and as I approached Dufferin, I observed a slightly intoxicated, slovenly dressed soldier. Soldiers were a common sight at any time of the day or night; the war was just over and the nearby Exhibition grounds were being used as a military depot, housing thousands of them awaiting discharge.

But this particular soldier attracted my attention mainly because of his less than soldierly appearance. When I pointed him out, the sergeant immediately ordered me to turn left and stop on Florence Street. He told me to get out of the car. He would take over, he said, and drive around the block in order to approach this suspected armed man from the rear. I stepped onto Queen Street, facing east. I could see the slightly staggering soldier rapidly approaching me. I glanced back at the street – no sign of my fearless leader! When the soldier realized I was walking toward him, he stopped and proceeded to throw at me a long string of obscenities that included a more than cursory reflection on my war service, or lack of it. When he slid his hand inside his battle-dress blouse, I leapt on him, knocking him to the pavement. He fought furiously, and it was only after a vicious exchange of punches and a roll over on the sidewalk and roadway that I was able to subdue and disarm him of a fully loaded German P.38 pistol, which he had in the waistband of his trousers. Quite a crowd of civilians had gathered by this time, gawking at me kneeling on the soldier's chest and holding the pistol in my hand. Before long, the crowd started to get noisy; then they began shouting for me to let him go, or they would take him from me. It was only with the support of two waiters from the Gladstone Hotel, who had followed the soldier, that I was able to hold my prisoner until my absent sergeant finally arrived at the scene. We put the prisoner into the car and took him to our nearby station.

At the police station, I experienced for the first time something that I was to see over and over again. It happened to me and to other young officers: a young policeman makes a good arrest only to have the credit and accompanying glory stolen by sly, experienced veterans. I am sorry to say that my later adventures would show me that some of the worst offenders were detectives.

When we arrived, the inspector was present, and he and the other old boys lost no time in congratulating the sergeant, shaking his hand and commending his bravery. As for me, I was directed to go into the guard room and bring my memo book up to date. While I was doing this, I could hear the newspaper reporters arrive. They were out there taking the sergeant's photograph while he proudly displayed the seized weapon. When the newspapers appeared the next day, there were front-page pictures of the sergeant and the firearm, but only one article made the slightest mention that the hero sergeant had been accompanied by a rookie constable.

I never forgot this injustice, and the fact that it was subscribed to by the inspector made it that much worse. The memory has always made me careful not to let anyone give me credit for the efforts and successes of other officers; and because of the many checks and balances introduced in recent years, I'm happy to say that it is now almost impossible for an arresting officer to be deprived of the credit he deserves.

ONE NIGHT IN LATE AUGUST I was on the midnight-to-8:00 a.m. relief, and I was instructed by the parading sergeant to spend some time in the vicinity of the Edgewater Hotel, at Queen and Roncesvalles, when that watering hole closed at midnight. I was to keep the drunks moving and not allow them to congregate in front of the hotel and create a disturbance.

I arrived at the hotel shortly after midnight, and it wasn't long before I observed two soldiers, who had obviously had too much to drink, making a nuisance of themselves to a young woman who was at the streetcar stop, waiting for an eastbound King car. I approached the two soldiers and ordered them to leave the lady alone. They then turned their attention to me, and called me a coward and a zombie, and asked what I was doing when the war was on. Without further ado the shorter of the two threw a punch at me. His fist struck my cheekbone; I felt a sudden sharp pain, and I staggered. My helmet flew off my head, and the other soldier gleefully kicked it out onto the roadway. They were both laughing now, and as I grappled with the soldier who had struck me, the other one jumped on my back, knocking me to the pavement. What frightened me most was their heavy army boots: I had served long enough in the army to see hundreds of fights, and knew full well how boots were used to kick a fallen opponent senseless. In sheer desperation, I rolled against the hotel wall – in that position, there was only one direction from which the blows could come. The circling spectators were all on my assailants' side, which was usual when a serviceman was in a fight with the civilian police.

The thought flashed through my mind that I was done for, but at that very instant my old friend, the sixty-year-old English TTC inspector, suddenly came charging through the crowd, shouting and swinging his metal-clad time book, and with him came a middle-aged TTC motorman who promptly struck one of the soldiers in the face with his closed fist. The soldier started to scream as he saw the blood streaming from his nose. The crowd quickly began to thin out. The fight was over.

Two police cars arrived shortly after, and my assailants were bundled off to the station in one, and my TTC saviours and I in the other. By the time we reached the station, my right eye was swollen and had begun to discolour, and my whole body felt as if it had been pulled through a washing machine wringer.

The military police arrived and took custody of the two soldiers. All the police officers present thanked the TTC men for their timely intervention, and they were returned to the car barns at Roncesvalles and Queen. The sergeant asked me if I wanted to book off duty and go home, but I said no, because I knew my early arrival home and my slightly less than perfect appearance would only alarm my parents unnecessarily, so I returned to the beat. Thankfully, it was night and my black eye did not cause any comments from citizens. But when I arrived home the next morning, my mother took one look at my beat-up appearance and begged me to quit the force.

I HAD BEEN ASSIGNED TO one, two and three beat, which was a long walk and a large area of responsibility; the patrol was both sides of Queen, from Dovercourt on the east to Roncesvalles on the west. I had to check all the properties on both sides of this long stretch and inspect the rear of the buildings as well. One particular night I felt I had religiously performed my duty, and when I reported off at 8:00 a.m. I was tired. After taking the long streetcar ride home to my parents' house, and soaking my aching feet, I demolished the poached eggs and toast that my mother had prepared for my breakfast and fell into bed, where sleep instantly overtook me.

After what seemed only moments I was awakened by my mother, who informed me that the station was on the phone. I jumped out of bed and raced downstairs. A sergeant ordered me to get into my uniform and return to the station. The inspector, he said, wanted to see me immediately. Despite my mother's protests, I dressed and hurried back to the station. On my arrival I was paraded before the inspector and the desk sergeant. The inspector read off my assigned duties from my last shift and inquired, in a hostile manner, whether I had in fact inspected all of my properties as I was required to do. I replied, "Yes, sir, fronts and backs."

Quickly jumping on my statement he asked, "Then how come you failed to find a broken window in a service garage situated right next to this police station?"

I was speechless. I distinctly remembered checking the doors and windows of the building and taking special care just because it *was* next to the station. Seeing my confusion, the inspector told the sergeant to take me to the gas station and show me what they were talking about. It was a small, levered window, about eight feet off the ground, that opened into a washroom. It was so small that even a large cat would have found it almost impossible to enter through that window. When we got back to the inspector's office, I was informed that as a penalty I would be deprived of my weekly day off for the next month, and that if such carelessness happened again, I would be dismissed from the force.

When I arrived home again, suffering from sleep deprivation and absolutely exhausted, I told my mother what had happened and what they had done to me. My dear mother reverted to the language of the Glasgow slums to express her feelings. After a ten-minute tirade against the "Canadian bastards," she again begged me to quit and find another job. I assured her that things could only get better and went off to bed, where I was asleep again within seconds.

AROUND THE MIDDLE OF SEPTEMBER 1945, I was working the four-to-midnight shift, and I was walking the Dundas Street beat near Sorauren Avenue when, at about 8:00 p.m., I observed a passenger in a passing taxicab throw a bottle from the cab window. The bottle smashed to pieces when it hit the pavement. The taxi was eastbound on Dundas and I promptly commandeered a passing auto, stood on the running board and ordered the surprised motorist to follow the cab. We were able to catch up to the stopped cab at Dovercourt. As I approached the car, the taxi driver jumped out, shouting, "Don't blame me, officer, my two passengers are crazy."

I yanked open the back door of the taxi. Two slightly inebriated, very tough-looking guys were sitting there, both smiling. I shut the door, got into the front seat and ordered the cab driver to take us to Number 6 Police Station. During the ride, the two passengers kept begging for a break, offering to sweep up the broken glass if I would only return them to the scene. I refused and told them to save their pleas for the desk sergeant. At the station, I took them in through the rear door to the booking area to wait for the sergeant. When he and the station duty operator appeared, the sight of my prisoners seemed to give them quite a shock. They both turned pale, and the elderly station operator actually began to quake and shiver.

The sergeant drew me outside the booking room and in an incredulous voice asked, "Do you know who those two *are*, constable?"

"No," I replied, "but I do know they threw a whisky bottle from the window of a moving cab. Surely they should be charged with something."

Dropping his voice to a whisper, the sergeant told me that they were members of the notorious Polka Dot gang. In fact, the big guy with the broken nose was the leader of the gang, one Kenneth "Budger" Green. Their photographs (the sergeant further informed me) were in every police station guard room in the city, with instructions that any officer approaching these men should be very cautious and never attempt to deal with them alone. It usually took six to eight police officers to bring in Kenny Green. But to-night, for some reason, he had let one skinny rookie cop bring him and one of his pals in without a fight. What was more, I had been sitting in the front seat of the cab, with my back to them the whole time, and all they had done was beg for a break for smashing a bottle on the roadway! Ignorance is certainly bliss.

After a reprimand by the sergeant, Green and his associate were released. As they left, they gave me a hearty handshake and bid me, "So long, see you around, copper!" The Lord was watching over me on that particular occasion, because for some reason the two hoodlums had decided to treat the whole episode as a joke rather than as an occasion to pound the stuffing out of someone.

On October 31, 1945, shortly after nine o'clock in the evening – on Hallowe'en, in fact – several hundred youths, male and female, started a series of bonfires on the streetcar tracks near Queen Street and Hammersmith. They were joined in their Hallowe'en exuberance by several soldiers and sailors. Within a short time, the destructive mood of the mob escalated. Nearby wooden fences were torn down to feed the rapidly enlarging fires, and store windows were broken. Frightened storekeepers telephoned the police and fire department, who were quickly on the scene.

The firefighters set to work to extinguish the major bonfires, but the mob continually obstructed and then began to assault them. Police reinforcements were hurriedly called to help establish some control over the rioting youths. During the half-hour confrontation that ensued, thirteen of the more vocal and resisting youths were arrested on charges of obstructing police. They were transported to Number 10 Police Station, at the corner of Main Street and Swanwick Avenue. The crowd, which now numbered about 2,500 shouting and screaming male and female teenagers, decided to march in a body to the police station and rescue their thirteen associates.

When word of this threat reached the inspector of the station, he notified the acting chief at home. Apprised of the potential seriousness of the situation, John Chisholm, the acting chief, issued a "riot call" to all twelve of the city's police stations.

When the call reached Number 6 Station, I and three other officers were speedily transported to Number 10, which by this time was already under attack by the uncontrolled mob. When we got there, we had to draw our batons and literally beat a path through the crowd in order to reach the front steps of the station. Two high-velocity fire hoses, manned by firefighters and police officers, directed steady streams of ice-cold water at the hundreds of noisy and violent youths. Without the hoses they would not have been able to prevent the mob from storming the undermanned police station. A constant rain of rocks, stones and other missiles hurled by persons in the enraged crowd pelted the police and firefighters. Whenever one of these objects struck one of the defenders, a loud cheer would ring out from the mob.

Inspector Charles Greenwood was the man in charge at the scene. With quiet, cool courage, he commanded like the veteran officer he was. Several firefighters and police officers had been injured by the unrelenting projectiles, and were bleeding profusely from head and face wounds. Yet Inspector Greenwood, undaunted, calmly formed us into a phalanx three deep. We then managed to form a cordon on the front and north sides of the police building. I was in the front line of the cordon and I could hear the windows being smashed in the station house behind us and in the fire hall, which was next door.

The mob was pressing very close to our thinly manned ranks. Suddenly a young man took hold of my uniform belt, which held my holster and firearm, and tried to pull it from my body. It was only after I was able to manoeuvre myself into a position where I could strike him several blows with my baton that he released his grip on my gun belt. (The following day, this youth's mother complained of police brutality, and I was ordered to submit a report concerning my actions.)

More police reinforcements arrived, and with continued help from the fire hoses, we gradually drove the crowd back across the street. They eventually dispersed, still shouting and screaming, and walked north and south on Main Street. Although the most serious part of the confrontation only lasted for about forty minutes, it seemed to us, who were being pelted with rocks and stones, to have lasted for hours.

A dozen firefighters and police officers received injuries that required hospital treatment, and frankly, it was a miracle that there were not more and worse injuries. Many of us had cuts and bruises, of course, but we didn't feel they were serious enough to warrant attention at the very busy East General Hospital. This was my first experience of working shoulder to shoulder with firefighters in a dangerous situation and I have been an admirer of their courage and dedication ever since.

GRADUALLY, AS THE MONTHS PASSED, I became more proficient at the job of being a policeman. Of course, like many others before me and many more after, I made mistakes that were embarrassing not only to me personally, but to the police force as well. But if I made serious errors in judgement from time to time, I think I can honestly claim that I had the wisdom to learn from them.

I also did some things right. It wasn't long before I had a reputation at the summons issuing office for the neatness and accuracy of my printing on my parking tags and traffic summons applications. I received several commendations for this from police headquarters, and from my own divisional inspector, and I believe – in fact, I have been told – that it was because of this minor achievement, together with a few arrests I made for a variety of offences ranging from auto theft to robbery and assault, that I came to the attention of the Traffic Division commander. On March 17, 1946, I was transferred to the Traffic Division on Strachan Avenue. This was a step up in the world, and with it my days of walking the beat came to an end.

Like most ambitious young men, I was eager to put the first stage of my career behind me and move on to the next. With cocky pride, I figured I had paid my dues. I didn't know then that the long adventure had only just begun.

CHAPTER FOUR

Motorcycle Cop

T HERE ARE LOTS OF KINDS *of robbers, but in general, they fall into two cat-egories: sneaky and flamboyant. Before he ran into the men who would make up his notorious gang, Edwin Alonzo Boyd was basically a lone ban-dit. Though he was used to dodging whizzing bullets, he kept his business to himself. Later, though, things changed. With the help of his henchmen Lennie Jackson, Willy Jackson, Steve Suchan and Norman Boyd, Edwin be-came famous as the leader of a gang with fearless style. He and his boys broke into banks dramatically and athletically, specializing in a flying leap that got Boyd up onto the counter with his gun trained on bank staff, while the rest of the gang raided the cash.*

The story of the Boyd gang — their heists, their countless tricks, their escapes — filled newspaper pages for months. The cold-blooded shooting of Sergeant of Detectives Ed Tong on College Street, where he was left mor-tally wounded, added an element of cruelty to the legend.

Jack Webster was still in the early days of his life as a policeman, and had no personal involvement in the investigation. His sole connection with the investigation leading to the arrest and trial of Edwin Boyd was as one of the uniformed police constables assigned to guard him while he was locked up in the court's holding cells during his trial. His actual contact with Boyd was brief, but it was memorable, and it afforded Webster an op-portunity to reflect on the irony of life, because guarding Edwin Alonzo, Jr., was not the first time he'd found himself in the presence of this family.

Some years before, when he was just starting out as a cop in the sum-mer and fall of 1945, Webster had met a veteran police constable, Edwin

Boyd, Sr. The older man took a liking to this young colleague at Number 6 Police Station and insisted on giving Webster a ride home whenever they were on shift together, even though it took Boyd Sr. out of his way.

The older officer was a religious man, and driving through the deserted streets at the end of a long shift, he was given to counting his blessings, chief among which was his son, Edwin Jr. Proudly, he told Webster how his kid had been overseas serving in the army since the beginning of the war.

Edwin, his English war bride and their young child were living in the father's house. Boyd Sr. told me his son had secured a position as a streetcar motorman for the TTC.

During the trial, Edwin Jr. showed none of his father's willingness to chat with Webster, but eventually, after several days of guard duty, Webster found he could speak to him freely enough to admit having known his father, and to tell the son of the older man's kindness. Unable to contain his sense of sorrow, Webster told the younger Boyd how proud of him Officer Boyd had always been.

The bank robber responded wryly that his father had every reason to be proud of him now. There wasn't a paper in Canada that didn't have his name and picture on the front page.

The comment was tragically ironic at the time, but perhaps Boyd Sr. was not ultimately disappointed. For Edwin Jr. paid his debt. He served twelve years, got parole, and disappeared back into the life of an ordinary, law-abiding citizen. It began to be thought that the gang that bore his name might in   reality have been more actively led by one or two of the other members. His flamboyance, like the flamboyance of many another bank robber, may have been only a phase ...

IT WAS 1946, AND I had never operated a motorcycle before. On my first reporting day, I was joined by two other young prospective traffic officers who shared my ignorance. Of course, we optimistically expected to begin our motorcycle training immediately, but instead, we three were assigned the task of washing the windows of the entire Traffic Division, which contained hundreds of them. This building was situated at Ordnance Street and Strachan Avenue, and also contained the entire repair facilities for the police motorized fleet. The traffic unit was an elite and prestigious section of the force. In later years – most notably the fifties and sixties, when there was a rapid expansion – there would be a decline in the energy and efficiency of the division, but in my day, an officer had to prove himself worthy of the duties of attending at car accidents and all the other difficult skills necessary to the motorcycle cop.

Still, washing windows was insulting work, and after two days of it we confronted the sergeant and informed him that if we were not going to receive our motorcycle training at once, we wanted to be transferred back to our divisions. This rather arrogant ultimatum proved to be successful. Right after lunch that same day, we were individually taken out on the city streets by a veteran officer. We travelled sitting in the sidecar, until our less than enthusiastic instructor found a quiet, unobstructed street to begin our instruction.

After two days, we were deemed ready to go out alone, though not on solo machines, since it was March and the roads in many places were still snow-covered and icy. With a sidecar-equipped machine, which was easier to balance, we were able to survive the next few weeks. By the time May rolled around, we considered ourselves veteran motorcycle traffic officers.

Unlike the sleek modern machines young traffic officers ride today, with their push-button ignition and automatic gear shift, our Harley-Davidson overhead valve machines had a kick-starter, a foot clutch, and a manual gear shift. It was a tremendous thrill to be a motorcycle police officer. Sitting amid thousands of moving motor vehicles, you felt a sense of tremendous power when speeding motorists saw you and quickly slowed down to an acceptable level. You were almost a hero to children, who would surround you and your machine whenever you stopped and dismounted. I suppose one of the drawbacks was that there always seemed to be a smell of gasoline and oil fumes, especially after you arrived home upon completion of a shift.

I thoroughly enjoyed my traffic experience, mainly because, not being confined to the beat, I was no longer restricted to a small area. Now I had the opportunity to explore three or more divisions and to seek lawbreakers of all kinds, a task I approached with great enthusiasm – most of the time.

One occasion that I particularly remember was at a major fire on Commissioners Street, not far from the waterfront at Cherry. About nine o'clock that night, I was assigned the traffic point at Lakeshore and Cherry Street, and my job was to reroute the eastbound Lakeshore traffic north onto Cherry. It was a cold night, and I was less than happy with this duty. When I had been at it about an hour, a car travelling at a high rate of speed failed to obey my pointed directions, emphasized by my red-lensed flashlight.

Instead of turning, as I expected, the vehicle headed directly towards me. I was able to jump to one side, but with less than a second to spare. The driver flew over the curb onto a patch of roadside mud, then abruptly turned north on Cherry Street and sped away.

I ran to my machine, shouting to the sergeant, who was sitting in a nearby police vehicle, to take over my post. It took me only a matter of seconds, after kick-starting my motorcycle, to reach speeds of forty, fifty, sixty and then seventy miles per hour. I caught up with him on Eastern Avenue, where I was able to force him to stop, and remove his car keys from the ignition. A concerned motorist stopped and I asked him to call Number 4 Police Station, at Parliament and Dundas, to request a car and tow truck.

A scout car soon arrived and transported the obviously inebriated driver and his rather frightened female companion to the station. I waited for the police tow truck to arrive, and after giving the necessary details to the driver for the towing of the car to our central police garage on Strachan Avenue, I proceeded to Number 4 Station to charge the driver with dangerous driving, if not drunk driving. When I arrived I found the arrested driver weeping and pleading with the desk sergeant to release his female companion. We agreed to do so, and she left the station in a taxi. The driver was still crying, pathetically attempting to bribe the desk sergeant and me.

We managed to get him booked on the driving charge, then lodged him in the cells. In those days, long before the present-day Bail Reform Act, an arrested person would be held in custody at the station until his court appearance the following morning. Patrol wagons, or what people commonly refer to as paddy wagons, would make pick-up calls at the various stations early in the morning, and transport the arrested persons to the "bull pen" at City Hall for a ten o'clock appearance before a magistrate. The bull pen was a large holding area (as opposed to individual cells), and bedlam reigned there on any given morning prior to the court sitting. (The police station cells of today are little more than temporary detention facilities, meant to hold accused persons for a period of an hour or two, until the usually very busy desk sergeant is compelled to release them as directed by the Bail Reform Act. The amount of recognizance required for bail varies according to the seriousness of the charge and the person's reputation and standing in the community.)

While I was contemplating the necessary paperwork for our weeping detainee concerning the details of his offence, the desk sergeant received a telephone call from the sergeant at the police garage, who reported that the recently arrived vehicle had been searched by garage employees, and that when they opened the trunk, they found a sea of ten-cent pieces. Besides loose dimes, there were bags and socks just filled with them. I informed the detective office, then headed out to the central garage. By the time I got there, they were already removing the hoard of money to an upstairs office. After several hours of counting by night-shift constables under the watchful eye of a traffic sergeant, it was revealed that the total amounted to over $7,000. Seventy thousand dimes!

The accused was questioned by investigating detectives, who learned that he held a supervisory position with a major department store. Soft drink machines were then a new phenomenon, and techniques for the proper accounting and control of the deposited ten-cent pieces were not yet perfected. The department store's machines were emptied under the supervision of the accused, who would take possession of the money and secretly skim off the top for himself. His present problem was compounded by the fact that he was a married man, and his lady friend that evening was a fellow employee. They were out for a sneak celebration of a recent promotion the thieving supervisor had received.

This is just one example of the many such cases I encountered during my career as a uniformed police officer. A motor vehicle would be stopped for a simple offence, such as "no rear tail light" or a "dirty licence marker," and other illegal activities, trivial or serious, would come to light. Most young police officers learn early in their careers that such routine matters can lead to major criminal apprehension – as well as to considerable danger!

AT THE SOUTHEAST CORNER OF Bay and Queen streets, there was a restaurant called Bowles Lunch. It was one of a chain of old established restaurants, where one could obtain plain, wholesome food at reasonable prices, cafeteria-style, without frills of any kind. The counter help, dishwashers, and table cleaners were usually alcoholics, or former alcoholics, and in general were mostly unfortunates at the lower level of the employment scale.

The Bowles employees, who were always friendly and easy to converse with, welcomed uniformed police officers, including motorcycle cops, to partake of a free cup of coffee, a piece of pie, or even a bowl of their hot, nourishing soup. One spring evening I was sitting in the basement staff dining area, having a coffee and a piece of pie, when I observed one employee sitting eating by himself. He was not talking to anyone, and his looks and general appearance set him apart from the others. He had a hint of suntan on his face, which was unusual for that time of year; his light-coloured hair was neatly combed and his moustache was well trimmed. By his appearance, he might have been a recently discharged serviceman, as thousands of us were, but it puzzled me that he would be working at this type of employment, with this rag-tag bunch of co-workers.

I engaged him in small talk, asking him if he had been in the army. He said yes, he had – for a short time. He had been an artillery man and had lost the hearing in one ear as a result of a training accident, and for that reason, he claimed, he had been discharged early in the war. When I inquired about his tan, he said he had recently been working in the tobacco fields at Delhi, Ontario, and it was probably more of a wind burn.

Something about this man intrigued me. But whatever it was, it was not suspicion of any sort of criminality. I finished my coffee, said goodbye to the staff, and resumed my motorcycle patrol.

About two months later, I was sitting on my motorcycle at the southeast corner of Bloor and Spadina when my mysterious friend from Bowles Lunch walked up to me, and said, "Hello, officer, remember me?" I of course recognized him immediately, and asked him if he was still working at Bowles Lunch. No, he said, he had quit shortly after our meeting and was now teaching tennis at the exclusive Granite Club. He certainly looked the part, wearing white running shoes, white pants, and sport shirt. During our brief but friendly conversation, he told me that he had just finished visiting his girlfriend, who worked in the drugstore on the north side of Bloor, just east of Spadina. After a few more minutes of small talk, I said goodbye and continued on my patrol.

About two weeks after this meeting, I was working the day shift and was eating my lunch in old Number 5 Police Station, which was then situated at Belmont and Bay streets. At that time, every police station guard room had posted Royal Canadian Mounted Police bulletins, which showed names and photographs of escaped German military prisoners of war who were still at large. I was casually leafing through this bulletin, when I was startled to see the face of my new-found friend, the dishwasher from Bowles Lunch. Along with his photograph was his name, Wolfgang Friedlander. He had been a major in Field Marshal Rommel's Afrika Corps!

With astonishment, I read how he had been at large for some months, having escaped from a prisoner of war camp in western Canada. The bulletin warned that caution must be used in the event of his recapture, because he had a brilliant mind and would use his above-average intelligence to escape again. I immediately left my lunch and very quickly drove my motorcycle to the Granite Club on St. Clair Avenue. (It has since been relocated to a beautiful setting on Bayview Avenue.) I inquired at the reception desk where I might find the tennis instructor. The attendant informed me that they were without a tennis professional because the previous teacher had resigned two weeks before. The Granite Club's office records were not available, and they were unaware of his new employer.

I then raced to the drugstore on Bloor Street at Spadina, where he had told me his girlfriend worked. I went into the store (in full uniform), and inquired of the two young ladies on duty which one was the friend of the young tennis instructor. I explained that I was a friend of his and wanted to contact him for some private lessons that he had promised me.

One of the pretty young ladies excitedly said, "He's my boyfriend, but he just moved out of Toronto and is now the tennis professional at the Seignory Club, near Hull, Quebec." (This beautiful resort is now known as the Hotel Montebello.) I thanked her and said I would telephone him and make some arrangements about my tennis lessons. Trying to act nonchalant, I strolled out of the store, then leaped on my motorcycle and raced to the RCMP headquarters, which was then located on Sullivan Street.

I spoke to an RCMP inspector and imparted all the information I had about the escaped prisoner of war. The inspector told me that they would have their Ottawa detachment attend at the Seignory Club immediately, to effect the arrest. I was also told that I would be informed of the results. I left my home and office telephone numbers with the Mounties.

When I arrived home at my parents' house at about five o'clock that afternoon, my mother told me a staff sergeant had called, and I was to telephone him as soon as possible. I did so, and learned that his Ottawa detachment had missed the escaped prisoner by less than an hour. The wanted man had fled in such haste that he left behind most of his clothing, including his tennis shoes.

I have no doubt that his innocent girlfriend had either telephoned him, or he had telephoned her, and she had informed him that his policeman friend was looking for him. That, of course, would be enough of a tip-off for him to take flight immediately.

I never saw him again, nor did I hear anything further concerning his whereabouts until, about ten years ago, I was reading a magazine (which is no longer published), the weekend coloured supplement of the *Toronto Star*. There he was, in a feature story on escaped German prisoners of war, and especially the ones who had been recaptured and returned to their homeland after the war, but had returned to Canada as landed immigrants. The point of the article was to show how well several of these ex-prisoners had done in their adopted country – many of them succeeding handsomely in a variety of businesses and occupations.

But the most interesting item to me was the photograph of my old friend, Wolfgang Friedlander. I saw a smiling, distinguished-looking man, who (using an assumed name) had climbed the corporate ladder to become a senior executive in one of Canada's largest lumber and paper corporations, with headquarters in British Columbia. Then he had decided that he should declare his true identity to the other executives of the company, and get a fresh start. He hoped that his record of good citizenship and the influence of the large corporation he worked for would persuade the Canadian government to permit him to stay in Canada. His further advancement in the higher echelons of the corporation was assured, and I suppose he felt that he should make a public acknowledgement of his past before someone else did, so that supporters of his would not suffer embarrassment.

I never heard the results of this highly publicized request for citizenship, but I do recall that the magazine article finished with the statement that the Department of Immigration had ordered that he must return to Germany and make application from there. To this day I don't know what happened to Major Friedlander, but if he or any of his friends should read of the events I have related here, I'd like to remind them that I knew this high-powered business executive when he was a dishwasher in a beanery known as Bowles Lunch!

AS MOST TORONTONIANS OF THE older generation will recall, there used to be several cruise ships operating out of the Port of Toronto. The crew members of these ships were all members of the very militant Seamen's Union. They were on strike in July 1946, and when the steamship companies began bringing in non-union replacement crews for the ships, the strike became violent.

It was at the height of the holiday season, and the companies were determined that two of their ships would depart from the Toronto docks as scheduled on a Saturday. In anticipation of the trouble that we feared would result, the entire Traffic Division was assigned to duty at the steamship docks. We were lined up three feet apart on Queen's Quay in front of the dock entrances, to prevent any rush by the strikers and their many supporters to invade the pier areas and possibly to damage the ships.

About one o'clock in the afternoon there was a sudden charge of about two hundred seamen, and several of them were successful in getting over the fences. I apprehended one of the invaders and while a police inspector was attempting to put handcuffs on his wrists, I was standing up with the struggling man's ankles under my armpits. As he violently attempted to pull free of my grip, I was momentarily pulled off balance and my right foot was lifted off the ground. At that very second, a *Toronto Star* newspaper photographer snapped a picture of the action.

The photograph was on the front page of all editions the following Monday, and in this case the camera lied. In the picture I seem to be about to kick the striker in the groin. My number, which was 27, was clearly visible on my right shoulder. Of course, the labour organization made much of it. They distributed thousands of pamphlets showing the photo, under the caption THIS IS HOW TORONTO COPS TREAT THE WORKERS. People remembered the photograph for a long time, and for many months I had to endure being called a dirty bastard every time someone noticed my shoulder number and remembered the false picture.

DURING THE YEARS THAT I spent on motorcycle duty I was able to make a continuous series of significant arrests. Most police officers will tell you that in order to be successful in apprehending criminals you need three qualities: energy, constant alertness, and luck. I often seemed to be blessed with all three. There was one thirty-day period in which I arrested a man for armed robbery, nabbed a young person on thirty-odd charges of purse snatching and theft, and apprehended a well-dressed businessman on several charges of indecent exposure. The latter had plagued the area of a nurses' residence, terrorizing the young women for some time. (These arrests were all in addition to my regular traffic enforcement and accident investigation duties.)

During this same thirty-day period, I was standing at the corner of Queen and Yonge at about two-thirty one afternoon when I was approached by an excited citizen, who informed me that a man had just entered a theatre on Queen Street, a little east of Yonge. The man was wanted, I was told, on numerous fraud charges. My informant operated a jewellery store in the area and claimed to have been one of the fraud victims; he cautioned me that the wanted man was an escape artist who on several previous sightings had eluded all efforts at apprehension.

Armed with this information, I entered the theatre with the jeweller and spoke to the manager. I instructed the manager to give me two minutes to go into the theatre's rear exit door, then turn up the house lights. The victimized jeweller would then begin to walk slowly down the aisles, looking at faces. My ruse worked. Seconds after the lights were turned on, the wanted man bolted out of the back exit, right into my arms. He was subsequently charged with fraud offences perpetrated all over Canada and the United States.

The police department recognized my numerous arrests during these months by awarding me a merit mark, which came with three months' promotion toward my next rank. That meant that my required two years as a second-class constable would now be two years less three months. I would attain the rank of first-class constable, and the raise in pay that went with it, that much sooner.

THE CASE OF THE JEWELLER in the movie theatre could not have come at a more opportune time. I was planning to get married, and the grateful jeweller sold me the engagement and wedding rings that are still in my wife's possession forty-four years later. I got them wholesale!

For some unknown reason, I had always believed that the girl I would marry would be a redhead who wore glasses, and in the spring of 1947, I was fortunate enough to be introduced to a lovely auburn-haired girl, who (you guessed it) was wearing glasses. The introduction took place at a hastily convened party to which I and two other young police officers had been invited. I attended without a female companion, and the beautiful redhead of my dreams was escorted by one of my police buddies.

To say that I was smitten by this girl would be an understatement. My pursuit of her was relentless, and when I learned where she was employed, I haunted the area in the hope that I would get a glimpse of her, and if I was really lucky, a chance meeting.

Although my lovesick actions could almost be described as "watching and besetting," they proved successful. I finally did meet her, accidentally on purpose, during her lunch hour on busy Bay Street. She was my girl from that moment on, and we were married in October of that same year. Our small but beautiful wedding was attended by many of my police friends, but (you guessed right again) the policeman buddy from whom I had stolen my bride was noticeable by his absence.

In the forty-four years of our marriage, my long-suffering wife, Marion, was in fact a police officer without a badge. She endured the impossible hours, the dangers, the threats, even the smell of death that sometimes permeates a homicide investigator's clothing. She coped with the worry that every police officer's wife knows. She did all this without complaint, and with very little reward.

WE YOUNG MOTORCYCLE OFFICERS WOULD sometimes be assigned temporary duty on the accident-investigation cars while the regular, and in most cases senior, constables were ill or absent on leave. One bright, sunny spring day in March 1947 I was assigned car duty with another young constable. I was only casually acquainted with him, but I knew he was an energetic go-getter who sometimes got into trouble for being overzealous in the performance of his duties.

In those days, there would be three two-man accident cars on patrol for the day relief. One car would be designated for the downtown area, one for the east end, and one – which on this May day was ours – for the western part of the city. We were assigned to personal injury accident investigation, and at about ten o'clock that morning we were slowly patrolling the High Park area when our police radio crackled with the information that a hold-up had occurred at the Purity Dairy, on Dundas Street in the neighbourhood known as the Junction. We duly noted the description of the two wanted men, while the dispatcher informed us that both were armed and dangerous, and that all officers should exercise extreme caution. A few minutes after this report, the dispatcher advised all west-end units that one of the robbery suspects was being chased by plainclothesmen in the cattle-pen area of the stockyards, at Keele Street and St. Clair Avenue.

My partner and I joined the chase. With our siren wailing we tore through the streets, soon arriving in the area of St. Clair and Ryding Avenue, where we immediately saw a good deal of police activity. We parked our vehicle and commenced a search of the dozens of cattle pens on foot. The smell of manure that I remembered from the Toronto streets of my boyhood was a far cry from the barnyard atmosphere my partner and I were now wading through! We were a little distressed to see what the mud and cattle droppings were doing to our shiny boots and leggings, but we walked on, carefully looking into every nook and cranny that could conceal a man. We hadn't been on the search very long when I stood on one of the cattle-pen fence rails and peered over the fence; as I did so, I could see into the backyard of a house on Ryding Avenue. In the yard was a police inspector in full uniform, with his hands up in the air. In front of the inspector was a man with his back toward me. He was pointing a nickel-plated revolver at the officer. I can still remember how the bright spring sunshine reflected off the weapon.

Unobtrusively, I was able to draw my partner's attention to what was going on, and we both slowly and silently climbed over the fence. We snuck up behind the gunman, holding our breath. By the time he heard our approach and started to turn, I was close enough to touch him and in that instant I leapt on his back and pinned his arms to his sides. My partner twisted his wrist, and the revolver fell to the ground. With the aid of the much-relieved inspector, we handcuffed the struggling gunman, as other officers arrived on the scene. He was transported to the police station, where my partner and I basked in the congratulations that were showered upon us for our good work.

But all that ended with the arrival of the police inspector, whose skin we figured we had saved. He gave us supreme hell for endangering his life by jumping on the gunman's back – an action, he pointed out, which might well have caused the gun to go off. His thinking was probably correct, but when you are young and eager, the quickest, most immediately effective approach is the most appealing one.

The second hold-up man was arrested later that day in a rooming house on Spadina Avenue, by headquarters detectives. He and his accomplice were tried in county court on several armed robbery charges, and sentenced to a term of twelve years in Kingston Penitentiary.

After the trial my partner and I were summoned to headquarters one morning, and there, in the presence of our inspector, we were congratulated by the chief constable and the deputy chief constable. (It would be quite a few years before this "chief constable" designation would be discontinued and replaced by today's title of chief of police.) The chief told us that he was recommending us to the Board of Police Commissioners for the Medal of Honour. This medal was seldom awarded and would have been a highly prized and valued tribute, but our inspector had another idea. He suggested to the chief that as both my partner and I were still only second-class constables, with time to go to achieve the rank of first class with its accompanying raise in pay, it might be financially better for us (who were both making marriage plans) if we received merit marks with some months of promotion toward our next rank, instead of the medal. The wisdom of this appealed to both of us.

When the chief presented the circumstances of our arrest to the board, they awarded us a merit mark with an accompanying unheard-of *twelve months'* promotion toward our next classification. This automatically brought us to the top constable rank of first class. We were highly gratified by the award, and the newspapers made a big play of it, with stories and photographs of our alleged heroism, and it was not until some years later that I found out that the board could have awarded us the Medal of Honour *and* a certain number of months' promotion toward the next rank as well.

I sometimes feel cheated when I think that, but for this well-intentioned but incorrect advice, I might have had that Medal of Honour, but I still managed to receive more meritorious service awards, with their accompanying months of promotion, than any other officer in the history of the

Toronto and the Metropolitan Toronto Police Force, so perhaps I can afford to be generous with the mistakes of others. (It was a very great honour for me, on my retirement, to be awarded the Medal of Merit by the Board of Police Commissioners. This is also a seldom awarded decoration.)

AFTER MY MARRIAGE IN OCTOBER 1947, my life looked wonderful. I had a beautiful young wife, a steady and most interesting job, and many years of future glorious happenings on the way. This worry-free period of our lives came to an abrupt end on a Saturday evening at the beginning of July 1948. I was directing traffic at the Sunnyside Amusement Park in the Parkdale area. About 6:30 p.m., I was approached by a veteran accident squad officer, who informed me that I was wanted at the office of my Traffic Division. I was about to get on my motorcycle when he told me to leave the bike and get in the car. At that moment, I knew something was wrong with my family. I was not able to think what it might be, except that my father, who was only sixty, might possibly have been struck by some sudden illness.

On arriving at the second floor of our traffic unit, I was surprised to see my inspector there, wearing shorts and a T-shirt. He was not on duty but had casually dropped in at the station, and thus happened to be present when a call was received from the Ontario Provincial Police detachment at Bracebridge. The inspector told me to sit down. "Do you have a brother named James Peter Webster?" he asked. I replied, "Yes," but before he could tell me the rest, I already knew that my brother, Jim, was dead. In shock, I listened to the brief, grim details. He had been drowned at a summer resort in Muskoka, where he had been spending a long summer weekend with his wife. In the difficult hours that followed, while my family grieved, I learned the full circumstances of my brother's death: he had died assisting two non-swimmers to safety. It was a tragic end for a fine twenty-seven-year-old man, the eldest in our family, and a joy to everyone who knew him. As my mother used to say, "It's the good who die young."

It was an almost unbearably sad taxi trip that my wife and I, accompanied by Jim's sister-in-law, took to the town of Bracebridge to make official identification of Jim's body, and to return his shocked widow to Toronto. It was a tragic period of my life, and the life of my young wife, that we have never forgotten.

After my brother's funeral, my father lost all desire to live and was unable to attend to his business. My mother asked me if I could get a leave of absence from the force and take over, at least until my father could regain his will to continue with life and its responsibilties. I applied for a three-month leave of absence without pay. In those days, there was no provision for such an arrangement as there is today, and my application was refused. However, the deputy chief constable, on the recommendation of the training inspector, Edward C. Dunn, gave me a letter stating that if I resigned from the force to attend to my family's business problems, I could make application to rejoin when matters were straightened out, and the application would be given favourable consideration. There were two conditions: I must re-apply before my twenty-ninth birthday, and I must pass the medical examination.

It was a sorrowful day for me when, in July 1948, I tendered my resignation to the Toronto City police department and took over the running of my father's company. I had no interest whatsoever in the trucking business, but I felt I had a duty to my parents, and I was determined to do the best job I could in my new position. Then, when the situation appeared to be reasonably resolved, I would rejoin the police.

It was hard work, with staff and mechanical problems arising every day. We were operating seven trucks, and most of them were badly in need of replacement. I drove a truck and worked twelve hours a day, plus weekends, until we were able to purchase four brand-new vehicles, at considerable initial cost, with the inevitable monthly payments. Although my father no longer took an active part in the management of the business, he put in many late hours and weekends doing minor repairs, and occasionally filling in for an absent driver.

With the long hours, increasing insurance costs, and less than reliable employees, my wife and my mother both felt it would be far better to sell the business and try some other line of endeavour, and after twenty months of operation, I did so. The business, with its reasonably new equipment, was bought by a large Toronto cartage operation. The sale included trucks, contracts, goodwill, and the name of J. Webster Cartage Company, which my father had used for so many years.

The morning after the sale was finalized I presented myself at Toronto Police Headquarters, armed with the letter that I had received regarding favourable consideration, and applied to rejoin the force.

This was on April 19, 1950, and as luck would have it, the inspector in charge of the training school was Edward Dunn himself (who had written the letter of recommendation), and he welcomed me back. The medical officer was examining new recruits that very morning, and I was sent to the Toronto General Hospital for a chest X-ray, then presented to the police doctor for examination. After the strenuous physical work I had been doing for the past several months, my body was as hard as a rock, and the doctor

Jack, holding his baby daughter, Rosemary (aged six months), 1950, now Rosemary Vodrey, a Conservative MPP in the Manitoba Legislative Assembly.

told me there was not an ounce of fat on my entire frame. This did not surprise me, because at nearly six feet, one inch tall, I weighed only 165 pounds.

I passed the medical examination with flying colours and was taken personally by Inspector Dunn to the basement of headquarters, where the clothing and equipment stores were located. After being supplied with a second-hand motorcycle uniform, leather coat and leggings, and a .32 calibre firearm, I was escorted to the chief's office on the ground floor, and asked to wait outside while the inspector spoke privately with the chief. About three minutes later, I was called into the large, high-ceilinged room, and asked to take the Bible in my right hand. For the second time in my life I was sworn in as a constable on the Toronto Police Force.

The chief told me he had reviewed my previous record and that it was a fine one, and he welcomed me back. He then told me to work hard, live a good family life and some day I might be sitting in the chief's chair. I thanked him for his kind words of welcome, but in my heart I knew, from past experience, that the remarks about eventually reaching the position of chief of police were part of a ritual that most recruits went through. Nevertheless, I was more than happy with my reception, especially when the training inspector told me that it would not be necessary for me to undergo recruit training again; I was to report in uniform to my old Traffic Division on Strachan Avenue, that very afternoon, to parade for the 3:45 p.m. relief. It was now 1:30 p.m., and I had to rush home to my house in the High Park area to wash and dress and prepare myself for a return to police duties.

It was like Old Home Week at the Traffic Division, with most of my previous comrades still there. I received the warmest welcome from them. There were also many new faces at the division, but enough of my old friends, both sergeants and constables, were there to smooth my re-entry.

At 3:45 p.m., I was paraded with the rest of the relief, and much to my surprise, I was assigned a solo motorcycle and detailed for the busy traffic point at Dupont and Davenport. It was a somewhat shaky Constable Jack Webster who rode his motorcycle out of the Strachan Avenue garage that day, but after several blocks of careful driving, I found that the old motorcycle operating skills came flooding back. The most important of these skills is to remember to lean your body when making a turn. Within minutes, I was leaning and the Harley was responding in the old familiar way. By the time I had finished my first shift, it was hard to recall ever having been away.

CHAPTER FIVE

Accident Investigator

S HORTLY AFTER HE BECAME A *detective, Webster had to shoot himself out of trouble. The incident proved to him that if no man is a prophet in his own country, the opposite applies to cops, who get no respect outside their own territory.*

It started when Webster and his partner were assigned an arrest warrant for a man charged with stealing his employer's truck and converting company funds to his own use. There was nothing particularly special about this duty, except that the man named in the warrant was an out-of-towner.

In the fifties, there was nowhere near the traffic up to the country north of Toronto as there is now. For one thing, it took a couple of hours to get to Barrie, a trip that today can be done in forty-five minutes under ideal conditions. The length of time it used to take, plus the fact that there was just a lot less city to Toronto than there is now, meant that Webster and his partner had a long way to go through foreign – rural – territory between the familiar city streets and the tiny community on the outskirts of Barrie where the wanted man lived.

When they pulled off the main road, they suddenly found themselves in a village as isolated, and as hostile, as any they might have imagined existed in places like Kentucky or Tennessee. There was only one thing they knew for sure about this place, and it was that strangers were about as welcome as snakes, tornadoes and unemployment, which had also been known to visit the area.

Webster and his partner, dressed as usual in their impeccable suits, sensed they were in trouble the moment they arrived at the clutter of homemade shacks and abandoned car wrecks that made up the village. It was about six-thirty on an evening in early spring, and, granted, the country air was sweeter than what they'd left behind in Toronto, but that was all that was sweet.

The two detectives couldn't help but notice the dress of the residents when they stopped to ask the whereabouts of the man they were after. And as city cops, of course, they stood out like sore thumbs. Fashion isn't the primary concern of the farmer; self-preservation is. Almost immediately, everyone in town was aware that outsiders were asking questions. Within minutes, Webster and his partner found themselves completely encircled by an ever-growing crowd of shouting, taunting people.

The circle got quickly larger and the space in the centre where the two detectives were trapped got smaller. It didn't take either of them long to realize that their country brothers were armed. A spiky halo of bats and pieces of steel pipe rose above the circle of angry villagers.

One thing a police partnership gets good at over the years is unspoken communication. The glance of an eye, the slight tip of chin, the almost invisible rise of brow. A cop's life can depend on a little movement like that. Without anyone else seeing or understanding the signal that had passed between them, Webster and his partner simultaneously drew their firearms and fired two warning shots into the air.

The stunned crowd ceased its advance at once. The detectives took advantage of the resulting silence to warn the ringleaders that the first person who resorted to actual violence could expect to be shot.

Nobody moved, but nobody backed down either. Then, in a moment of face-saving drama, a man stepped forward. The crowd fell back as he declared that he didn't want anybody to get hurt because of him. He was the one they wanted, and he was turning himself in. True to his word, the man went along without a struggle, but Webster and his partner weren't taking any chances. Backing up, step by step, they kept both the prisoner and the crowd covered as they inched their way toward where they had parked the car. It was only after they'd got the man into the car that Webster saw that one of their tires had been slashed completely flat, the wheel resting on its rim.

Without hesitation, Webster swung into the driver's seat, manipulating the damaged vehicle as best he could while his partner covered the mob with his revolver. They hobbled along over three miles of rough terrain before they felt secure enough to stop. At that point, they got their prisoner out of the car and kept a close eye on him as he changed the tire before the three of them set off for the safety of the city.

Years later, Webster remembered two things about this "hillbilly" experience. That it was funny. That it was utterly terrifying.

IT WAS 1950. AS THE city of Toronto grew, the number of accident cars increased along with it, and it wasn't very long before I was assigned almost full time to one of these bright yellow vehicles. Our mandate was to investigate motor vehicle accidents whenever personal injury was involved. With thousands of automobiles and commercial vehicles constantly on the roadways and thoroughfares, we were always busy.

During my three years of accident car assignments, I had the experience of investigating many fatal motor vehicle occurrences, and have seen, time and time again, the carnage and human misery caused by drivers who drink alcohol and then operate a motor vehicle. One that I can never forget was the case of a young father of two little girls, who took his daughters along while he visited his brother. He and his brother began by having a few sociable drinks, which led to more and more, until the brother fell asleep, and the twenty-seven-year-old father put his two children into his car and commenced to drive home. He had travelled only about four blocks when he failed to observe a stop sign at a busy intersection and struck another vehicle. The impact tore his door open and he was thrown from the car onto the busy highway, where he was run over by another vehicle, whose driver had swerved desperately trying to avoid the original collision. When my partner and I arrived on the scene, we found the two uninjured children, screaming hysterically and cradling their dead father's head in their arms. If this experience has stayed with me, what must it have done to those two children?

OUR ASSIGNED ACCIDENT INVESTIGATIONS OCCUPIED so much of our time that patrol for possible criminal apprehension was often out of the question. Yet any veteran police officer will tell you that a police constable who has wide exposure to investigations of accidents and the hundreds of other types of traffic violation often finds that, in the process, he is becoming a first-class criminal investigating detective. The very fact that he is continually dealing with all levels of the court system puts him in a position to gain an advantage over police officers without such experience. One becomes very proficient in report writing and develops an expertise in the gathering and preservation of evidence.

I believe that, in my own case, the career path that took me into the detective department in early January 1953 was the direct result of a near-fatal fail-to-remain accident that I investigated in December of 1952.

The accident involved an eighty-four-year-old lady who was knocked down and badly injured by a hit-and-run driver. Upon examination of the victim's clothing, I determined that the tire tread markings on her dark cloth coat criss-crossed in a way that indicated she was struck twice by a vehicle first backing up then proceeding forward and running over her a second time. Observing the amount of snow and other debris near where the victim was found, I had a strong hunch that the motorist might have been unaware that he had struck the woman. This reasoning was not subscribed to by my superior. Yet when a lengthy report containing evidence that supported my theory was submitted to the Centre of Forensic Sciences, and they considered it along with careful examination of the clothing, they agreed with me.

My next step was to check a nearby automobile repair shop for all vehicles that could have left the premises on the evening of the accident. After tracing and checking several cars and questioning their drivers, I took possession of one automobile and had it taken to the forensic centre for expert examination. I wasn't surprised to learn that on examining the underside of the vehicle, the centre found hairs and fibres that could be traced to the victim.

I went back to the driver and questioned him for hours. I was convinced that he was unaware that he had inadvertently hit her when he was backing up out of a laneway adjoining the repair garage. The Crown attorney nevertheless decided to lay a charge of fail-to-remain against the driver, but his court appearance was brief: the presiding magistrate agreed with my original findings and the charge was dismissed.

I was glad I had stuck to my guns on this one, because my written reports and stubborn investigation of the case came to the attention of a newly appointed headquarters inspector by the name of Adolphus J. Payne. He was a well-publicized member of the Criminal Investigation Branch, who had achieved country-wide fame and the stature of a hero for his investigation of the Boyd gang and arrest of Edwin Alonzo Boyd.

Payne recommended me to the chief of detectives to fill a vacancy on the auto theft squad, at headquarters. After being interviewed by senior detective personnel, I was made an acting detective on January 15, 1953. This indicated not a rank, but an appointment, which meant that I would remain a plainclothes police constable for as long as it took to prove myself. If I did well, I would at some future date be promoted to the rank of detective, and to earn that much-sought-after and prestigious rank, I was certainly willing to put in my time as an "acting."

As it turned out, I would remain an acting detective until January of 1957, a period of four years. But I was lucky. Some of my fellow officers had been "acting" for seven and eight years. In any event, my appointment to the Criminal Investigation Branch was the first step into the area of policing that was to claim me for decades to come.

I was twenty-nine years old, with a total of six years of police experience. In police circles, this rapid rise was considered phenomenal, and I had to endure plenty of winks and nudges, implying that I must have known people in high places to get so far so fast. These suspicions were wrong. I loved my job, and I did it as well as I could. Anyone who does the same nowadays will find that those two principles are just as effective today as they were then in assisting advancement in one's chosen profession.

My first assigned partner in the detective office was a handsome, forty-year-old, university-educated bachelor. He held the rank of sergeant of detectives, and had been a naval officer during the war. At the time I was assigned to work with him, he had had sixteen years of police service. Sergeant of detectives was a very high rank in the Criminal Investigation Branch, one step below that of an inspector. There were some who felt that the rank of inspector was one step below God!

Two police officers who work as a team over a lengthy period of time usually become closer than brothers. Sharing dangers, trials and tribulations creates a bond of respect and affection that lasts for a lifetime. I was fortunate in that throughout my career I was always partnered with first-class people. They were not only top-notch police officers; they also showed dedication and incredible courage.

In the close-knit world of the detective office, it did not take me long to learn that my partner, though respected, was not considered to be a first-class investigator. But he had other attributes that set him apart from most of the others. His commanding appearance was a definite asset: he was, as I have said, very handsome, over six feet tall and an immaculate dresser. I don't remember ever seeing him, on duty or off, without a business suit, white shirt and tie, and fedora hat.

I worked over four years with this officer, and I learned from him many important lessons that would stay with me for the rest of my career as a member of the Criminal Investigation Branch. One of these was: always dress well, and when you are on duty, always act and speak in a manner that will be respected by the general public. This tends to bring about a level of co-operation that can only be helpful in whatever investigation you may be conducting. Another important thing is never to lose your sense of humour. I was fortunate in this regard, because I always have had a better than average ability to see the humorous side of things, and that has stood me in good stead during many difficult and trying times.

As a detective, I was attached to the auto theft squad, a very busy unit, working three shifts out of headquarters – days, afternoons and nights.

Because our main area of responsibility was stolen cars and other vehicles obtained by false pretences, we were continually travelling out of town to bring back thieves who had been arrested far from Toronto. Thus, as early as during the first twelve months of my detective service, I had occasion to visit most of the major cities in Canada and to work with police officers of many municipalities. These personal associations were very valuable to a working police officer and they soon grew into a national network. When an investigation arose in which a contact was needed in a particular city – Montreal, Winnipeg, Vancouver or any other – I could pick up the phone and talk to just the man I needed, in the assurance that the inquiry would be handled with dispatch and in a thorough and professional manner. The same out-of-town contacts remained with me throughout my career in many cases, and I was pleased, as the years went by, to see them reaching high ranks in their respective forces.

In my many years on the force, I have only been involved in two actual gunfights, but in several situations I found it necessary, sometimes in company with a partner, to draw and even discharge my gun in order to get out of a set of particularly dangerous and volatile circumstances. The story of one such occasion is told at the head of this chapter, but it was not the only dangerous situation in which my partner and I found ourselves during the years 1953 through 1956, and either by ourselves or in the company of other officers we participated in the arrest of hundreds of criminals for just about every offence named in the Criminal Code of Canada. Ever vigilant, the press seemed almost another partner sometimes, because many of these arrests were high-profile occurrences that made their way to the front pages. Nor were the radio people slackers. It wasn't long before I had gained a certain public recognition and respect (or notoriety!) as a result of my name continually appearing in the newspapers and on radio newscasts.

In the summer of 1954, there was an armed hold-up of an employee of a finance company in the west end of Toronto. The wanted man had been dressed in what was thought to be a police uniform. He had shown up at the office of the financial institution one morning, slightly in advance of the time when a local police officer normally arrived to escort the employee to a nearby bank with a routine deposit. After questioning this person a little, the bookkeeper was satisfied and she accompanied the culprit out of the building.

As soon as they hit the street, the man drew his revolver, threatened the young woman with death and grabbed the satchel, which contained several thousand dollars in cash. There was a car ready and waiting at the curbside, with motor running and a driver at the wheel. Clutching the money bag, the hold-up man jumped into the front passenger seat of the automobile and it sped off. Despite being frightened and in a state of shock, the female employee had the presence of mind to observe the first two digits of the licence number and the colour and make of the getaway car.

When my partner and I reported for duty that day at the 3:45 p.m. relief, we read the latest teletype information about the major occurrences of the previous twenty-four hours, including the details of this robbery. Naturally, we were interested in the description of the getaway car, and as members of the auto squad, who had continuous dealings with the auto rental agencies in the city from our investigations, we knew that the two licence-plate digits identified by the victim were the beginning numbers of a series owned by a large car-rental firm. Not only that, but the entire fleet of this particular rental company was the same make as the getaway car!

My partner and I agreed that we should get down to the main office of the rental firm, which was located at Dundas and Yonge, in the heart of town. Because we were in almost daily contact with the rental agencies, we knew the rental employees well and they were happy to help.

The manager assisted us in checking the rental records for the previous day. We noticed one in particular: the renter had identified himself by name, and stated that he was an employee of a very large security agency, with a business address in Toronto. We knew that the security guards employed by this company wore a navy blue uniform not unlike an official police uniform.

We took possession of the rental records, and requested that the clerks stall any person returning the vehicle in question, and get in touch with us at once should anything develop. I have often found that when you have to enlist the aid of a civilian in an investigation, he or she becomes very professional – especially when you impart some secret or confidential aspect of the case. They become part of the chase, and many times they prove to be more valuable to you, the investigator, than some police officers.

When we got back to headquarters, we had a civilian clerk telephone the security company and ask to speak with the person named in the rental agreement. We felt that even if he was a legitimate guard posted to a satellite assignment elsewhere in the city, we could get his location by using the pretence of an urgent family problem. Our inquirer was informed that the employee had reported sick the previous evening and was probably at home. His address was readily supplied to our clerk.

We lost no time in driving to the house, which we found to be a rooming house with a number of tenants. When we asked to see our suspect, we were told he'd moved out the previous day and left no forwarding address! Further questioning of the landlady revealed that the wanted man did have a very close friend who was a police officer on a suburban police force, in the same municipality as the financial institution that had suffered the robbery. Immediately sensing that we were on to a conspiracy beyond a single bank job by our robber, we got back to headquarters to seek additional manpower to mount what might have turned out to be a lengthy investigation.

Back at our office, we informed Inspector Adolphus Payne and his partner, Kenneth Craven, of our findings and suspicions. Payne was a shrewd and capable investigator, who to this day is considered by many knowledgeable people to be the finest detective Canada has ever produced. (After many years of acquaintance with the gentleman, I fully subscribe to that opinion.) He readily agreed that our leads should be followed. It was now approaching midnight, so Payne and Craven, who were working the night shift, took over the investigation. My partner and I would rejoin them at eight o'clock the following morning.

When we reported for duty the next day, we learned that Payne and Craven had worked hard during the night, and had three men under arrest for robbery and conspiracy. The questioning and subsequent arrest of the security guard had led to the arrest of a police officer of the small municipality where the hold-up had taken place, and of a second security guard who was the actual hold-up man. Our investigation continued all that day, and it soon developed that the disgraced police officer had been a close friend and fellow countryman of the two security guards. He had acted as money escort for the financial institution on many occasions, and that had given him the idea for the robbery, which ended in failure. The result: all three received terms in Kingston Penitentiary.

There was a further sad commentary to this case. After lengthy questioning of all three arrested men, we were informed that the money obtained from the robbery was buried out of town. One of the robbers took us to the hiding place, which was in a cemetery. The money was recovered from a hole that had been dug on top of the grave of the infant child of the escorting robber. When we made no attempt to hide the anger we felt at the desecration of a child's grave, he told us that it was his idea, and that he had been sure no one would suspect the hiding place. A callous and desperate man.

In 1955, there was an epidemic of car thefts in which only 1955 Chevrolet automobiles were being stolen. The disturbing part of these motor vehicle thefts was that none of the automobiles were being recovered. This strongly suggested the operation of a car theft ring.

It had to be presumed that the stolen vehicles were being relicensed, with the aid of forged bills of sale, and then sold. My partner, a veteran auto theft investigator, suggested that it was possible that the motor vehicle identification plates, which were installed on the fire wall of this particular type of car, were being stolen from other 1955 Chevrolet vehicles and re-attached to the fire walls of the stolen vehicles. A slightly less than honest car dealer, possibly of the used-car variety, could then easily forge new, false documents.

Unknown to most automobile owners, their vehicles have two identification numbers. One is on the plate attached usually to the fire wall, which is quite visible when the hood is raised. The other is a secret number, the location of which is known only to the auto manufacturer. It's usually located in a hidden but permanent part of the vehicle's structure, such as the chassis, axle, or wheel disc. The location of this hidden number can be disclosed only to bona fide police agencies to assist them in theft investigations.

We started at the Ontario Department of Highways, where, with the assistance of employees in the vehicle registration department, we made thousands of checks of motor vehicles and sales involving 1955 Chevrolet cars. Thirty recent registrations of such vehicles showed up. We then visited General Motors in Oshawa, Ontario, and consulted with some of their top production people, who supplied us with the location of the hidden numbers of all 1955 Chevrolets. They were very co-operative – they also told us about a numbered code on the fire wall, which indicated the original colour of the vehicle when it left the factory.

Armed with this valuable information, we began visiting the homes of the thirty recently registered owners of 1955 Chevrolet cars, who had purchased the almost new vehicles as re-sales. At first we restricted our vehicle checks to registered owners in the Metropolitan Toronto area. Our modus operandi was to request the co-operation of the new owners and have them attend at the central police garage, where, in a specially designated area, we would have the garage foreman (who was sworn to secrecy) put the vehicles up on a hoist and remove the necessary part to reveal the hidden serial numbers. We would then compare this number with the number on the fire wall plate.

After ten such examinations had disclosed identical hidden and fire wall numbers in every case, we were disappointed and began to feel we might be on the wrong track. It was only when the eleventh vehicle was examined that we struck pay dirt. The two numbers were completely at variance.

The owner of the car had purchased it from a small north Toronto used-car lot. We visited the Department of Highways again, where we took possession of a photocopy of the vehicle registration papers and the bill of sale. It was then a simple matter to go to the used-car lot, question the owners and seize their records on a warrant.

Our investigation was concluded with the arrest of the two car lot owners. We also traced and took into custody some twenty 1955 Chevrolet automobiles from the surprised and profoundly annoyed owners. These seizures were made in Ottawa and Windsor, as well as To-ronto. Since the vehicles were stolen property, they had to be held in po-lice custody until the lengthy court proceedings were completed. The hold-ing of the vehicles was further complicated by a dispute as to their legal ownership. Did they belong to innocent new owners, or to the various in-surance companies who had already paid off the original owners for the thefts?

Besides these problems, out-of-town vehicles had to be stored in the police garages in Ottawa and Windsor. Because the trial was a long and in-volved one, with many witnesses subpoenaed from all over the province, the automobiles were becoming older with each passing month, and the in-surance companies took civil action in the courts to retrieve them.

The interesting part of this is that the writs sued the mayors and chiefs of police of Ottawa and Windsor, as well as the mayor and chief of police in Toronto. My partner and I were not named anywhere in the court action, al-though we were responsible for the entire episode.

Needless to say, the telephone lines between Ottawa, Windsor and To-ronto were burning with not too many compliments for the two of us, al-though at the conclusion of the very lengthy trial, we were highly commended by the presiding judge for our thorough investigation and me-ticulous preparation of the case. This certainly took some of the heat off us, especially from our own chief constable, who called us down to his office, and after adding his own congratulations for a job well done, informed us that at no time was he ever worried about the several-thousand-dollar law-suit against him as a result of our actions. We learned later that this was not true, because he had been contacting the chief of detectives on a twice-daily basis, asking for progress reports.

As a footnote to all of this, it is worth mentioning that for all the motor vehicles that had their fire wall identification plates stolen, not one owner had noticed. Perhaps we should all check from time to time – when having an oil change or washer refill, for example – just to make sure the vehicle identification plate is still there.

IT'S A FACT THAT CARS and crime often go together. As a result, the auto theft squad was often involved in major crime investigations. One such occurred in 1955, when a bank at the corner of Dundas and McCaul streets was held up by three men. During the getaway, there was a gunfight between senior bank employees and the hold-up men, and a bank teller was shot and fatally wounded. At first it was unclear whether the bullet that killed the teller had been fired by one of the bandits, or if in the heat of the melee the bank manager had accidentally shot his fellow employee. Subsequent ballistic testing indicated that the fatal shot was fired from the manager's revolver.

The hold-up men made good their escape, although blood at the scene – other than the poor teller's – indicated that one or more of them had been wounded. Alarms were issued to all police personnel to use caution when attempting to apprehend these individuals, who were described as armed and dangerous. Fortunately, the licence number and description of the getaway car had been obtained by a bank employee.

Later that same afternoon, my partner and I observed the wanted vehicle parked on Dovercourt Road. We radioed a call for assistance and began a search of the neighbourhood, canvassing nearby homes. It wasn't long before dozens of uniformed and plainclothes police officers were on the scene, and this included the chief of detectives and senior personnel from headquarters.

One of the canvassing officers, speaking with a lady in a house near the abandoned car, was told that yes, she had observed a man park the vehicle and leave the car, and he had appeared to be hurt. She had watched him enter a house, which she pointed out.

With this important information, our investigation moved into high gear, and a plan was devised. Four detectives would enter the house, with firearms ready to shoot at the slightest sign of resistance. Because it was broad daylight, we assumed that most of the police activities would be under observation from inside the house involved.

I was selected to be one of the raiding officers, and on this occasion I was partnered with a fine veteran, Detective Frank O'Driscoll. Our planned approach was to cross the lawns of the neighbouring houses, get onto the veranda, and kick in the front door to create an element of shock and surprise.

Our entrance went beautifully. As we stepped over the broken door, Frank O'Driscoll shouted to a woman in the hallway on the ground floor, "Where is he?" The woman pointed upstairs, and Frank and I bolted up the narrow staircase, fully prepared for a gunfight. When we reached the second-floor landing, with two of our associates immediately behind us, we headed for the front room while the others took to the rear.

Frank and I burst into the front bedroom, ready to shoot if necessary, and found a man lying on a bed clad only in his shorts. He had been bleeding profusely from a neck wound, and although we recovered a loaded revolver nearby, he offered no resistance, saying, "Don't shoot, fellas, I'm done for."

Other officers entered the room, and we managed to get the suspect on his feet. Although he was weak from loss of blood, he walked with our assistance. We handcuffed him, and he was taken to hospital for treatment of his wound, which proved to be not life-threatening, needing only a few stitches.

The other two bandits were still at large. A massive dragnet was set in motion throughout the city, with raids conducted by dozens of detectives at known criminal hangouts. Within two days, they were both apprehended in separate incidents. Neither man offered any resistance to heavily armed officers. All three eventually appeared at trial, and after each pleaded guilty to the charge of armed robbery, they were all sentenced to lengthy penitentiary terms.

MY REGULAR PARTNER AND I were of similar build, and both over six feet tall. That, plus the fact that we both took pains to be at all times well dressed, earned us a certain renown and popularity with the various police station desk sergeants and station duty people. Most of the time, we were good-humoured and willing to share a laugh or two with our uniformed associates in the twelve uniform divisions that made up the Toronto City Police Force. On night relief, after 1:30 or 2:00 a.m., when the city was asleep and calls for our attention at a standstill, we would make a point of visiting at least two different stations every night, and have a coffee and a little fun with our divisional comrades.

Being attached to headquarters, we were expected to possess little tidbits of secret information that had not filtered down to the field divisions. There was no real truth to this, but in order not to disappoint them we would sometimes make up stories about future promotions and proposed retirements in the ranks of the top brass. This nearly always satisfied our gossip-hungry friends who, after our departure from their station, would fill the long and idle night hours by discussing our erroneous information among themselves and on the internal telephone lines to other stations. Their calls were usually prefaced by, "Don't ask who told me, but this, or that, is about to happen, so keep it under your hat." Very often we would arrive some time later at another station on the other side of the city, and our false information would be confidentially imparted to us, with the admonition "Keep it under your hat." My partner and I became masters at spreading these fabricated stories, and I am sure many unsuspecting officers are still wondering why that reported promotion never took place. Many long-serving and senior members of the force were put off their food by reports of their premature retirement or impending transfer.

We considered all this harmless fun, and I don't believe any real damage was done by our exercises in hoodwinking our colleagues. But we may have overplayed our acting abilities on one particular occasion, when, in answer to a subpoena, we attended at Montreal to give evidence in the trial of a person whom we had arrested in Toronto for an offence committed in Montreal. We took the train from Toronto, then went by taxi to Montreal Police Headquarters, where we were welcomed by old friends on the force.

It is considered good manners in police circles for visiting officers to be appropriately entertained when their official duties and responsibilities have been attended to. There is usually a small party, quickly assembled, with good food, good drink, and friendly conversation between brother officers. On this occasion, our friends informed us that they had arranged for a get-together to be held after court had concluded for the day. They said that the food and drink had already been seen to, and the party would be held in the manager's suite of a downtown hotel.

Court commenced, with a very precise and veteran judge presiding. As my partner and I waited to give evidence, we were both appalled at the demeanour and dress of the Montreal police officers who were in the witness box before us. Some of them were wearing red plaid shirts, some were minus ties, and nearly all slouched or leaned against the sides of the witness box. My partner whispered to me that when our turn came, we should show the Montreal authorities how Toronto police officers presented themselves in a court of law, and he told me to watch him and then do the same when my turn came to testify.

When the court clerk called for my partner, he stood at attention, made a military-like left turn, walked briskly to the aisle, than strode to the front of the court. Upon reaching the witness box, he stopped and bowed from the waist to the surprised judge. He then stepped into the box, took the Bible in his right hand, held it in the air and when the oath was administered answered in a loud, ringing voice, "I do." As he gave his evidence before the packed courtroom, my buddy stood straight and tall, slightly inclined toward the judge, and spoke in a loud, clear, respectful manner. When he stood down, the clerk called for Detective John Webster. I imitated his performance in every particular.

At the conclusion of my evidence I returned to my seat, whereupon the very proper and crusty old French Canadian judge halted further proceedings and announced in accented English, "I hope the last two gentlemen from Toronto will not be embarrassed if I say that it was a pleasure to see and hear you both today. In my twenty-five years on the bench, I have not seen or heard police officers comport themselves so well and give such precise and accurate testimony. It was a pleasure to have you both in my court, and I only wish some of the Montreal officers could do half as well."

My partner and I stood up and bowed to the judge. When we adjourned to the corridor of the courthouse, not one of our Montreal police friends was in sight. Needless to say, the party was off.

The following day the front page of the Montreal newspapers had articles quoting the judge, and the Toronto papers followed up with similar news reports. It was some time before *any* Toronto police officer could attend on business in Montreal and be received as a welcome comrade. But I am happy to say that the incident was eventually forgotten, and I as well as many other Toronto officers have since been in the wonderful city of Montreal and the co-operation and the kind social reception that were extended to us could not have been better. The Montreal City Police was in my day most certainly an excellent force, with many brave and dedicated officers who willingly shared dangers with us in effecting the arrest of various notorious Toronto criminals hiding out in Montreal.

It was high spirits and our sense of humour that led us into that episode. An example of a different kind of difficulty I got into occurred in 1956. My partner and I were working the four-to-midnight shift, and at 11:15 p.m. the duty desk sergeant of detectives handed us a Province of Quebec coroner's warrant for the arrest of a wanted man. The Montreal police had forwarded the address of the man's brother along with the warrant. We were somewhat vexed at being given this assignment a scant forty-five minutes before we should have been reporting off duty, but at least we would have no trouble locating the man.

Cursing our bad luck for being available at this time of night, we reluctantly drove to the address on Wellesley Street East. After identifying ourselves to the man who answered our knock at the door, we were admitted to the premises.

Once we were inside, we asked for the person named in the Quebec warrant. A young man, about twenty years old, who was sitting having a beer at the kitchen table said, "That's me." When we showed him the warrant for his arrest, he said, "I've been expecting it – will you be taking me to Montreal?" I informed him that he would be lodged in one of our police stations, to await the arrival of the Montreal officers, who would escort him back to that city. The wanted man put on his suit jacket and top coat, and told his brother not to worry. We then left the house. Before we got into the police car, I gave our prisoner a quick body frisk, and then we drove to Number 51 Police Station, where we booked the man on the out-of-town warrant. After leaving the necessary documents with the desk sergeant, we returned to headquarters, telephoned the Montreal police and informed them that the wanted man was in custody. We asked them to send the return escort as soon as possible. By the time we booked off duty, it was 2:30 a.m.

The following morning my partner and I both received a telephone call at home from the assistant chief of detectives, who ordered us to report to his   office immediately. Something in the sound of his voice made us think that we should waste no time in presenting ourselves at headquarters. When we were ushered into the assistant chief's office, he demanded to know whether we had searched our Montreal prisoner after his arrest.

I replied that yes, I had searched him before placing him in the police car, with negative results.

"Why is it, then," the assistant chief asked, "that when the arrested man was searched by a station duty constable, prior to being placed in a cell, he was found to be carrying a fully loaded .38 calibre snub-nosed revolver taped to the small of his back?"

This came as an absolute shock to us, and especially to me, because I was the one who had given him the pat-down search. We had to write out lengthy reports for the chief of detectives, detailing the procedure we had taken during the arrest. The assistant chief hinted about possible disciplinary action being taken against both of us. Because I was only an acting detective at this time, I could see the distinct possibility of being returned to uniform duties.

Happily, our punishment was limited to a serious dressing-down by the chief of detectives, who finished his tirade by saying, "I hope this will be a lesson to you both, and especially to you, Webster."

Well, it certainly was a lesson to me. For the rest of my career, I had a reputation of practising absolutely meticulous searches of prisoners and other suspected persons! We were not thought of too kindly by the desk sergeant and his assistant at Number 51 Police Station for a long time. Our moment of inattention or carelessness could have cost them their lives.

Despite this incident, in January 1957 my partner was promoted to the rank of inspector and I finally attained the rank of detective. I was very proud and more than glad to now be able to drop the word "acting" from my title.

My old partner was transferred to another area of the force, and I received a new partner. He was a twenty-eight-year-old six-footer, well built, with dark Irish good looks, by the name of Charlie Gordon.

Charlie had joined the force in January 1951, shortly after his twenty-first birthday. Prior to joining us he had been a milkman, operating a horse and wagon for a large Toronto dairy. Surprisingly, he still moved with the quick, almost shuffling step of an experienced milk salesman. His elevation from uniform patrol and motorcycle duties to the detective office of the prestigious Criminal Investigation Branch, in such a short time, was entirely due to his energetic and brilliant achievements while still a young and comparatively new officer. He was now given my old title of "acting detective," and it was my turn to be the senior partner, with the responsibilities that went with that role.

Acting Detective Charlie Gordon and I were to remain partners for the next four years. We got along famously, and although we did have disagreements, they were quickly resolved. We shared the responsibilities – neither of us acted like the boss – and I believe that was one of the reasons why Charlie and I had a record of arrests over the next few years that has seldom been duplicated.

The first two arrests that Acting Detective Gordon and I made as partners were almost comical. The first was when Charlie spotted an expensive, high-powered automobile being driven by a very young male, with an equally young-looking male passenger. Our suspicions aroused, we followed the car until we finally pulled the driver over on Dundas Street, at Bay.

We ordered the driver and his escort out of the vehicle, and were shocked to find ourselves (both six foot one) completely dwarfed by what turned out to be a six-foot, five-inch fourteen-year-old driver and a six-foot, six-inch, fifteen-year-old passenger. Luckily, they turned out to be docile young boys, who readily admitted to stealing the car from a west-end used-car lot. When we delivered the two giant youngsters to the juvenile shelter, on Jarvis Street, the lone attendant took one look at them and said, "To hell with you guys, take them to a police station." He then slammed the door in our faces. Our two young car thieves spent the rest of the night sitting behind the desk in a nearby police station, with the desk sergeant advising them to join the police force when they reached twenty-one.

The second arrest that Charlie and I made as new partners could have been painful for us, if it had not turned out to be almost like a Charlie Chaplin comedy. It was about nine o'clock at night, and we were patrolling Queen Street near Spadina, when our radio alerted any car in the vicinity of the Paddock Tavern at Queen and Bathurst streets to proceed there as quickly as possible to "assist the P.C." The dispatcher also stated that there was a large fight in progress. We were not surprised to be called upon to attend at a tavern fight, but the fact that a police constable was in trouble electrified us into an immediate response. Because we had been relatively close to the scene, we were the first police unit to arrive. We observed a large crowd outside the Bathurst Street door of the tavern, and Charlie and I pushed our way through the mob and into the lobby of the hotel that housed the pub.

As soon as we entered the lobby, we found ourselves in the middle of what resembled a battleground. There were waiters and patrons lying on the floor, bleeding, holding their heads in their hands. In the centre of the scene was a huge middle-aged man, stripped to the waist, with bulging muscles that would do justice to a professional wrestler. Our police constable comrade, minus his hat and with a torn tunic, was imploring this raging giant to calm down and come along with him quietly. Each time the officer put his hands on the man, he would be pushed away.

Acting Detective Gordon and I now took charge, and we each took hold of one of the giant's wrists. His wrists were so thick that it was almost impossible to get two hands around them. As we did this, the man let out a growling roar, and started lifting Charlie and me right off the floor. We knew we were in deep trouble.

When our feet were lowered to the floor, we both at the same moment struck him in the stomach with our fists (both Charlie and I feel that this was the most powerful punch we have ever thrown). His stomach was as hard as a rock and the impact caused my partner's watch to fly off and break into a dozen pieces. Our victim didn't even blink after receiving these blows, but he said to us with a hurt look in his eyes, in heavily accented English, "Please, I no fight the police. They are good boys, they no steal my money like these bums. Please take me home."

You could hear the sigh of relief from Charlie and me all the way to Queen Street! As we left the hotel with the now quiet hulk walking between us, the crowd, who had not witnessed the events inside the hotel lobby, cheered and clapped their hands. Some of them even slapped us on the back and said, "Boy, are you two cops ever tough. I wouldn't want to mix with you."

We took our prisoner to the local police station and booked him. It turned out that he was a Ukrainian-born brewery worker, who was normally quiet and law-abiding, but who had become incensed when someone stole his money off the beer-soaked table in front of him.

When Charlie Gordon and I returned to headquarters, both still shaking from the ordeal, I said, "Charlie, I think our partnership is going to be fun." And he agreed.

BOTH MY PARTNER AND I made ourselves available at any time of the day or night, on duty or off duty, for the pursuit of criminals. There was no paid overtime for the long hours that we worked and, like many other detectives of that era, we would be wealthy men today if they ever decided to pay us retroactively, even at straight time and at what was then the going rate of pay! It has been said that a detective is only as good as his information, and that is partly true, but there are two other necessary ingredients: energy and dedicated hard work. Detective Gordon and I had more than our share of dedication and energy, so we set about developing a string of informants – or in police parlance, finks.

I suppose there are many ways that a detective can go about developing sources of information, but Charlie and I soon realized that more frequent and accurate information would be received when your "fink" was "hanging on a hook." This is detective's slang, meaning your informer has been arrested on some charge, is now free on bail, and is willing to barter his inside knowledge of criminal activities for a more lenient disposition of his case when he appears in court. The value of services rendered by the informant, of course, depends on the seriousness of the crimes he is able to assist in solving and the effect of those crimes on the public at large. An informant providing inside information on a big case can carry tremendous weight in a police officer's presentation to the Crown. When such an informant requests a reduction in sentence for his own wrongdoings, the court will usually take his valuable assistance into careful consideration. Both the cop and the fink know this well.

As a general rule, all of the pre-trial discussions are held not in open court but in the judge's chambers, with the defence attorney, the Crown attorney, the involved police officers, and of course the judge present.

The judge will decide what degree of amnesty the accused person has earned as a result of the information he or she has provided to the authorities, and how much this information benefited the public at large. Of course, the verbal submissions by the defence and the Crown greatly assist the judge in arriving at his decision. The obvious reason for the secrecy surrounding this perfectly legal manoeuvre is to protect the informant, whose life would, very likely, be forfeit if his co-operation with the police and the Crown became public knowledge.

My experience with persons wanting to exchange "information" for money has not been very rewarding, and I always avoided that type of volunteer informant.

Some of the best information that a working police officer can get, however, is from the "woman scorned," be she wife, lover, girlfriend, or landlady. She is the easiest type of informant to deal with, because in most cases she demands nothing in return but a promise that you will "put that son of a bitch in jail and throw away the key."

We were highly successful in our efforts to develop a string of informants, not only from persons we had arrested, who were still facing criminal charges in the courts, but from people we had previously arrested, whose charges had long since been disposed of. In these latter cases, where the person was no longer "hanging on a hook," they would provide information from time to time because they perceived that my partner and I had treated them fairly and in a humane manner. Whether this was for providing a desperately needed cigarette, a cup of coffee, or a sandwich, or for allowing them several telephone calls to contact relatives or friends, or whatever, it was mostly forgotten by us – but not by the person or persons arrested. Many times a simple kindness would be rewarded with valuable "case-cracking" information many years after the encounter.

For a police officer to achieve success in developing sources of information, he has to do two important things. The first is to treat the informant confidentially and with the utmost fairness. The second is to keep the informant, who is in most cases a criminal (past or present), at arm's length at all times. My partners and I made a point of never associating with them, or in fact treating them like friends. In meeting with them we always documented our arrangements and, if possible, advised a senior officer of our dealings in advance.

These precautions are for the protection of the police officers involved with the informant, because, as one can imagine, not many finks are honest and upright citizens. It is very simple for eager and energetic police officers to be led into a trap, where injury or death may result, or – and this is even more prevalent – where a suspicion of criminal behaviour may be cast upon police officers, in a "set-up."

In my years as a high-ranking police official, I found it necessary to ensure that all my police officers assigned to criminal investigation work identified their sources of information to their inspectors. The inspectors were required to record the informant's identity by a code name and start a file on him or her in which all police contacts were documented. This information was secured by the commanding inspector, and was available only on a need-to-know basis. All this is very important to the officers involved, to prevent double-crosses and accusations of wrongdoing.

IN THE FALL OF 1957 there was a theft of some very valuable paintings from one of Toronto's most exclusive galleries. The articles stolen were valued at about $50,000, perhaps a quarter of a million dollars in today's terms. A special squad of detectives was formed at headquarters, and directed to work full time on the case. Detective Gordon and I were not part of this special team, but about one week after the theft we received a telephone call from an anonymous citizen, who stated that although he did not know us personally, he had a friend who claimed that after being arrested by us, he had been treated fairly. Our unknown informant said that the stolen paintings were impossible to sell because of the newspaper publicity about the theft, and if we wanted them back, we were to go to a certain phone booth on a deserted street, at a specific time. We agreed to do this and arrived at the designated phone booth at the specified time. True to the man's word, the paintings and sketches were jammed into the narrow booth. It was pouring rain, and with the door open, the stolen material would soon be drenched.

Although Charlie and I were both ignorant about paintings and the care needed for their protection and preservation, we decided that we had better remove them from the exposed area they were in. As we stowed them away in the trunk of our police vehicle, we shone a flashlight on the various works of art. Most of them made little sense to us, and I remember we laughed and joked about the reported value of these masterpieces and said we wouldn't pay twenty dollars for the whole lot. As it turned out, we were not alone in our lack of appreciation for these artistic treasures. After receiving the stolen property at headquarters detective office, where it was stored until the following morning, the chief of detectives held a press conference which was widely covered by television and radio, as well as by representatives of the three Toronto daily newspapers. The recovered paintings were on display for examination by the media.

In his statement, the chief of detectives said to all and sundry (in his pronounced Scottish accent), "I know when you look at these things you will think the same as me, and say I wouldn't pay five cents for this pile of garbage."

For connoisseurs of art, it may be interesting to know that this so-called pile of garbage contained at least two original Krieghoff masterpieces. Of course, the news media of the time had a field day with the quote from the chief of detectives, and in response the police force received hundreds of phone calls and letters condemning our lack of appreciation for the finer things in life. The chief of detectives' response to this criticism was a typical, "Fuck 'em."

ONE OF A POLICE OFFICER's best friends on the street is the taxi driver. If I may retrace my steps just a bit and go back to late 1946, when I was on the motorcycle beat, I can give you an example of their much-appreciated assistance. It was an early fall evening and I had stopped my bike at the corner of Jarvis and Dundas. Any person who is acquainted with Toronto, especially in those days, will know that the area centred around Jarvis and Dundas was notorious and could have been called, I suppose, "gangland." There were about eight cheap beer parlours within a two-block area, and these so-called "hotels" catered to the lowest level of prostitute and their ever-present pimps. The dozens of rooming houses catered to these business girls, as they preferred to be called, and rooms were rented over and over again in a twenty-four-hour period.

Jarvis Street was the dividing line between two different police precincts. Old Number 2 Division, which had a 100-year-old station house at Bay and Dundas, was responsible for both sides of Jarvis Street and points west of there to Spadina Avenue. Number 4 Division, with a 115-year-old station house, situated at Parliament and Dundas, had the responsibility of policing everything east of Jarvis, including both sides of the Don River. These two police divisions were the toughest and roughest areas of Toronto. Although I had never been attached to either station, I had the opportunity to patrol both of them on many hundreds of occasions as a wide-roaming motorcycle officer. Officers on foot patrol in the Dundas-Jarvis-Gerrard-Carlton areas normally patrolled in pairs. I can't recall any other area in the city where this was necessary, with the exception of Queen and Bathurst streets, in old Number 3 Division.

To return to my story of helpful taxi drivers – I had alighted from my motorcycle and was about to ring at the police call box, which was on a pole at the southeast corner of Jarvis and Dundas. Before I could do this, a middle-aged lady excitedly informed me that two young girls were being bothered by two obviously intoxicated men around the corner, just east of Jarvis. When I looked around the corner, I saw the two roughly dressed men holding two young girls by the shoulders, shouting that they wanted to get screwed and would pay five dollars each. Both girls were about fourteen years old, and each of them was carrying a pair of roller skates. This was not unusual for the area, because the roller rink was nearby, on Mutual Street. The girls were crying and doing their best to escape the pawing hands of the two individuals who obviously thought that every female any-where near that corner was a prostitute.

I ran thirty feet or so to seize one of the men, and when I shouted, "Let the girls go," the men released the girls and began to threaten me, vowing they would beat me so badly I would be hospitalized for a year. I drew my billy from the back pocket of my uniform and by swinging it in wide arcs, I was able to fend off one of the men, while dragging the other to the police call box on the corner. By this time, a large crowd had gathered and circled us.

It was a hostile crowd of thugs, pimps and prostitutes. Rather than offer any assistance, they were screaming for me to let the man go. It was a touch-and-go situation, because I knew that if I were knocked down, the usual rain of kicks would fall on me, ceasing only when I was unconscious.

Just when I was convinced I was doomed, a man broke through the crowd and yelled at the threatening hoodlums to stand back or they would have to deal with him. They drew back slightly, and this Good Samaritan quickly grabbed the call box key from my pocket, and without any instruction pulled the lever for "an assist the police constable" alarm. He continued to keep the crowd at bay until police vehicles began to arrive from both divisions and took control, making several arrests on charges of obstructing the police.

I charged my two prisoners with assaulting a police officer, obstructing the police, and creating a disturbance. It turned out that both men were steelworkers from the Lakehead district, and had been told by fellow workers at home to go to Jarvis and Dundas if they wanted a woman. The next morning in court they pleaded guilty before Magistrate R.J. Browne and were given sentences of three months each.

It may be of interest to know that my saviour on this occasion was a taxi driver by the name of Sammy Luftspring, one of Canada's finest and most popular boxing champions. Sammy and I have been friends ever since this incident.

The second time a taxi driver saved me from serious injury or even death was in 1957. Detective Gordon and I were on the night shift and, on this particular night, Charlie had a bad case of the flu and had telephoned to the desk sergeant that he would not be reporting for duty. As there was a shortage of personnel on duty that night, it was decided that I would work alone. Shortly after midnight, the sergeant of detectives on duty received a call from the Buffalo, New York, police department. The caller informed the sergeant that a tavern in Buffalo had been held up by four armed and dangerous men. The licence number of the car was given to our duty sergeant. It was now about 12:30 a.m., and as I was leaving to go out on patrol, the sergeant told me to be on the lookout for this car and four men, but not to attempt to approach it alone. I was to keep it under observation and put in a call for assistance. I agreed, and left the building.

I drove west on College to Spadina Avenue and turned south. One block south of College, where vehicles were angle parked (Spadina is a very wide street) I observed a car bearing the New York State licence number of the wanted vehicle. Inside it were four black males. The driver was in the process of backing out of a parking space. I pulled my police car across the back of the wanted car and jumped out with my firearm drawn. I stood back from the driver's door, pointed my gun at him and ordered all four to get out of the car with their arms raised. The four got out very slowly, but did not put their hands up. Even though I had my revolver at the driver's head, all four began to advance on me.

At that time in Toronto, Spadina and College was one of the few areas where blacks congregated. Although it was now about one in the morning, an increasing number of both black and white spectators began to gather, to view what they thought would be a white police officer shooting a black man. I shouted several times to people in the crowd to call the police for help. No one made a move and a few called out, "Fuck you, copper." One of my hostile prisoners shouted to me in a deep southern United States accent that they were going to "take the gun off me and stick it up my ass." I had only a few seconds to decide to shoot, as they continued to advance on me, but the difficulty was that I had not observed any firearms on any of them.

There are difficult times in a police officer's career when he knows that if he makes the wrong move, he will be criticized and possibly face criminal charges as a result of faceless people clamouring for his neck, without knowing or even wanting to know how extremely tense the situation was at the time.

Just as I had decided to fire a warning shot into the air, a taxi roared up and skidded to a stop beside me. The driver jumped out and said in a loud voice, "It's okay, officer, there's about ten police cars coming along College Street." This sudden diversion halted the advance the four hoodlums were making, and they appeared satisfied just to hurl verbal abuse at me. There were no ten cars speeding to the scene, but it gained me enough time for the taxi dispatcher to call the police station for reinforcements, after being alerted by the driver, whose action I know prevented the situation from developing into a no-win proposition for me.

Two police units did arrive shortly and the four suspects were transported to nearby police headquarters. The wanted vehicle was searched, and a large sum of American money and a fully loaded automatic pistol were located in the glove compartment. Within a matter of hours, the suspects had waived their right to deportation or extradition hearings and were returned to the United States by Buffalo detectives.

DURING MY DAYS AS A headquarters detective, I had my first experience in the use of tear gas. It was less than successful.

Detective Alvin Sproule and I were working together for a period of two weeks while our respective partners were on leave. It was about 11:30 p.m., and we were heading back to headquarters at the conclusion of our shift. The police radio sparked with a message that an armed man was firing random shots through the door of a room on the upper floor of a downtown hotel.

We were close to the hotel, which was situated at Bay and Dundas streets (it has since been demolished), and so were the first to arrive on the scene. We entered the lobby, and the terrified hotel employees informed us that a man had barricaded himself in his room on the eighth floor and was periodically firing shots through the door. At one point he had emerged from his room and fired a shot at an employee in the corridor.

While Detective Sproule called for reinforcements, I called the room on the house phone. A man answered, and I identified myself as the hotel manager. I asked him about his bill. He answered me in a foreign language; then, in English, he told me to go to hell.

As other police officers arrived, Detective Sproule volunteered to go along the hallway armed with a machine gun that had been brought to the scene, and kick the door in, while spraying the room with gunfire. (Alvin Sproule was a fearless police officer, with a reputation for bravery. He had been a paratrooper in wartime, with the elite Canadian-American Special Service Force, and had been wounded in the Italian campaign.) His suggestion was vetoed by a detective inspector who arrived at the scene and took charge of the investigation. He was right to forbid us to enter firing, because we had no way of knowing whether the occupant was alone or had an innocent hostage with him.

There was continued gunfire from the room. Periodically, the gunman would emerge into the corridor, where both Alvin and I would fire at him from either end. After one of these gunfire exchanges, the man screamed and re-entered his room. We were sure that one of us had wounded him, but he continued to fire through the door, all the time shouting unintelligible words. Then, a final shot was heard from within the room, followed by complete silence.

Not knowing if this was a ploy, the inspector called for tear gas shells to be brought from headquarters. The large, artillery-shell-like tear gas canisters soon arrived, but it turned out that there was no police officer present who had any experience in their use. The shells were designed to be fired by a short, stubby-barrelled rifle. After much discussion, the inspector ordered a detective to fire the shell through the window of the room, which was accessible from across the open inside courtyard of the hotel. This detective, who was an experienced infantry soldier from the war, took careful aim and fired the canister. It was an accurate shot and went directly through the window into the room.

Within a matter of seconds, smoke was pouring out of the now smashed window, and seeping into the corridor through the bullet-riddled door. The entire hotel, filled with hundreds of guests, had to be evacuated, along with dozens of crying police officers: the gas was so strong and in such quantity that even spectators and firemen in the street were affected.

Detective Sproule and I, accompanied by two other detectives, all wearing Second World War gas masks, entered the smoke-filled room, only to find the gunman dead from a self-inflicted gunshot wound to his stomach. A follow-up investigation of the identity of the dead man revealed him to be a usually quiet, friendly twenty-two-year-old European immigrant, who had become despondent with his new life in Canada.

Our inexperienced tear gas action was responsible for the complete closing of the hotel for a number of days, at great expense, I am sure, to the owners and their insurance companies. Experienced tear gas handlers later explained to the officers involved that a single tear gas bullet, about the size of a .38 calibre shell, would have been sufficient to accomplish our task, and that the canister used was large enough to clear that famous ice hockey arena, Maple Leaf Gardens.

Before this incident it was thought that tear gas was not likely to be needed except by police forces south of the border, or possibly in prisons. Certainly no one thought the police in Toronto, a city that was considered a model of law and order, would ever be called upon to use it. But after this unfortunate demonstration of our lack of preparedness in the use of emergency weapons, the situation changed immediately. Most of us in the Criminal Investigation Branch were sent to the army base at Camp Borden for a one-day crash course in how to use tear gas weapons (and how much to use). In later years, with violence increasing in our community, I had more experience of such situations, but, thankfully, we now have in place a highly trained emergency task force, whose members are expert in the use not only of tear gas and other such weapons, but also of a variety of sophisticated high-powered firearms designed for emergencies.

As YOUNG DETECTIVES IN THE 1950s, Charlie Gordon and I loved our work. The excitement, the challenge of the chase, never knowing what was going to happen next – all this was heady stuff for two young men from poor, working-class Toronto families. I remember one experience, however, which was not an enjoyable one for Detective Gordon.

We were approached by a veteran detective sergeant, Robert Bamlett, who was working on a major investigation of a case of alleged bribery involving a driving-school operator and a driving examiner employed by the Department of Highways. Sergeant Bamlett wanted our help in securing evidence necessary to arrest the driving-school operator. A good way of accomplishing this, he suggested, would be to have Charlie hidden in the trunk of a vehicle, armed with a pen, a flashlight and notepaper. It was hoped that poor Charlie would thus be able to record the offer of money to the Highways employee by the driving-school operator. Bamlett and I would be in a nearby car with binoculars, viewing the money exchange, if any. These arrangements were agreed to by me and a not too enthusiastic Detective Gordon.

It was a cold day in the late fall that the plan was put into operation, and the Department of Highways employee had to keep the motor of the car running. With Charlie curled up in the confined area of the trunk, Bamlett and I watched for any movement that would indicate the passing of money. The two occupants of the car took longer than we had anticipated to arrive at a point where we could move in and make the arrest for attempted bribery. After what seemed to be a long time, we observed a hand movement by the suspect that allowed us to move quickly to the car and seize the money and make the arrest.

We placed the arrested man and the witness in the police car. Then we retrieved the ignition keys, after shutting off the motor. When we opened the trunk, we found an almost unconscious, purple-faced Detective Gordon. We had to assist him out of the trunk, and it was only after long minutes of breathing fresh clean air that he was able to regain his full senses. What had happened was that the vehicle's exhaust system was faulty. Carbon monoxide fumes had crept through the floorboards. In another few minutes or so, Detective Gordon would have probably been beyond revival.

All's well that ends well, and the accused driving-school operator appeared in court. After Charlie Gordon gave his testimony of the notes he had made in the trunk, the man was convicted, and Charlie was highly commended for the unique manner in which he had gathered the necessary evidence. The commendation did not placate Charlie, however. He maintains to this day that Bamlett and I had wandered off for a coffee and forgot all about him as he lay scrunched up in the trunk plying his trade as a headquarters detective.

CHAPTER SIX

The Hold-up Squad

J ACK WEBSTER WOKE UP ON the morning of July 4, 1958, looked out the window, and decided that his partner had picked the perfect day to go to the dentist.

As Webster made his way through the teeming rain, he reflected that Charlie Gordon's dental appointment would probably result in some minor scheduling changes. He was right. When he ducked into headquarters, partially drenched, he found that Charlie was already on duty, partnering Detective Inspector Bolton. Jack was assigned to work with Detective Sergeant Frank O'Driscoll, which was fine with him. As the two patrolled the city, watching a few straggly pedestrians sheltering from the downpour, it seemed almost cozy inside the cruiser.

Suddenly, the two were jolted out of the lethargy of the wet summer day. Over the radio blasted the command for all cars in the area to attend at High Park. A mounted constable was in some kind of trouble.

Splashing through the west end, Webster and O'Driscoll were there in no time. The first thing that caught Webster's eye was his partner, Charlie Gordon, who was already at the scene. Raindrops were skidding off Gordon's hat, falling onto his shoulders, his hands, his shoes. The look on Gordon's face kept Webster from taking the time to ask questions. Quickly he observed the scene. What he saw made him sick.

A number of officers stood around a parked car. At the bottom of one of its doors, a faint trickle of blood mixed with the rain and flowed away into the park. Webster's eyes travelled up toward the window of the car. As a cop, he knew he couldn't touch anything, but he didn't want to anyway. On the front seat, slumped on its right side, lay the body of a man. The body was dressed in ordinary clothes. No hat was visible. Despite the blood that had seeped out of the car, the wound in the man's head had stopped bleeding. He was dead. Beside the man was his gun.

Webster fought hard for control. As he stared at the body, it was as though time had stopped. Scenes from the past flooded his mind, countless scenes in which this man had been the main actor. It was he who had set the tone for the impeccable work of the detectives on the Toronto force, who had reminded them they were professionals, who had hounded them when necessary, who had been everywhere all the time checking on "his" force. Jack wouldn't have been surprised to see this man in the middle of the night finalizing some small detail, but he was shocked beyond reason to see him here now.

Slowly, the words of one of the other attending officers finally reached Webster's conscious mind. "It's the chief," someone was saying. "My God. It's Chief Chisholm. What the hell are we going to do?"

Call headquarters, that's what. It didn't take them long to set things in motion, even though Jack could hardly feel himself move – as if he were standing in the park in February instead of July. Getting the facts clear, he established that the patrolling mounted officer, while checking parked cars in the park, had observed blood trickling from the car. Requesting a citizen to phone for back-up, the officer had briefly inspected the body, which he had no doubt was dead. This constable had not the slightest notion that the corpse was that of one of the most respected chiefs in the history of the Toronto force, John Chisholm. To the headquarters detectives, the chief was familiar, a friend, but the constable who discovered him might only have seen his chief in person once or twice during his entire career.

Almost incapacitated by shock and grief, Detective Gordon and Detective Inspector Bolton took charge of the investigation and reports, while Webster and O'Driscoll took charge of the scene.

Jack worked as fast as possible to cordon off the area of the park surrounding the car, fighting off his own feelings as well as the intrusion of the quickly gathering crowd. It wasn't really that hard to piece together the puzzle of this tragedy. John Chisholm, once the unchallenged head of the Toronto force, had been through hell in the past couple of years.

On January 1, 1957, the police force of the city of Toronto had amalgamated with twelve other police departments from surrounding municipalities to become the Metropolitan Toronto Police Force of today. The job had been a huge one, and it hadn't been done without a great deal of conflict. Everybody had an axe to grind: the public, the politicians, the individual police officers, and especially men like Chisholm, that is, the top brass from

*the integrating forces. It didn't help that the forces ranged in size from To-
ronto, with a strength of about 1,300 sworn personnel, down to Mimico,
which proudly boasted 10 officers, including all ranks. In time, the new
force would have nearly 6,000 sworn officers, but the creation of one out of
so many was no easy task.*

*The power behind the amalgamation rested in Fred "Big Daddy"
Gardiner. There are plenty of people around today who still remember
Metro Toronto's first chairman. He was down-to-earth, gruff, a tough lawyer and a relentless politician. Under him was his friend Charles Bick, the
full-time chairman of the newly formed police commission.*

*At first glance, it would have seemed hard to find a less likely police
commissioner than Charles Bick. By trade, he was an optometrist. He
looked more like a scholar than anything to do with law enforcement, and
his most significant contribution to public life before that had been to serve
as the reeve of the Village of Forest Hill.*

*As soon as he became chair, Bick was appointed a magistrate, a highly
unusual honour for a man who was not a lawyer. The provincial government of the time seemed to think that a person in the top position of such an
influential body should have a title, even though it in no way permitted him
to carry out the duties of the bench.*

*Despite his total lack of police experience, despite the harsh criticism
he received from both inside and outside the force, Charles Bick did the job
he had been chosen to do, and he did it outstandingly. Without him, it is
doubtful the force could ever have achieved amalgamation, but with him it
had been able to use the union as a base for growth, flexibility and strength.*

*But the amalgamation had a victim, and that victim was John
Chisholm. Jack Webster and others who were close to the senior levels of
police administration at the time of John Chisholm's suicide became convinced that the extreme pressure Chief Chisholm had been under trying to
get a still-fragmented collection of police forces operating at an acceptable
level was just too much for the man. And no one could deny that the frequent confrontations with Judge Bick over policy decisions had worked on
Chisholm until his strong will failed him.*

*There was no doubt that both Bick and Chisholm gave all they had to
setting up the force. It was for the sake of the job at hand that Bick was so
adamant in pushing for his own views, but for Chisholm it was more than
just a job.*

*Many figured Chisholm would retire. He was sixty-two. He'd put in
thirty-eight years. He'd paid his dues. But suicide is a silent partner in
every police cruiser, and as some wit has pointed out, there are fates worse
than death. Before his self-sentenced execution in High Park, John*

*Chisholm had been acting totally unlike himself. He'd even engaged in un-
explained wandering. He had ceased to be a cop. To some that means you
might as well cease to be a man.*

JOHN CHISHOLM'S POLICE FUNERAL WAS massively attended, but even as the
dead chief was laid to rest, the rumour mill was working away in earnest,
speculating on who would be the next chief of police. Many senior officers
of the force started gathering political friends together, hoping to find the
support in government circles they knew was necessary for appointment to
this very prestigious post.

The names of the supposed front-runners would change daily, and it
was even suggested that an outsider would be brought in to head the force.
This particular rumour was not well received by the rank and file. Most of
us believed that in an organization as large as the Metropolitan Toronto Police Force, there must be at least *one* serving member who had the experience and ability to lead us.

It is interesting to note that an almost identical situation arose in July
1989, when the retirement of Jack Marks was announced. A group of new
and – in some ways – inexperienced members of the current police commission voted to advertise across Canada for a new chief of police. Fortunately, the more experienced and knowledgeable members of the commission voted for, and were successful in appointing, a serving member of the
force in the person of Deputy Chief Bill McCormack. Chief McCormack is
a fine man, with vast police experience, and he has the advantage of an inti-
mate knowledge of the workings of the force as well as long personal acquaintance with many of its thousands of members, something that no outsider, whatever his good qualities, could claim. I know, too, from my over
forty years of service with this police force, that the appointment of an outsider would have brought an uncontrollable upheaval among the rank and
file, and that many brilliant and dedicated senior officers would have resigned.

To return to 1958: many people were surprised, even shocked, by the
appointment of James P. Mackey to the position of chief of police, simply
because, although he was forty-five years old and a veteran criminal investigator, he was very junior in the ranks of the many uniformed inspectors at
the time.

He was a tall, fine-looking, popular officer who had more than his share of "smarts." Although he was friendly and approachable, he had a serious business-like view of police work. He seldom smiled, and had no time for jokes, wisecracks, or frivolous time-wasting activities. A non-smoking, non-drinking, church-going man, he divided his life almost equally between his family and the job. He had been a star athlete in his younger days, and during the Second World War had been commissioned in the Royal Canadian Air Force, in which he served as a pilot instructor.

The choice of James Mackey as the new chief of police was a popular one, and was acclaimed by members of the bar and judiciary as well as the vast majority of the Metropolitan Toronto Police Force. I am proud to have had the privilege of working with him.

A FEW MONTHS BEFORE THESE events, during the late fall and Christmas season of 1957, there had been an unprecedented rash of armed robberies. The newspapers and politicians were screaming for the police to do something to halt the violent crime wave.

The top brass of the Toronto City Police decided, for the second time in the history of the force, that a special, handpicked group of detectives would be selected for a unit to be known as the "hold-up and safe squad." I say for the second time because there had been a small group of dedicated and experienced detectives assigned to a previous, unofficial, and not too well publicized hold-up squad. For a period of about two years, from 1954 to 1956, this squad had operated with such efficiency that they were soon feared by members of the criminal community, but it was disbanded in 1955 as a result of a steady stream of complaints to the Board of Police Commissioners. The complaints came from some less than reputable members of the criminal bar and a few badly informed politicians, who alleged that the squad was using violence against armed and dangerous bandits after they had been arrested.

The accusations were never supported by any evidence, but because of their persistence, the chief of detectives was ordered to disband this highly effective group of police officers.

Of course, what the accusers failed to take into consideration was the fact that these experienced, veteran detectives were dealing on a daily basis with some of the most dangerous criminals in North America. They were not your ordinary fraud artist, car thief, and housebreaker; they were armed with every conceivable type of firearm, which they did not hesitate to use in the course of their crimes. Violence begets violence.

The decision to reactivate a reorganized, official hold-up squad was received with applause by the business community, and the newspapers gave it plenty of space in their pages when it officially came into existence on January 1, 1958. Detective Gordon and I were proud to be two of the first officers selected as members. It was commanded by the veteran headquarters detective inspector, William Bolton, with two senior detectives to assist him: Harold Genno and Frank O'Driscoll. One could not have chosen three more experienced and admired leaders. Besides Charlie Gordon and me, the other officers selected were Jack Nicolucci, Vic Henderson, Bob Coghill, Ken Harris and Bob Stirling. A major robbery occurred the very day the squad was formed. It spurred us on toward what we would come to be proud of as a long list of arrests.

In the early spring and summer of 1958, there was a series of armed hold-ups of drugstores. During these hold-ups, violence or the threat of violence was used by the three-man gang. At about five-thirty one evening the gang held up a drugstore in the Beaches area of Toronto. On this occasion they fled the scene, but did not go far: they had the temerity to sit down in a booth in a nearby restaurant, where they were soon observed from the outside by two police officers.

While one of the officers telephoned for assistance, the other kept his eye on the culprits. The leader soon realized he was being watched, and by a series of clever moves, managed to leave the restaurant and, at gunpoint, disarm the officer. The first officer returned after phoning for assistance and a gun battle ensued. During the furious fight, one policeman was shot and seriously wounded by the gang leader, who was shot in turn as he and his two accomplices escaped. They were quickly traced to an apartment above a store on Queen Street, and countless detectives and uniformed officers, including the chief of police himself, converged on the scene.

Chief Mackey had been on his way home, driven by his usual chauffeur, when the news came over the car radio that the gang was holed up and still exchanging gunfire with the police. He ordered his driver directly to the scene, where he took charge in the manner of a veteran of many gun battles, which he was. (I am happy to say this fearless and much loved leader survived them all and is now living in comfortable retirement at his home in Muskoka!) Eventually, officers were able to storm the room and arrest the wanted men without further injury.

The subsequent criminal trials were newspaper-headline events, and all three received lengthy sentences in penitentiary. The leader got life. During sentencing the presiding judge told the man he was the most dangerous ever to appear before him, so it came as no surprise when the Crown attorney and senior police officers reached the conclusion that this prisoner was too dangerous to be escorted to Kingston Penitentiary on the train by the usual civilian sheriff's officer. They decided he must be escorted by armed detective personnel. Detective Gordon and I had been off duty at the time of the gun battle, and were about the only members of the hold-up squad who were not known to the prisoner. That was thought to be an advantage, since the proximity of the arresting or testifying officers might incite the man to further violence, and so we were detailed to escort him to prison.

On the appointed morning, Detective Gordon and I took possession of the prisoner at the Don Jail, and were then transported to Toronto's Union Station for transfer to the Kingston-bound train. We were being lifted on a freight elevator to the departure level, when our prisoner – even though he was handcuffed – started to fight both Gordon and me. He was not a large man, but he was extremely strong and desperate. He put up a vicious struggle (which was captured on film by an enterprising newspaper photographer) but with an effort, we controlled our prisoner and got him calmed down enough to continue to the train.

After boarding, we were seated in a somewhat isolated area of a passenger coach. By isolated, I mean that there were very few civilian passengers on the coach, and those present were seated by the conductor some distance away from us. As the train pulled out of the station, I informed our prisoner that as far as anyone else was concerned, he didn't know us, and we didn't know him. Even handcuffed to Detective Gordon, he could be as comfortable on his train journey to Kingston as anybody, as long as he behaved himself. But I warned him that if he failed to heed this advice, my partner and I were prepared to use whatever force was necessary. I reminded him that we both knew he felt he had nothing to lose. Nevertheless, he should make no mistake about it, we were prepared to use our firearms.

The prisoner remained quiet for a while, but Charlie and I figured we were in for another violent eruption before long. Instead, the man suddenly put out his shackled hand for me to shake and then did the same to Detective Gordon. We had no further problems with him. In fact, he spent the rest of the three-hour train ride talking about his home town of Ottawa. As the train pulled into Kingston, he removed his necktie and handed it to me saying, "Here's a souvenir for you from the most dangerous man in Canada." I purposely "forgot" the somewhat loud necktie on the seat as we left the train, but some time later Gordon produced it and I am told it is still in his possession.

When we left the man in the charge of the Kingston custodial officers, he shook hands with both of us, saying we had been very fair to him, considering his past demonstrations of violence against the police. Needless to say, Detective Gordon and I were much relieved to be rid of this explosive individual, and we adjourned to a local tavern for two or three beers before the train trip home.

SUCCESSFUL CRIMINAL INVESTIGATION SOMETIMES involves a tremendous amount of leg work. If a detective is not prepared to be patient, accept disappointments, and still carry on with the utmost determination, he might as well explore some other line of endeavour.

A case in point was a bank robbery that Detective Gordon and I attended one spring morning in 1958. The bank was in the west end of the city, and had been robbed of several thousand dollars by a lone hold-up man. Although no firearm had been seen during the robbery, the man had claimed to have one. After completing the usual investigation and interrogation of the bank employees, my partner and I knocked on the doors of several houses adjacent to the bank. One householder told us that it was probably not important, but she had noticed a blue truck parked near the bank at different times during the morning. By different times, she explained, she meant that the truck would go away and then come back again. When we asked if there was anything unusual about the truck, she replied no, it was just a plain blue truck carrying a supply of what looked like wire screening in the open back. The description of the wire screening suggested to us that it could have been a plasterer's truck.

We checked the Yellow Pages under plastering contractors and noted each one that was located in the west end, then proceeded to investigate each address. After routinely checking at thirty-one plastering firms, we finally received information from one proprietor that he owned a small blue pick-up truck and that at the moment, it was out on the road with one of his employees.

He supplied us with the name and address of the employee, and because it was close to the time when the employee should be getting back with the truck, we waited. When 6:00 p.m. arrived, the owner told us the individual was long overdue and it wouldn't surprise him if he had stopped at his favourite beverage room, the Clinton Tavern, for a few beers.

Charlie and I set out for the tavern, and as we turned onto Clinton Street, we saw the blue truck parked just south of Bloor. In order to draw our suspect out of the crowded beverage room, we spoke to the manager and asked him to announce to his patrons that a small blue truck had been struck by a passing motorist, and would the owner please go out to his vehicle.

In a matter of minutes, a man left the tavern and ran to the truck. We immediately apprehended him, and the three of us proceeded to Number 7

Police Station, at Ossington and Bloor. The young plasterer loudly protested his complete innocence. A thorough search of his person turned up nothing but a few paltry dollars.

Although it was now 7:30 p.m., we planned to bring the bank teller to the police station and hold an impromptu identification parade. In the meantime, having given the truck a cursory search, we had it towed to the central police garage, with instructions for garage personnel to make a careful search of the vehicle. But just before we sent a police car to pick up the witnesses, we received a telephone call from the garage foreman. As his men were removing a section of the leather lining of the truck cab roof, several thousands of dollars had rained out on them. When informed of this, our suspect confessed immediately. He was a first offender, but he was sentenced to a penitentiary term.

We got no congratulations from our boss, Inspector Bolton. Instead he gave us supreme hell for not making a more meticulous search of the vehicle ourselves. Despite our protests that we had to interrogate our possibly innocent suspect without delay, the reprimand still stood. An on-duty police officer can't afford the luxury of being careless, or less than alert, while performing his or her duties. It is a dangerous profession, and a few moments of inattention can very quickly bring death or serious injury.

My partner and I were guilty of another such procedural lapse during our hold-up squad years, this time with near-fatal results. It was the summer of 1959, and Detective Gordon and I were patrolling in the downtown area. Our police radio reported that there was an attempted robbery taking place in an alleyway near John and Queen streets. We weren't far from there and were able to respond quickly. We arrived on the scene in a matter of minutes.

We found two wine hounds going through the pockets of a third, less than sober gentleman of the streets. The two would-be robbers had obviously been drinking, but were in much better shape than their victim. Detective Gordon and I, thinking we were dealing with two ordinary alcoholic bums, broke a cardinal rule and placed both of them in the back seat of our vehicle. With my partner driving and me sitting in the front passenger seat, we set off for the nearest police station.

We had travelled only three blocks when the man sitting immediately behind Detective Gordon threw his arms around Gordon's neck. Gordon slammed on the brakes, but his head was forced back, and his knees became locked under the steering wheel. The prisoner kept squeezing tighter, while screaming obscenities at us.

My immediate reaction was to reach into the back seat and try to pull the thief's arms away from my partner's neck. To my shock, I found that our prisoner had wrists twice the size of mine, and his arms were as hard as steel. Detective Gordon's face was turning a deeper shade of purple by the second. A large blue vein protruded grotesquely from his forehead. He couldn't utter a sound and both his eyes were bulging out.

Our police car was a two-door vehicle and there wasn't room to climb over the seat into the back, bearing in mind that we had a second prisoner there, who, thankfully, was not taking any part in the assault.

The berserk prisoner was frothing at the mouth and trying to bite Detective Gordon's ear. There was nothing I could do except draw my leather billy. With very little room to manoeuvre, I swung it in a wide arc, and was lucky enough to connect with the side of the prisoner's head. Blood flew in every direction, but he released his death grip on my partner.

During the few minutes it took for Detective Gordon to catch his breath, I covered the now injured man with my revolver. I am sure that if he had renewed his violent behaviour in the close confines of the automobile, with my partner temporarily immobilized, I would have had to shoot him. But the blow to his head had apparently taken the fight out of him temporarily, and we were able to place him in handcuffs. When I say "temporarily," I mean just that, because at the police station, while still handcuffed, he suddenly kicked the desk sergeant in the testicles, which I'm sorry to say caused him permanent injury.

The prisoner was not your ordinary, unemployed street alcoholic. He was a recent arrival in Toronto, a stevedore from the docks in Halifax, Nova Scotia – which certainly accounted for his thick wrists and strong arms.

As I recall, it was over a week before Detective Gordon could swallow solid food. We had certainly learned a lesson the hard way.

IN JULY OF 1959, Charlie Gordon and I investigated an attempted hold-up of a streetcar-type diner, located on the south side of Queen's Quay, near York Street, and frequented by police officers, streetcar operators, and truck drivers from the many large trucking companies that occupied the nearby warehouses.

As a favour to his steady customers, the transport drivers, the friendly owner of the diner often cashed their pay cheques at no charge. To do so he had to keep a large amount of cash on hand, and he usually withdrew several thousand dollars from the bank the day before the drivers' payday. He had been doing this for a long time, and word eventually reached a pair of hardened veteran criminals, who had only recently been released from Kingston Penitentiary. They were both very big men, well over six feet tall, and on this particular day they entered the diner wearing disguises and armed with heavy-calibre handguns. They ordered the owner to hand over the money.

What they didn't know was that one of the customers sitting at the counter having a cup of coffee was a recently retired veteran detective sergeant from the force. He was fifty-two-year-old Arthur Keay, who during his police service had been involved in some of the most high-profile criminal investigations of the preceding thirty years, and who was quite used to dangerous situations.

When he and several other restaurant patrons were ordered by the hold-up men not to move, Art, a former star athlete, pretended that he was as frightened as the others. When he saw his chance he leapt at the man nearest him, knocking him to the floor, where he straddled the criminal and disarmed him.

At that moment the second hold-up man, seeing the difficulties his partner was in, struck the former police officer over the head with his .357 Magnum revolver. Keay felt a stinging blow at the side of his head and heard a deafening noise. The firearm had discharged. The bullet struck the disarmed bandit in the head, killing him instantly. At that point, the other one took to his heels and fled the scene.

Although bleeding profusely from his head wound, Art Keay attempted to pursue the man, but lost him when he escaped in an automobile that had been left with the motor running. Fortunately, Detective Sergeant Fred Maxwell and Detective Stan Henderson had just left the City Hall courts, and were in the immediate vicinity of Queen's Quay on their way back to their west Toronto police division. They caught their police radio reporting the hold-up, along with a description of the wanted car.

Almost immediately, they observed a car being driven in a reckless manner, and it matched the description of the getaway vehicle. Officers Maxwell and Henderson drew their firearms, and after a short chase, were able to force the car to a stop. They arrested the driver without a struggle. A search of his person revealed the .357 Magnum revolver, which contained five live rounds and one spent cartridge.

On our arrival Detective Gordon and I took over the investigation, and officers of the homicide squad charged the suspect with murder. Deservingly, ex-detective Sergeant Arthur Keay was awarded many honours by the force and the public for his heroic action. (This exceptional man died recently at the age of eighty-two.)

I believe that I and other police officers involved in this investigation and subsequent court trial remember not only the brave actions of Art Keay, but also the rude and offensive behaviour of the presiding Supreme Court of Ontario justice. From the outset he made no attempt to hide his dislike of police officers. He would not recognize police department ranks. For example, when the homicide squad inspector was in the witness box, he continually addressed this very respected and veteran police commander as "constable."

When the Crown attorney, Mr. Arthur Klein, suggested to the justice that the witness was in fact a very senior police officer with the rank of inspector, he replied,"They are all constables to me. If the police force wants to bestow some fancy, unimportant titles on its members that is their business, but in my court they are all constables." Ironically, this belligerent man was removed from the bench shortly after this trial by cabinet order, after facing highly publicized conflict-of-interest charges arising from his activities while he was both a politician and a jurist.

The "diner" gunman was convicted of murder by the jury and he was sentenced to be hanged. The sentence was subsequently commuted to life imprisonment.

As THE MONTHS AND YEARS passed through 1958, 1959 and 1960, the day-to-day activities of the hold-up squad continued to be hectic. Even then, we were alarmed by the increasing use of narcotics by the criminal element. More and more of the people we arrested for armed hold-ups and other firearm offences were drug addicts. We were also experiencing a new phenomenon in violent criminal offences: an increasing number of our wanted suspects were female, and when arrests were effected, most of these accused were also users of hard drugs.

One must remember that during the '50s, widespread marijuana use had not yet taken hold. Most of the addicted people we were dealing with used cocaine and heroin, and the fact that more and more drug-crazed individuals were in possession of firearms, and were prepared to commit violent crimes to support their very expensive habit, made our area of policing all the more dangerous. We had to develop a more cautious approach in our investigations of people even suspected of committing armed hold-up offences. We had once been gung-ho, rushing to attack our criminal adversaries; now we had to move carefully. We were dealing with individuals whose foolhardiness was greatly increased by drugs – when they knew what they were doing at all – and whose desperation was often nearly total.

With regard to fighting crime in the age of drugs, I feel obliged to remind the reader that the police officer of today, male or female, uniformed or plainclothes, has a far tougher job now than we had. During the latter years of my police service as a senior command officer, I continually admired, and still do, the dedicated young men and women who daily face the possibility of death or serious bodily harm at the hands of an ever-growing drug-taking public. It is not a job for the faint-hearted, and I sometimes wonder if I would have had the fortitude to do as they have to do, especially in the face of the verbal and written abuse to which they are continually subjected. But then, being showered with abuse has always been the police officer's lot.

IN LATE 1959, A DOWNTOWN bank was held up by two armed men. An intense investigation came up with the identity of a female who had driven the getaway car. She was arrested, and as a result, the identity of the two men was established. One of the suspects was originally from Montreal, and it was reported that he had returned there, immediately after the robbery. Another detective and I were sent to Montreal to search for him. Upon our arrival we asked for and obtained the assistance of detectives from the Montreal hold-up squad.

Accompanied by these officers, we attended at the home of our suspect's father. It was a second-floor flat in a working-man's district of the city. We were admitted to the flat by the father, who was a fiery Irish Canadian; he gave us hell and called us every name anyone could ever think of. We did not have a search warrant, nor did we have probable grounds to obtain one. Just before we left, one of the huge Montreal detectives noticed that despite the winter cold outside, a Quebec heater type of stove in the centre of the kitchen was not in service. The officer winked at us, and said to the father, "Here, let me help you, pop, to get some heat in here." With that, he lit a match and lifted the lid of the stove and pretended to be about to drop the match in. Leaping toward the detective, the father screamed, "Don't you do that, you stupid French bastard. I don't need any heat." The officer reached into the stove and removed a newspaper-wrapped package. Inside it he found six thousand dollars, still in bank wrappers. The man broke down and told us his son had hidden the money in the stove the previous day, and had then returned to Toronto. He supplied us with an address for his boy, and we notified our people. The suspect was arrested within the hour. My associate and I returned to Toronto with the recovered money, which we knew was only about half of what had been taken in the hold-up.

When we arrived back at our office, Detective Sergeant Frank O'Driscoll told me not to bother unpacking, because we would be returning almost immediately to look for the second man, who was known to be still in Montreal. I rushed home for a change of clothing, and Frank O'Driscoll and I took the afternoon train to Montreal.

When we arrived we booked into our usual downtown hotel and then proceeded to Montreal Police Headquarters. Although it was now almost nine o'clock in the evening, Inspector Joe Bedard, the commander of the Montreal hold-up squad, was still in his office. Inspector Bedard was an old friend of ours, and after we'd spent an hour bringing him up to date on our investigation, he offered us a ride back to our hotel.

A few minutes later, Inspector Bedard stopped at a night club on Mountain Street, suggesting that we adjourn for a nightcap before heading back to the hotel. As we entered the club, Bedard showed a photograph of our suspect to the doorman-bouncer of this slightly notorious establishment, and told him that if he saw the individual in the photograph, he should call the hold-up squad right away. The three of us then took the elevator to the second floor, where the door opened directly into the club manager's office. We were welcomed by Inspector Bedard's friend, who phoned downstairs for drinks all around.

Just seconds after this, the doorman burst into the office and excitedly reported that the guy in the picture was downstairs at that moment. Although Sergeant O'Driscoll and I did not really believe it could possibly be our wanted man, we took the elevator down to the lobby of the club. When we got there, the doorman pointed out a short young man wearing dark glasses, who was standing just inside the front door. The man glanced in our direction. He didn't know us, but he smelled cop and took off, running down the snow-covered street. Naturally O'Driscoll and I lost no time in taking after him, and after a short chase, Frank gave a flying tackle that brought the wanted man down. We handcuffed and searched him, and found several thousand dollars of the robbery loot.

We returned to Toronto on the morning train, where Sergeant O'Driscoll's football-like tackle had made the front pages of the newspapers, just as it had in Montreal.

IN 1959 AND 1960, THE city of Montreal seemed to be the home base of many of Toronto's bank robbers. During this period, we had several hold-ups of financial institutions perpetrated by an especially vicious gang of criminals. Their modis operandi was to smash the front window of a bank with a sledge hammer, run into the building shouting obscenities to customers and employees alike, vault the counters, and remove the money from every cash drawer. If their instructions were not obeyed quickly, they wouldn't hesitate to pistol-whip a customer or employee and in some instances they would fire a shot or two into the air to instil greater fear. This hated gang was wanted for robberies all over the city of Montreal.

Their violence was legendary. During one noon-hour robbery of a downtown Montreal bank, the gang was escaping with their loot when the bank manager, returning from his lunch at a nearby restaurant, saw the gang rushing out of his bank, each of them wearing a Hallowe'en mask and cowboy hat. The unarmed manager ran up to them, shouting and flinging out his arms to stop them. He was shot several times, and as he lay on the sidewalk, the robbers calmly stepped over him, climbed into their getaway car, and sped off.

We were prepared for a shoot-out when we confronted these unscrupulous crooks, and for the first time we began to carry bulletproof vests and heavy-calibre weapons in our squad cars. The gang struck again one bright, sunny morning at a bank in north Toronto. On this occasion two detectives, who were in the immediate vicinity, gave chase to the escaping bandits. After a hectic pursuit on foot they managed to capture one of the suspects.

Our hold-up officers were summoned to the scene, and we questioned the arrested man. We were able to learn the names and addresses of the rest of the gang. All of them lived in Montreal. After a brief conference it was decided that four hold-up detectives should fly to Montreal to track them down. We were warned by the arrested man to be prepared for a gunfight, because the leader of the gang was never without his firearms, which included a deadly sawed-off shotgun. Detectives John Mitchell, Bob Stirling, Doug Barclay and I were selected to go, and we took the first available flight to Montreal. At Montreal Police Headquarters, we conferred with senior officers and hold-up squad personnel. We went over detailed reports of the numerous crimes the gang had committed in that city, including the bank manager's murder, but unfortunately because the bandits were always masked no witnesses linking the crimes had ever come forward.

It was decided that we would raid the apartment of the leader, which, I recall, was on Decarie Boulevard. The Montreal officers lent us bulletproof vests. These were the old type that covered almost the whole front of the body, and although this was a good safety feature, the down side was that they weighed about seventy-five pounds!

Our planning for the apartment raid was meticulous. We even obtained floor plans from the building's owner, in order to have advance knowledge of the room layout before crashing through the door. We were well aware that we were dealing with a person who had demonstrated absolute ruthlessness on many previous occasions. When we arrived at the apartment building, we entered from the rear, using great stealth. The apartment superintendent was a very co-operative Englishman, who told us he was a British army veteran of the First World War and quite used to danger and gunfire.

We knew the suspect was at home. The superintendent had seen him go into his apartment shortly before our arrival. The old soldier now volunteered to knock on the apartment door and inform the suspect that he had to check the bathroom plumbing, because a tenant directly below had complained about water leaking through his ceiling. It was decided that Detective Stirling and I would stand on either side of the door, and the moment the wanted man opened it, the apartment superintendent would jump out of the way, and Stirling and I would crash in, wearing the bullet-proof vests and armed with machine guns supplied by the Montreal police.

After some protests that his water system was not leaking, the suspect agreed to let the superintendent in. As we heard the door being opened a crack, Stirling and I hit it with full force, aided by the additional weight of the vests. Our sudden move bowled over the wanted man and he was overpowered and handcuffed. As luck would have it, he had just got out of the shower and was wearing only a towel around his waist. A search of the apartment revealed a sawed-off shotgun resting on the toilet seat, fully loaded, with the safety catch off. We also found seven handguns of various calibres, thousands of rounds of ammunition, and other types of explosives.

Detectives Stirling and Barclay removed our prisoner to Montreal police headquarters, while Detective Mitchell and I, along with two Montreal detectives, remained behind on a stakeout, in case the other wanted man arrived at the apartment.

We didn't have to wait too long before there was a knock at the door. We opened it and at once seized a very surprised and shocked young man. After a brief interrogation of this person, we satisfied ourselves that he was not one of the wanted men, but he was able to give us valuable information as to the possible location of the other two suspects. He supplied the address of one of them, which we telephoned to Montreal headquarters, and the suspect was apprehended without incident. Our new informant somewhat reluctantly told us that he did not know the address of the one man still at large, but he could point out a European café on lower St. Denis Street where our suspect often played chess of an evening.

At this point Stirling and Barclay left, taking the two men now in custody back to Toronto. Mitchell and I stayed in Montreal to check out the café.

Shortly after 8:00 p.m., with a Montreal detective driving us, we were slowly moving through the lower St. Denis area, looking for the café, when our informer suddenly said, "There he is, don't let him see me." I instructed our driver to pull ahead two blocks and let me out, then circle the block and let Detective Mitchell out. My plan was to walk toward the suspect while Detective Mitchell moved in on him from the rear.

When I drew abreast of him, I took hold of his shoulder, half turned him around and showed him my police badge. I said, "Police. Let me see some identification." A slow smile came over his face, and he replied, "Sure, no problem." As quick as a flash, he reached into his inside pocket and brought out a silver object, and was about to point it in my face when Detective Mitchell struck him a thunderous blow to his jaw. The silver object fell to the sidewalk as he slowly sank to his knees. We handcuffed him, then picked up and examined the object. It looked exactly like a fountain pen, but it was a tear-gas gun, loaded with a .38 calibre tear-gas bullet. If John Mitchell had not intervened at that precise second, I would have received the full force of the gas in my face. Weapons experts later told me that at such close range, I probably would have been badly burned, and would have received permanent damage to my eyes. This unusual weapon is still on display in the Metropolitan Toronto Police Museum.

We returned to Toronto with our prisoner on the first flight the following morning, but that was not the end of the story of this vicious gang of criminals. While he was in custody in Toronto's Don Jail, the gang leader wrote a letter, which was intercepted by the jail authorities, requesting a friend in Montreal to visit him and smuggle in a firearm so that, at the first opportunity, he could shoot his way out. He also informed his friend that when he made good his escape he was going to kill detectives Webster, Stirling, Barclay, and Mitchell. The prisoners were of course under heavy guard during their many court appearances and eventually all were sentenced to lengthy penitentiary terms.

The gang leader was represented by a high-profile criminal lawyer, who successfully persuaded the trial judge to have his client examined at a psychiatric facility before beginning his term in the penitentiary. We on the hold-up squad were absolutely dismayed at this decision of the court, because we knew from past experience that the security at the provincial assessment centre at Penetanguishene, Ontario, was not adequate to contain such a dangerous individual for long.

We delivered the prisoner to the hospital, but Detective Sergeant Frank O'Driscoll told the doctor in charge not to trust the new patient to any degree whatsoever, and he suggested to the worried psychiatric officials that if the man received any parcels they should be opened or at least X-rayed to prevent his receiving weapons of any kind. The letter written by the prisoner when he was in the Don Jail was shown to the doctor in charge to impress upon him that our request was not unreasonable.

As a result, the authorities remained on the alert, and a good thing, too. Shortly after the man began his incarceration at the hospital, a parcel wrapped in Christmas paper was received at the institution's mail office. It was addressed to the gang leader and bore the address of a female in Montreal (a subsequent check of this address revealed it to be fictitious).

After a brief consultation, the hospital X-rayed the parcel with a normal medical-ray machine. The parcel contained a Christmas cake, but concealed inside it, the X-ray revealed, were a .38 calibre short-barrelled revolver and nine .38 calibre bullets, along with six .38 calibre tear-gas shells. When we were notified of this by the hospital officials, Sergeant O'Driscoll went to Penetanguishene, and on breaking open the cake, discovered that, in addition to the loose ammunition, the revolver was fully loaded with six bullets.

Shortly after this incident, the gang leader was assessed as mentally fit to serve the remainder of his sentence in Kingston Penitentiary, but when he had served only a fraction of it, he was released under the normal parole procedure. Detectives Mitchell, Stirling, Barclay, and I became ever vigilant because of the death threats he had made against us. However, it wasn't long before we were notified by United States authorities that the paroled convict had been shot to death by a New York City detective while attempting to break into a doctor's office in that city. We were all much relieved.

THE HOLD-UP SQUAD SOMETIMES investigated cases of robbery in which the victims had been violently attacked even though they had offered no resistance. Frankly, we could hardly wait to get our hands on the cowardly criminals who could commit such acts, to bring them before the courts and do everything in our power to get them lengthy prison terms.

On one such occasion, in September of 1960, four heavily armed men were in the process of robbing a finance company, and the manager and staff were obeying their instructions. There was one customer on the premises: a frail lady who had come in to pay her monthly loan bill. One of the bandits ordered this innocent woman to get away from the counter. In her shock and nervousness, she apparently did not move quickly enough to satisfy the robber, and he angrily pistol-whipped her several times over the face, causing severe injuries.

When we arrived on the scene and observed what these cowardly gunmen had done to a defenceless woman, we were enraged, to say the least. But justice triumphed. In searching the immediate area of the hold-up scene, Detective Sergeant Jack Nicolucci and Detective Frank Barbetto found a fedora hat that one of the bandits had dropped while making his hasty escape. Inside the hat, on the hatband, was the robber's full name. It was a simple matter to check the name through our criminal record system, come up with a recent address, and take the culprit into custody.

We then fanned out over the city and soon had his three accomplices behind bars. We were were able to recover the firearms used in the hold-up as well as all the cash. The four robbers appeared in court and pleaded not guilty, but halfway through the trial they changed their plea to guilty, and they got what they deserved from the presiding judge.

I had had previous experience with gratuitous violence. In the late 1950s, the proprietor of a small trucking company had been held up at gunpoint by one man. The sixty-year-old victim, with his hands raised in the air, told the criminal to take anything he wanted and indicated where the cash box was stored. The owner also begged the hold-up man not to hurt him, because he had only recently been released from the hospital after suffering a serious heart attack.

For no reason whatsoever, the bandit reacted by striking the owner several times over the head with the barrel of his firearm. The gunman then ran from the premises with about thirty dollars, still in the cash box. He had his getaway car parked on a nearby street, but in his haste to escape, he drove into a fire hydrant, knocking himself unconscious. When a police officer arrived at the scene of the accident, he found the firearm, the intact cash box, and of course, the bandit – who, as we later discovered, was also wanted in several states in the U.S.A. for a variety of criminal offences.

The sad part of the story is that two weeks after the hold-up the victim died, after suffering a second heart attack.

DETECTIVE CHARLIE GORDON AND I were driving south on Avenue Road one day, and while we were stopped for a traffic light at Bloor, a citizen knocked on the car window and asked if we were cops. When we replied that we were, he said, "There's a guy with a gun in the bar of the Park Plaza Hotel." We pulled up to the curb and questioned our informant.

He said that he had been having a drink at the hotel bar when he caught a glimpse of a large gun in the waistband of another customer at the bar on the ground floor of the hotel. He pointed out that there was an entrance off Bloor Street.

When Detective Gordon and I peered through the door window, we could see about thirty customers sitting on stools at the bar. We asked our informant to walk slowly down the bar, and when he was opposite the suspect's back to nod his head and keep on walking. He agreed, and when he had passed about twelve bar patrons, he gave the signal with his head and continued to walk into the dining room of the hotel.

My partner and I then quickly walked into the bar. When we reached the suspect, we each gripped one of his wrists. Quietly, we whispered that we wanted to talk to him outside. Without speaking or even glancing at us, he instantly tried to break free of our wrist holds, and a violent struggle ensued. Shouting to the other customers in the bar to stand back, we wrestled him to the floor face down. We were then able to handcuff his wrists behind his back, and remove a fully loaded .45 calibre pistol from the waistband of his trousers. Not surprisingly, the customers at the bar had fled, and I'm sure some bar tabs were left unpaid that night!

We removed our prisoner to a nearby police station and searched him. We found a key for a room in a downtown hotel. He carried no identification and he refused to answer any questions. There were several hundred dollars in large bills in his pockets, but no wallet. When other officers from our squad checked out the downtown hotel room, they found a dozen discarded hold-up notes – he'd been practising the wording of the demands! – but the basic content was identical to those we had on file for hold-ups committed in Toronto and other Ontario cities.

He was tried before a county court judge and sentenced to fifteen years in prison. As Detective Gordon and I were leaving the courtroom, the father of the sentenced man attacked us verbally, and when we made no reply he attempted to attack us physically. It was only through the intervention of Sergeant Frank O'Driscoll that the confrontation was stopped before any harm was done. The tragedy of it was that the father was a respectable retired police officer, whose love for his son was obviously greater than his respect for the law.

BEFORE THE EMERGENCY TASK FORCE was formed, the hold-up squad was sometimes called upon for special service, because at the time the only police vehicles that were equipped with tear gas and heavy-calibre firearms were the three hold-up squad cars, and certain officers on the squad were trained in the use of this emergency equipment (eventually all of us were). We would be asked to intervene when, for example, a barricaded person was thought to be in possession of a firearm, and had demonstrated by action or words that he intended to use the weapon.

In the late spring of 1961, a man living in a third-floor apartment above a store on Bloor Street near Bathurst was sought on a criminal warrant. Two officers went to the apartment to execute the warrant, but the wanted man refused to open the door, threatening to blow the head off any person who dared to enter. The officers immediately backed off and called for the help of the hold-up squad.

When we arrived at the scene, our inspector, Bill Bolton, directed me to stand on Bloor and guard the front door of the premises while he and Detectives Stirling, Barclay and Mitchell crept up the rear stairs to make a surprise entrance. Inspector Bolton himself telephoned the wanted man from another apartment in the building. As he worked to coax the suspect into peaceful surrender, the other officers attempted to force entry at the rear door of the apartment. The wanted man heard the noise of this attempted entry, and fired two rifle shots in the direction of the door. At this, Bolton ordered a tear-gas canister to be thrown through the kitchen window. Within seconds, the apartment was filled with gas. The wanted man was forced out onto a window ledge at the front of the building.

A crowd of several hundred spectators had gathered on the south side of Bloor to view this exciting "cops and robbers" show. There was a collective gasp as they saw the man climb out onto the window ledge. Then a man in the crowd shouted, in a loud voice, "Jump, you son-of-a-bitch." Whether he was encouraged by this suggestion I don't know, but the subject did jump from the ledge, and landed right on top of me! The sudden impact knocked me to the sidewalk, with the wanted man sprawled over me.

Despite the shock, I was able to hold on to him until my fellow officers arrived to handcuff him after a small, futile struggle. The suspect was uninjured and – mercifully – except for a very sore neck and a torn trench coat, so was I.

The throngs of spectators clapped their hands and cheered, and all three of the Toronto newspapers acclaimed me as a hero for catching the man in my arms, thereby saving him from death or serious injury. But the truth is, if I had seen him coming, I would have moved out of the way as fast as I could to save my skin!

THE YEARS THAT I SPENT ON the hold-up squad were busy and happy ones. Working on a day-to-day basis with first-class, hand-picked officers, who constantly demonstrated conspicuous bravery, was an honour in itself. Most of my comrades of that particular time are either retired or dead, but we survivors do meet on rare occasions to talk about old times, when we were young.

In the early spring of 1961, a vicious attack was committed on a well-known Toronto gambler. This typical gangland attack took place in a nightclub in front of a dozen customers and employees. The scene of the crime was a large downtown Toronto establishment that served a respectable clientele of businessmen and criminal lawyers from the nearby law courts. But the place had another identity as a known hangout for organized-crime figures, who used it as their office. One well-known and feared Hamilton gangster, with supposed Mafia connections, continually conducted business there, surrounded by his henchmen, most of whom were notorious criminals in their own right.

The middle-aged gambler was beaten severely by his attackers, while the other gangsters who were present stood back in a wide circle. The gambler was a tough individual. Even though he was outnumbered, and his assailants much younger, he fought like a caged tiger and managed to inflict serious wounds on some of his enemies.

The police were notified of a tavern brawl, but when units arrived all they found was the victim, lying in a pool of blood. He was removed to hospital, where he remained for several days. No one, customers or employees, admitted to having seen anything. Although the attending detectives worked very hard and interrogated dozens of people, who had to have seen something, their inquiries were met with a stone wall of silence.

The newspapers the following day sported screaming headlines deploring the unprovoked attack on a citizen in a public place. They demanded police action to apprehend these dangerous people. The famous radio and literary personality Pierre Berton, was the most vociferous of those demanding action. Mr. Berton was a well-respected and well-read columnist on one of Toronto's huge dailies, and his outrage over the fact that such a thing could happen in Toronto the Good had its effect on Chief of Police James Mackey. The chief authorized a special squad of hand-picked detectives, under the direction of a veteran organized-crime-fighting inspector, Herbert Thurston, to further investigate the situation. Herb Thurston had been a classmate of Chief Mackey's in 1936, and he was a no-nonsense, criminal-hating, straight-arrow investigator. In selecting personnel for this special squad, Herb first named officers from the Number 1 Division detective office who had been working on the assault from the beginning, then chose several officers from homicide and two detectives from the hold-up squad, of which I was one.

My assignment in the investigation was to search for and bring in for questioning the ex-boxer doorman of the tavern, who had completely disappeared, out of fear, immediately after the assault. We found him, and he served as an important witness at the trial.

It was a long and extremely difficult investigation, but it was finally brought to a successful conclusion with the arrest and conviction of all the main participants, including the big-time Hamilton gangster. The sentences they received were considered light in view of the viciousness of the assault, but the determination of Inspector Thurston and his hard-working associates gave a loud, clear message to the organized crime community that Toronto was not ready to be taken over by criminals.

My own final written report on the aspect of the case I had investigated motivated Inspector Thurston to mention me to the officer who was then in command of the homicide squad, and in June of 1961, I was officially assigned to that organization. I had achieved my ambition to be a murder detective. My promotion created a ripple of pride in my immediate family. My wife, Marion, was a veteran police spouse by this time, and although she knew that the long and irregular hours of work would in fact be increased, she was well aware of the rigid standards that were in place before an officer was selected to serve in this very prestigious area of the Criminal Investigations Branch. She was proud of my achievements, and sure it was only the beginning of even more recognition.

My one and only daughter, Rosemary, was ten years old at the time, and I think at that early age she was firmly of the belief that the only real policemen were the ones who wore uniforms, but I am happy to say that as she entered her teens, she started to believe that I was the best detective in the world, and she commenced a sizeable scrapbook, recording my murder investigations. (I still have this book today.)

It was a whole new ball game for me to participate in, gathering the minutely detailed evidence needed when investigating the capital crime of murder. Capital punishement – death by hanging, in the event of conviction on this charge and the exhausting of all appeals – was still in effect in Canada. In view of that fact, even a non-police person, I am sure, will understand the care and attention to accuracy needed before an investigating homicide officer felt that he could shoulder the tremendous responsibility of putting a person on trial with his life at stake.

It was an awesome responsibility, but I was ready for it. Even though I knew that deep inside me there remained, and always would remain, the fearful repugnance that I had felt the first time I ever saw a dead man, in that seedy hotel so long ago.

Arthur Lucas, the last man to hang for murder in Canada.

CHAPTER SEVEN

Homicide Cop

ON DECEMBER 11, 1962, ARTHUR LUCAS *was hanged by the neck until dead, the last person ever to be executed in Canada. As with so many stories, this one started a long way from where it would end up . . .*

The drug trade in Detroit, Michigan, in the sixties wasn't any prettier than it is in Toronto right now. Then as always, there were small-time operators, big-time bosses and a thousand middlemen scrambling to stay in between. Therland Crater was such a middleman.

Crater was doing all right for himself until his luck ran out and he was hauled in on narcotic violation charges in November 1960. Rather than face a sentence he couldn't see the end of, he decided to squeal. He promised to help out the narcotics agents who'd arrested him by turning in a slew of Detroit kingpins. A lot of them went to jail, and since word had quickly got around that it was Crater who'd sent them there, his presence in Detroit began to seem a bit extraneous. About the only person who'd even talk to Crater was his pal, Arthur Lucas, a fringe member of the gang that Crater had so successfully ratted on.

The arrest of the major narcotics importers put quite a crimp in the street trade, and the Detroit drug supply began to dry up.

But not everyone was inside. There were still a few of the gang awaiting trial. Realizing that Crater remained the prime witness for the prosecution, and that his testimony would make the case a clean sweep, the Michigan State Bureau of Narcotics got concerned for Crater's safety. Without notifying any Canadian authorities, the Americans slipped Crater across the border and up into Toronto. They told him he could bring his girlfriend, a Miss Newman, which he did. They also told him to keep his mouth shut until they asked him to open it.

Once Crater got to Toronto, he had just what he needed – a base of operation from which to supply the Detroit dealers who were hungry for the product he'd caused to dry up. However, he needed a trustworthy runner. Arthur Lucas was a natural for the job.

The partnership was just about perfect. Crater used his considerable skills to make the necessary connections, and before long, he was buying large quantities of heroin and delivering them to Lucas. It was a good set-up for the whole crew, because when Lucas came up from Detroit for a drop, he stayed for a couple of days while his common-law wife plied her trade in the downtown Toronto hotels. This way, they had quite a substantial amount of ready money to give to Crater, along with big cash contributions from the customers waiting in Detroit.

By November of 1961, the Crater-Lucas enterprise was going full tilt with no complaints from any of the participants. Then things changed. Lucas came through with his thousands, but for some reason he wasn't ready to explain, Crater didn't come through with the goods right away. Lucas was a patient man, and he waited. After repeated delays, Crater finally handed over a quantity of heroin that Lucas lost no time in getting back to Detroit for packaging and distribution to the pushers.

It wasn't very long before reports from the street began filtering back to Lucas via the powerful traffickers he was dealing. The stuff he'd supplied was garbage. Someone ventured to suggest that the heroin had more baking powder in it than Lucas's mother's Sunday biscuits. It wouldn't have surprised anybody to find Lucas with his throat cut.

But nobody did. It was possible, though just barely, that Lucas had been double-crossed. At least, that's how the traffickers chose to look at it. They told Lucas to prove it was his supplier and not himself who was the double-crosser. All he had to do was come back with the real goods this time. Nobody, of course, knew that the supplier was their nemesis, Therland Crater.

Lucas wasn't crazy about getting back to Toronto right away. On his most recent visit, on November 10, he'd had a little run-in with the cops. A Detective Jim Majury had put two and two together and figured out that Lucas's ladyfriend wasn't just standing out on the sidewalk to catch the night air for her health. Majury had made a polite request that Lucas and his friend get the hell out of town. They had complied.

Lucas went back to Toronto in spite of his misgivings. He was determined to get the dope, the money or, if all else failed, the man. For three days Lucas tried to get Crater on the phone, without success. He had no way of knowing that Crater and Newman, who'd been picked up on a bawdy house charge, were safely ensconced in the Don Jail. Empty-handed and a little scared, Lucas headed back to Detroit.

He didn't have the nerve to stay there very long. During the evening of November 15, he managed to talk one of the traffickers into lending him a brand-new 1962 Chevy, using the excuse that he had to head over to Flint to settle the matter of the bad drugs. The next day, he slipped out of Detroit and through the Windsor tunnel into Canada, pausing long enough for the legal nicety of getting a traveller's vehicle permit from Canada customs for the Chev.

Lucas got to Toronto sometime between 3:30 and 4:00 that Thursday afternoon of November 16. As was his style, he checked into a sleazy hotel at College and Spadina. He parked the car, came up to the room, and stretched out for a little nap. The lumpy beds of cheap hotels were plenty good enough for him.

When he woke up, however, he got to work.

It took countless calls and several hours but he finally got hold of Crater by phone at nine that evening. If you were a fly on the wall, you might have heard this conversation:

"I've got to see you, man," Lucas told Crater, "this is serious and you know why – "

"Hey, take it easy, man. Take it easy. Me and the old lady been inside for the past few days. I made bail just an hour or so ago. I got plenty of stuff and you can have it, but – "

"No buts, man. No stalling. It's you or me, Crater, and it ain't gonna be me . . . "

"Easy, Lucas, easy. There's a lawyer coming over here in an hour – and he's bringing the bondsman. I can't screw up with these guys. I can't let them find me with anything – or find me with you. You dig, man? You understand?"

"What I understand is this, man. It's you or it's me."

"Okay," Crater answered, "okay. I can understand why you're maybe a little mad about the last load, but – "

"I'm coming over there, Crater. I'm going to be there in half an hour."

"No, man. That ain't going to do either of us any good. You call me back, Arthur. I'll get you the stuff. You just give me a couple of hours."

It was 3:00 a.m. before Lucas managed to again reach Therland Crater by phone at his place at 116 Kendal Avenue. He didn't take no for an answer this time. He said he would be coming over immediately, and within minutes, he was there.

But it did him no good. Crater refused point-blank to come up with either the money or any more drugs. He called Lucas a sucker. Lucas called him a few things in return. Before long they were at it tooth and nail. "I'm going to kill you, Crater. I'm going to cut your lousy, cheating throat."

But Crater just laughed. This wasn't Detroit, this was Canada, and as far as he was concerned, he was pretty safe. He laughed all the way to the front vestibule where he pushed Lucas out into the dead middle of a damn cold night.

Lucas returned to his hotel. He made two phone calls, both to Detroit. Then he checked out. It was 6:00 a.m.

When he got back to the house on Kendal it was morning, but it wasn't light. Lucas rang the bell. Like the cocky fool he was, Therland Crater answered the door himself.

Lucas took one small step into the vestibule and pumped four close-range shots out of his .38.

Crater slumped to the floor. But he was still moving. Lucas didn't waste a second. He lashed out with his knife and watched a deep red crescent smile up from the black skin of Therland Crater's throat.

It was then that he heard the heavy steps on the stairs from the second floor, heard the hysterical screams of Carolyn Newman. By the time he realized what the racket was, she was standing over him, staring at the mess he'd made of her man. She screamed over and over again, but she wasn't too shocked to try and save her own neck. She ran the hell up the stairs as fast as her legs would carry her – which was pretty fast. She was already on the phone to a Bell operator when Lucas came up behind her.

He heard her scream into the phone. But there weren't any words except, "Not my throat, not my throat . . . "

"Damn right, your throat, you stupid bitch." He grabbed her hair and yanked back her head. He cut her just the way he had cut her boyfriend – four deep gashes that did the job. The phone fell from her hand and she made a sound that sickened him, the sound of blood pumped hard by the heart but ending up where no heart would mean it to be – all over the cheap rug and the bed. He let her go. As he did so something flew from his hand. The idea of leaving something behind scared him, but nothing scared him more than the thought of sticking around for one second longer. He went into the bathroom and carefully washed the blood off his hands, then fled, jumping over the sprawled body of Crater and out the door. The sun was just getting ready to rise.

In fact, it still wasn't all the way up when some poor night-shift worker from the post office made his way home to 116 Kendal, where he, like Newman and Crater, was a boarder. He saw what had happened as soon as he opened the door. Without even dropping his lunchpail, he ran two doors south to the house where his landlord lived, and the landlord called the police.

———————————

O N NOVEMBER 17, 1961, I was temporarily partnered with Detective John Bassett. We were working the day relief, and when we reported for duty at about 7:15 a.m., we were told not to bother taking off our hats, because we were required at 116 Kendal Avenue, a house in the Bathurst and Dupont area of the city. Uniformed officers on the scene had reported that a preliminary observation led them to believe a double murder had taken place in the house.

We didn't lose a second. When we entered the house, we saw at once the body of a male black lying on the floor of the vestibule. Clad only in undershorts, the whole body was covered in dried, clotted blood. A red gash had been deeply cut into the dark brown skin of his throat. Upstairs we found the dead body of a black female lying with her back on the bed and her feet on the floor. This victim was clad in a white slip, which was gathered up to her waist. She, too, had had her throat slashed.

We sent for the coroner, and set about protecting the scenes of both murder areas. We posted uniformed officers at all entrances and exits to the premises, to prevent unauthorized persons from entering and possibly contaminating existing evidence, or evidence yet to be discovered. Unfortunately, some of the worst offenders in this regard were our own officers, most of them attending out of curiosity only. However, we could usually discourage them from entering by requesting their names and numbers, and suggesting to them that they would be subpoenaed to court as witnesses.

After the coroner had made his observations, Bassett and I proceeded with our examination of the vestibule. Despite the obvious distraction of the quantity of blood in the small hallway, we looked carefully around and were surprised to find a spent bullet. We examined the body more closely, and we discovered four holes – bullet entrances. So in addition to sustaining a badly slashed throat, our victim had been shot at least four times.

We took another look at the second-floor bedroom. There we found what appeared to be a man's gold ring, lying on the bed beside the right leg of the dead woman. This ring had a setting containing eight diamonds, and had several strands of string wrapped around it, as if someone wearing it had tried to make it smaller to fit his finger. We later tried it on the finger of the deceased man, but even with the string it was too big.

The rumpled condition of the bed sheets indicated that the murderer had lost the ring while in a frenzy of slashing. We figured that after completing the act, he'd hurriedly searched for his ring without success.

After the necessary photographs were taken, we had both bodies removed to the morgue for post-mortem examination. The pathologist confirmed that the male victim had been shot four times with a .38 calibre revolver. But the primary cause of death had been the slashed throat. The cut had completely severed the artery. Examination of the female victim resulted in a verdict of a cause of death similar to the male, but with no gunshot wounds.

A thorough search of the rooms occupied by the two deceased showed their identities as Therland Crater, male, forty-four, American, resident of Detroit, Michigan, and Carolyn Newman, female, aged twenty, American, also a resident of Detroit. There was ample evidence at the scene to substantiate our suspicions that the victim Newman was actively engaged as a prostitute in Toronto, and the victim Crater was living totally on her earnings.

When the particulars of the murders came to the attention of members of the various squads at police headquarters, a bright young detective by the name of James Majury remembered that he and his partner had questioned a black male and a black female on November 10, in a downtown Toronto hotel. At the time, Detective Majury and his partner had strongly suspected the female of engaging in acts of prostitution. On checking his notebook, Majury located the name of the questioned male. It was Arthur Lucas, fifty-four, with an address on Burns Street, in Detroit. Lucas had told the officers that he and his girlfriend were in Toronto to visit a friend, Therland Crater, who lived at 116 Kendal Avenue. Majury's meticulous notes on a routine investigation of a prostitute and her pimp were the first and most important breaks in what was to develop into an international murder investigation, ultimately involving major figures in American organized crime.

Further inquiries that afternoon revealed that both of the deceased persons had been arrested on November 12 on charges of keeping a common bawdy house at 116 Kendal. After appearing in court, they had both been remanded to the Don Jail for a medical examination, which at that time was the usual procedure when such charges are involved. Then they had been released on bail.

A meeting was held in the evening of November 17, and Chief James Mackey agreed with the suggestion that Bassett and I should fly to Detroit the next morning and attempt to locate the suspect, Arthur Lucas.

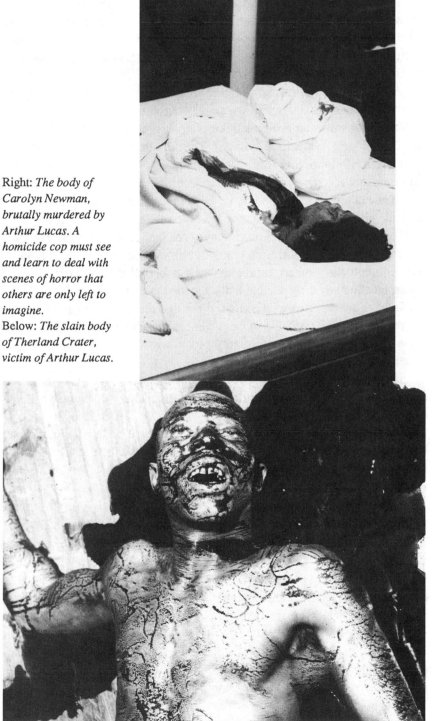

Right: *The body of Carolyn Newman, brutally murdered by Arthur Lucas. A homicide cop must see and learn to deal with scenes of horror that others are only left to imagine.*
Below: *The slain body of Therland Crater, victim of Arthur Lucas.*

When we got to police headquarters in Detroit the following morning, we were informed by narcotics officials that they'd located Arthur Lucas during the night and had already arrested him. He was being held for questioning by us. This was the beginning of a lengthy stay in Detroit for Sergeant Bassett and me, and it gave us a frightening first-hand look at Detroit gangland. In all the raids and searches of premises we took part in, there was not one house or apartment where the Detroit officers did not recover a variety of firearms and drug trafficking tools, such as scales, gelatin capsules, envelopes, needles and syringes. The drug trade was nowhere near as extensive in Toronto, and Bassett and I certainly had our eyes opened by the extent and volume of the problem in Detroit.

In one raid we participated in, we entered a house so quietly that heroin "capsule packers" were still hard at work at a long table, with an overseer perched on an elevated chair, watching to see that the packers did not take any free samples. We were informed by the man in charge that the only compensation the packers received was the periodic right to sniff their hands, inhaling any drug residue that happened to be left on them.

It was quite obvious to Bassett and me that the trafficking in narcotics and the operation of prostitution rings went hand in hand. Years later, in the late eighties, this seemingly foreign problem was to surface with a vengeance in Metropolitan Toronto.

Bassett and I worked very closely with the Detroit narcotics squad detectives, putting in sixteen-hour days until we could come up with enough evidence to bring a charge of murder. It wasn't that hard to find, but it took time. Lucas's lawyers, in the meantime, requested bail for their client. That was no problem, the presiding judge said, and he set bail at $1,000,000. Lucas remained in custody.

OUR INVESTIGATION AT THE SCENE, and the evidence we gathered in Detroit, left us in no doubt that Lucas was the killer, and we were able to reconstruct his actions in some detail. After the murders, he took time to wash his hands in an adjoining bathroom, dried them on a towel, and in his haste, left the tap running. He then left the premises and drove to the closest border-crossing point, which was Niagara Falls, New York, and then on to Detroit, via Cleveland, Ohio.

On his return journey to the United States border, while crossing over the Burlington Skyway Bridge near Hamilton, Ontario, Lucas attempted to get rid of the .38 calibre revolver by throwing it out of the car window, and over the high bridge. But the gun struck the railing and fell back onto the sidewalk. The cylinder was jarred loose, and it did go over the railing. As

A temporary investigation office was set up on the third floor of 116 Kendal Avenue after the double slaying of Therland Crater and Carolyn Newman. Left to right: *Inspector Bill McNeely, Deputy Chief George Elliott, Staff Superintendent Adolphus Payne, Detective Sergeant John Bassett and Detective Sergeant Jack Webster.*

luck would have it, a passing motorist noticed the gun lying on the sidewalk, and he notified the Ontario Provincial Police, who took possession of the firearm and turned it over to our force. The OPP had been alerted about our double murder, and thought the recovered weapon might have been involved.

Members of the homicide squad were dispatched to search the area, and the cylinder was located on the ground under the bridge. Both the gun and cylinder were badly bloodstained. Forensic examination revealed the stains to be blood type B, the same as that of both of the deceased persons. Ballistics examination of the weapon and the bullets recovered from Crater's body, as well as cartridges in the hallway at 116 Kendal Avenue, established positively that one of the bullets had been fired from the weapon. The markings on two of the other bullets indicated that they had also been fired from the same gun, but there were not sufficient points of comparison for positive identification. It was later stated in court that the markings on these bullets were consistent with their having been fired from this gun and the odds were astronomically against their having been fired from any other weapon.

In Detroit, Sergeant Bassett and I learned that Arthur Lucas owned such a gun, and the revolver was subsequently positively identified at the trial by two close associates of Lucas's. These same two witnesses also identified the ring found on the bed beside the deceased Newman as being the property of Arthur Lucas. One of the two witnesses testified that he was the man who accompanied Lucas to the pawn shop in Detroit when Lucas had retrieved his ring. He had also been present when Lucas wound the string around the base so that it would fit on his finger.

After Lucas was arrested by Detroit police, at our request, the borrowed automobile was also seized and taken to the Detroit Police Department's garage, where it was expertly examined by members of their scientific bureau, in association with experts from our own forensic laboratories, who had flown to Detroit from Toronto to assist the investigation. The vehicle contained bloodstains which were identified as blood type B. Blood-stained fingernail clippings were found on the floor of the front seat. An examination of Arthur Lucas's fingernails revealed that they had recently been clipped.

When Lucas first returned to Detroit, after the murders, he went directly to his estranged wife's apartment on Collingwood Avenue, where he informed her in great detail of what he had done in Toronto. He felt confident in doing so because she was his legal wife and was therefore not a compellable witness. (Even though she eventually was most co-operative with Sergeant Bassett and me, even coming to Toronto, by law we could not use one word of her testimony at the trial.) At his wife's apartment, Lucas washed his outer bloodstained clothing in a pail and telephoned an associate to bring him a change of clothes. When the associate arrived at the Collingwood Avenue address, he found Arthur Lucas standing in his undershorts. A later search of the apartment by Sergeant Bassett and me revealed the wet clothing, still in a pail of bloody water.

During this search, we also found a quantity of .38 calibre S & W Remington ammunition, and this was later identified as similar to, if not exactly the same as, that used in the shooting of Therland Crater. Shortly after his arrest, the hands of Arthur Lucas had been examined microscopically with the residual gunpowder nitrate test, and as a result, unburned gunpowder was found in the webbing of his right hand. Lucas was right-handed, and evidence later given by two ballistics experts showed that the residual gunpowder could only have become so embedded by the actual firing of the gun.

All of this information, including sworn statements from the associates of Arthur Lucas, enabled us to obtain a provisional warrant for Lucas's arrest on a charge of murder.

Formal extradition hearings were arranged. Henry Bull, the Crown attorney for the City of Toronto and the County of York, attended the hearings with Sergeant Bassett and me, to explain the laws of Canada as they pertained to the charge of capital murder and the possible penalties upon conviction. The proceedings were lengthy and both Bassett and I were uneasy about the many friends and obviously criminal associates of the accused Arthur Lucas who packed the courtroom daily, and made a habit of staring at both of us. On one occasion a very rough-looking black man, keeping his eyes compellingly glued to mine, ran his finger threateningly across his throat.

Our concerns were well-founded. Officers of the Detroit police department's Intelligence Bureau warned us to be on the alert, not to move about the city alone, and to call the police department for transportation at any time we went out, because their office had received reliable information that "Bassett and Webster are marked to be killed." The threats were motivated by more than just a desire for revenge. With the two Canadian investigators out of the way, there would be very little evidence against Lucas.

Heeding our colleagues warning, we checked out of our downtown Detroit hotel within the hour, and with the assistance of the police department in Windsor, Ontario, crossed the Canadian border and checked into a small Windsor motel. From that time until the conclusion of our Detroit investigation, we never moved without the companionship of two tough Windsor detectives and two huge Detroit narcotics officers.

Our presentation to the court for the extradition of Arthur Lucas was successful, and Sergeant Bassett and I returned to Toronto with him on March 1, 1962. After a brief preliminary hearing, he was committed for trial.

The trial itself was a strenuous event for Bassett and me. We produced a total of fifty-four witnesses, many of whom were from out of town, specifically Detroit. These witnesses from the United States had to be lodged and cared for, and Bassett and I had to organize that as well as our many responsibilities at the trial itself. A total of 105 exhibits were produced to the court by Henry Bull, Q.C., the Crown prosecutor.

On May 10, 1962, the case went to the jury. After only four and a half hours' deliberation, they returned a verdict of "Guilty of capital murder." The jury made no recommendation for mercy when asked to consider the possibility by the presiding justice, J.C. McRuer.

The chief justice sentenced Arthur Lucas to be executed by hanging, such execution to take place on July 25, 1962. The subsequent appeals leading up to the Supreme Court of Canada and the final deliberation by the prime minister and his cabinet delayed the execution until December 11, 1962. This made Arthur Lucas a significant man in history, for he was the last ever to be hanged in Canada.

About a week before his execution, Lucas sent word through his law-yer, Ross McKay, that he would like to see Sergeant Bassett and me. With some trepidation, we attended at the Don Jail, and Lucas was ushered into our presence in a room near the governor's office. We had talked with Arthur Lucas many times before, of course, and Bassett and I always called him "Luke." That was how we addressed him now. I said, "You wanted to see us, Luke?"

He replied, in the quiet voice we had come to know well, "I just want to thank you both for being very fair with me, and to say goodbye." He ended the conversation by adding, "You had a job to do, and I had a job to do." He extended his hand and both Sergeant Bassett and I shook it. He turned his back and walked away with the guard. That was the last time we ever saw Arthur Lucas.

IN 1961, MY FIRST YEAR on the homicide squad, my regularly assigned part-ner was a big detective – not only in physical stature, but in intelligence. His name? James F. Crawford. Big Jim had been a detective in the North York Police Force prior to amalgamation with Toronto. He and Ted Blakely, his partner in Number 3 District (as it was later named), were two of the finest thief-catchers anywhere in Canada. There were almost daily write-ups in the newspapers about their exploits, and at one time my partner Detective Charlie Gordon and I had a friendly rivalry going with them over which of our teams could make the most arrests. It eventually reached a point where the four of us had a meeting and called our unofficial contest a draw.

I was more than pleased to have this brilliant investigator assigned as my partner. Jim Crawford was my junior in service and rank at the time, he being a detective and I a detective sergeant, but I could fill a book with what he taught me in the proper and meticulous care that had to be taken in the investigation of death as a result of a criminal act.

Detective Crawford and I conducted several murder investigations when we were partners and in most cases we were able to bring them to a satisfactory conclusion. But not always. Two cases in particular remained unfinished, the culprits still at large.

One of these was the case of a two-year-old female child, who had been removed to the Hospital for Sick Children in an unconscious condition. Shortly after admittance, the little child died, and a post-mortem examina-tion revealed that her death was the result of a ruptured liver. The attend-ing pathologist was of the opinion that an injury of this type could only have been caused by a blunt instrument such as a closed fist, with direct application to the abdomen. In a death of this kind, with such findings by the attending pathologist, the homicide squad is automatically notified. Detective Crawford and I were the weekend duty officers and were assigned to the case.

We viewed the pitiful, fragile little body at the hospital, with the freshly made autopsy markings all too evident. Both Detective Crawford and I had young daughters at home, and to think that some person would fatally injure a beautiful and helpless child filled us with consuming rage. We were determined to bring the person responsible for this heinous crime to justice.

First, we talked to the parents of the child. The father was a booze-drenched, obese carnival worker, and the mother was a thin, work-worn young woman, who looked fifteen years older than her actual age. She would say very little, except that she knew no one who could purposely have harmed her child. One did not have to be Sherlock Holmes to see that this poor little woman was frightened out of her wits.

We soon learned what it was she feared. The father, when we questioned him, was insolent and abusive, punctuating his replies with profanity and generally behaving like the absolute slob he was. Despite his noisy protests, we took him to police headquarters to get a written statement. After several hours in custody, this so-called father of the murdered child did everything he could to obstruct our investigation. When we completed our questioning we knew he had signed a statement riddled with lies and misinformation, but we had no way of proving it. We had to return him to his downtown Toronto home.

Detective Crawford and I spent twelve- and fourteen-hour days on this case. We interviewed members of the immediate family: sisters and brothers of the father and mother, aunts and uncles and neighbourhood children. Time and again, we were met with almost complete silence. It was obvious that the word was out to tell the cops nothing. We attended the small, pathetic funeral, with its tiny casket. Detective Crawford and I stared pointedly at the father in the hope that we might shame him into remorse and an admission of his guilt, without success. For months after, we would attend at carnivals and street auction sites, stand at the front of the crowd and stare at this sub-human being. Stepping down from the platform he would walk past us, and out of the corner of his mouth, say, "Fuck you guys."

I should add that shortly after the child was buried, Jim Crawford and I received an anonymous call at headquarters, from a male person who identified himself as a relative of the child's mother. The caller told us that, although we would never be able to prove it, the father had violently attacked the little girl. He had been sleeping off a drunk on an old couch in the backyard. (It was summer, and Detective Crawford and I remembered such a couch.) Around eight o'clock on a Sunday morning, the child had tried to awaken her father, hoping that he would give her some breakfast. In his stupor, he was hard to arouse, but she continued to shake him. Suddenly awakening, enraged, he lashed out with a punch that struck her in the stomach.

This information had to be an accurate explanation of the series of events. It matched the pathologist's findings perfectly. Our informant went on to say that the wretch of a father was bragging that he had bamboozled Webster and Crawford, and that we had nothing on him and never would.

Jim Crawford and I have never forgotten this case, but unfortunately, what the murdering father said was true: we had nothing on him, though we knew he was guilty. Maybe when he faces his Maker, justice will triumph at last.

Many people have said to me that working on the homicide squad, and continually having to deal with violent death, must make one accustomed to it. This was not true for me personally or for most of my associates. As I have said, the murder of infants and children was particularly hard on us, because all of us had small children of our own. And it was always more than sad when, through mental illness or sudden depression, a mother or father who had decided to commit suicide would also murder their children or other family members, one after another.

One especially devastating experience that I recall vividly occurred about twenty-five years ago, in the east end of Toronto. We attended at a home where, upon our arrival, we found the severely battered bodies of a mother and four children in various rooms and in the basement. In the kitchen, we found the body of the father, with an obviously self-inflicted stab wound. With the exception of two older children who were away at the time, a lovely family was wiped out. The distraught father had left a letter stating that he had recently learned he had a serious heart problem, which would end his life prematurely. This dedicated husband and father of a close-knit and loving family felt that if he died, there would be no one left to look after his wife and children. With a tortured, unbalanced mind, he decided it was his duty to take the younger children and his wife with him, which he did.

I am sorry to say that I have investigated many such occurrences. My associates and I have always found that it took a long time before we could forget these terrible scenes of slaughter.

ONE EVENING IN APRIL OF 1962, Marion and I were dressed to go out to celebrate an anniversary; we had dinner reservations and were looking forward to a delightful evening. Just as we were going out the door, the telephone rang. My wife shot me a pleading look and said, "Don't answer it Jack, you're not on duty." I hesitated for a few seconds, but the telephone continued to ring, and I couldn't resist. The next moment, I was hearing my inspector order me to get to an address on Lakeshore as quickly as possible. Two young boys, aged three years and two years, had been found dead in a furniture warehouse. Of course, I had to go.

This wasn't the first time that our personal social life had been disrupted by the call of duty, nor would it be the last. But on this particular occasion, my wife was very upset. In another five seconds, she pointed out, we would have been gone. (This was before the age of the beeper.) I asked Marion to cancel our long-standing dinner reservations and I had to tell her I didn't know when I would be home. But the situation was old news to her!

At the Lakeshore address, as usual, we were briefed by the first uniformed officers to arrive on the scene. They told us a nineteen-year-old male warehouse employee, Gary McCorkell, had telephoned the police to report finding two obviously dead boys. This employee maintained that it was only the merest chance that he had made the discovery, since he didn't normally work in that particular area.

McCorkell was removed to the local police station for further questioning, while we made a minute examination of the scene. After the coroner's arrival it was discovered that the clothing of the boys was damp, and that the damp areas emitted a strong odour of urine. It was sickening. Two children dead, in a deserted warehouse, their deaths obviously having been caused by a perverted criminal act.

After extensive questioning at the local police station by detective sergeants Crawford and Alexander, McCorkell was shown several pieces of twine that had been used to bind the hands of the boys. He was reminded that this cordage was identical to a full roll that had been found at his work station, in an area far from where the bodies were found. This one piece of evidence in itself seemed to break his resistance. He confessed that he had lured the children into the warehouse to abuse them sexually, but when he began to molest them, they both had started to cry. He panicked, and in fear of discovery, smothered them. Not a difficult thing to accomplish for a strong young man, over six feet tall, with two children, only three and two years old. He further admitted that in order to satisfy his unnatural sexual urge, he had urinated on the dead boys.

This beast of a so-called human being was convicted and sentenced to hang. The sentence was subsequently commuted to one of life imprisonment. A large portion of his term of incarceration was spent at the Ontario Hospital for the Criminally Insane, at Penetanguishene, Ontario. He was eventually released from custody, and appeared to have quietly melted into the community.

But the story has a frightening postscript. Around 1985, I was the staff superintendent in charge of a police district comprising the whole city of Etobicoke, which included the Lakeshore area, with its many parks and recreational sites. My criminal investigators responsible for Lakeshore community reported a severe epidemic of sexual assaults on young boys. Some of these assaults were of a violent nature, and it was only by the accidental intervention of a passing citizen that one young victim was saved from being brutally slain. As it was, he received serious injuries, and I am sure the trauma of the assault will remain with the innocent boy forever.

The investigators, with the co-operation of the uniformed police officers, held many round-table discussions in an attempt to identify the dangerous sexual offender who was responsible for these attacks. As the senior command officer in the district, I urged uniformed and plainclothes officers alike to work as many overtime hours as necessary to capture this fiend before he attacked and possibly murdered his next defenceless victim.

It was at this point that a very bright middle-aged staff sergeant, Ronald Gillis, remembered seeing a small item on a released convicts bulletin, many months before, about the man who had killed the two little boys in the furniture warehouse. McCorkell had been released on mandatory parole. Twenty years had passed; he was now over forty, and it was nearly impossible for him to have avoided long exposure to sexual deviation while he was in prison. We checked the matter out and learned that his mother still lived in the Lakeshore area. Dispatched to her home, our officers were informed that yes, her paroled son had been living there, but he had recently left, and she did not know where he was.

An all-points bulletin was broadcast and distributed to police agencies in Canada and the United States, advising that this parolee was wanted for questioning regarding numerous sexual attacks on young boys. Almost immediately, a communication was received from a police department in the United States, reporting that they had arrested a man believed to be one and the same as the person we were seeking. We were further informed that he was facing charges of violent sex crimes in several central United States areas. Two of our detectives were sent to the city to interview him, and they were left in no doubt that he was the man responsible for our sexual assault occurrences.

At his trial in the United States, McCorkell received a sentence of 125 years, with no chance of parole, so it can be assumed that he will die in prison, and the world in general will be better off without him.

That, of course, is my private opinion on the case.

Top: *Law enforcement officers view the tragic scene in a furniture warehouse on Lakeshore Boulevard where two small boys were murdered. Left to right: Mr. John Funk of the Centre of Forensic Sciences; Detective Sergeant Irving Alexander; Detective Dave Saunders; Inspector Bill McNeely; Detective Sergeant Jim Crawford; the accused, Gary McCorkell; and Detective Sergeant Jack Webster.*
Above: *Gary McCorkell under arrest for the murder of two children on Lakeshore Boulevard, April 18, 1962. Detective Sergeant Jack Webster flanks McCorkell on the left; Detective Sergeant Jim Crawford, on the right.*

I have only told this story to illustrate the recidivism of criminals of this kind, and how common it is even after long periods of medical treatment and imprisonment. Despite stories like these, there were some happy times during my long service in the homicide squad. The Missing Persons Bureau was part of our squad's responsibility, and our investigations were sometimes long and intense, including such tasks as answering letters of inquiry from all over the world. It was always deeply gratifying to be able to reunite members of a family of long-lost loved ones.

Our unit was also responsible for the firearms section. Every firearm brought to the attention of the force had to be processed through us. This included registration checks and, very often, ballistic examination at the Centre of Forensic Sciences. Thousands of firearms of all descriptions passed through our unit, for one reason or another, but even though every member of the squad handled a continuous flow of these weapons, I do not recall a single one of us becoming a firearms collector, or what is referred to in police terms as a "gun nut." Homicide investigators constantly observe at first hand the serious injury and death that these weapons cause, and most of us hate the very sight of them.

Throughout my service in the military and my police career, I have had to tolerate being constantly armed with a deadly weapon. I very early learned a healthy respect for such death-dealing instruments, but that respect did not dilute my abhorrence of them.

ON MY THIRTY-NINTH BIRTHDAY, August 12, 1962, my wife and I were sitting comfortably with my mother and father, in their backyard. It was a sunny, warm afternoon and my mother had prepared some sandwiches and baked a cake for a small birthday celebration.

It was my duty weekend, and Detective Crawford and I were on call: that meant we had to be available by telephone from headquarters if a murder or suspicious death occurred anywhere in Metropolitan Toronto. If you had reason to leave your home, it was your responsibility to advise headquarters of a phone number where you could be reached. I, of course, had left my parents' telephone number, much to my dear mother's chagrin. She had never really accepted that my career as a police officer was the right one for me. (My father, on the other hand, was just the opposite. He was an intensely law-abiding man, and firmly believed that a law enforcement officer was just one step below the Lord himself.)

Before we had even had a chance to cut my cake, the telephone rang. My mother answered it, and of course, it was the office.

The duty desk sergeant informed me that the dead body of a young female had been found at the side of the road in the far northwest corner of

Metro. It was open country at that time, with some areas of dense bush at the sides of the road. The sergeant advised me that he had already notified Detective Crawford. I was to pick up the "homicide investigation kit" at headquarters along with "no entry" ropes and standards and meet my partner at the scene. The homicide kit was a black club bag, which contained rubber gloves, bottles and vials, occurrence forms, measuring tapes and a dozen other articles necessary for the preparation and preservation of evidence, both at the scene and at the inevitable post-mortem examination.

When we arrived, we observed the body of a young female lying in a ditch on the east side of the road. The body was nude from the waist up, and from the waist down she was wearing only a garter belt and nylon stockings. Even after a cursory examination, it was evident to us that she had been sexually abused. The body was removed to the coroner's building, where a post-mortem examination revealed that the cause of death was a .38 calibre bullet wound to the heart. The bullet was recovered and identified as being fired from an automatic pistol.

On checking the recent missing persons reports, we found the name of a sixteen-year-old girl who had been missing from her west-end Toronto home for five days. The girl's parents reported that she had been lured from her home after she had received a telephone call from a male person who had identified himself as a school teacher. When she had hung up, the girl had excitedly told her younger brother that she had to go to Yonge and Eglinton to undergo some type of examination, which was necessary for her high school entrance in September. The young girl waited for her mother to arrive home from work, and she repeated to her the directions she had received in the phone call.

The mother had tried to coax her to wait until the following day, when her father would drive her, but the girl said she had to go right away. Her mother gave her three streetcar tickets, in the event she lost one, and saw her walk over a nearby bridge to the streetcar stop. The next time her mother saw her was at the Toronto morgue.

We established a satellite homicide office in the local police division where the body had been found and commenced one of the largest manhunts in the history of the Metropolitan Toronto Police Force. At the peak of the investigation we had a total of fifty detectives working full time. Because the victim was from a Polish family who were active in all aspects of Polish culture in the city, we requested the assignment of Polish-speaking police officers to our investigation team. The officers proved to be invaluable to us in our questioning of hundreds of the victim's relatives and friends, who in many cases had recently arrived in Canada from displaced persons camps in Europe.

Hundreds of telephone calls and letters were received, and each and every piece of information was checked out. We sent out officers all over Canada and the United States to chase down leads. One letter, which was written anonymously, described in great detail a possible suspect who had very shortly after the murder returned to a city in Germany, where he had worked during the war as a conscripted Polish labourer. It was decided by our senior officers and the attorney general's department that Crawford and I would fly to Germany, and with the aid and co-operation of authorities in that country, locate and question this man. However, he returned to Toronto a few days before we were to depart. (He had gone to his brother's funeral in Germany.)

We questioned this red-hot suspect, but quickly determined that he was not involved in the murder. We and our associates interviewed and questioned well over a hundred prime suspects and in some of the cases, we could feel the excitement rise in our bodies thinking we had our man, but alas, at some point during the interrogation of every one of these suspects, facts were established or alibis checked out that meant that this one, like the last, had to be ruled out as our murderer.

I have been involved in hundreds of serious criminal investigations, and it has been my experience that time and money are no object where the pursuit of a deadly criminal is concerned. The public at large was most co-operative in this investigation. Their hearts were touched by the tragic end that befell the beautiful young girl. The fact that she had been in a displaced persons camp and had been entering upon a whole new life at the time of her murder captured the pity of all.

Despite our many months of full-time work on this one murder investigation, Detective Crawford and I and dozens of other veteran detectives were unable to bring it to a successful conclusion. During the years that have passed since our investigation was phased out, Jim Crawford and I have from time to time received sporadic tips relevant to the case. Even though we long since left the homicide squad and attained high rank on our force, we have personally checked out each item of information to the fullest possible degree.

This was the second of the two major disappointments that Detective Crawford and I had while we were working as partners. Despite the many successes we have achieved in our chosen profession, in the many years since the murder of this young girl, we are both still plagued with sadness at our lack of success in bringing the person or persons responsible to justice.

THERE ARE TIMES IN THE life of a working police officer when you honestly wish that you had chosen some other line of work. The worst of these has to be the occasion when you are called upon to arrest or investigate a relative, close friend or personal associate. It should not surprise anyone that these occasions do arise. Over the years, I have had the less than happy experience of arresting my cousin, next-door neighbours of my parents, old school chums and former army buddies. The charges against these people ranged from murder to lowly shoplifting. I have had the distasteful task of arresting a young man for the murder of his father, who was a former army captain in my old regiment. On two occasions I have arrested the sons of fellow members of the police force on murder charges. As someone once said, it goes with the territory.

For a police officer, there are many things that go with the territory. One of the most frightening is threats to the personal safety of your family. You learn to live with constant danger to yourself, but it takes on a completely new perspective when the safety and well-being of your wife and children are in jeopardy. Threats against innocent people are totally unacceptable, and my associates and I treated them with the utmost seriousness.

I once received a series of phone calls, made first to my wife and then directly to me, indicating that the callers were aware of the private school my daughter attended. They warned that if I failed to terminate a particular investigation, my wife and daughter would be harmed. Telephone calls of this type are usually punctuated by gross obscenities, meant to instil fear, especially in gentle and innocent civilians. (Though the families of police officers get very tough as the years go by!) At the time, I was still a member of the hold-up squad, and for a period of weeks, my daughter was escorted to and from school by my comrades on the squad. Rosemary was very young at the time, and she enjoyed the special attention, and soon became the centre of attraction with her school friends. The quiet, unassuming Anglican nuns who taught at the school, however, were less than delighted by these security measures.

When a close friend or relative of the neighbours or friends of a police officer is arrested, there is often a backlash of feeling directed against the officer in question. You may have had no part in the arrest or investigation, the arrest may have taken place in some other jurisdiction, but you as a police officer represent law enforcement, and therefore you are held responsible. When I first encountered this type of behaviour it made me sad, but when it spilled over and affected my wife and family, I became quite angry.

I SUPPOSE MOST POLICE OFFICERS have at one time or another investigated what can only be described as stupid, senseless criminal acts. I had to investigate one such occurrence in January 1963. It happened early on a Sunday morning, in a two-storey rooming house on Bathurst Street. The house was entirely occupied by recent immigrants from Europe. Three of the male occupants had made plans to go skiing, and they wanted to get an early start.

Two of them were waiting for the third to get out of bed in the basement of the house, and they commenced drinking tea – liberally laced with wine. At 10:15 a.m., when their sleeping friend had not yet made an appearance, they decided to awaken him by a method they had used successfully in the past. The alarm clock, as it were, was a .410 gauge, double-barrelled shotgun, which they would fire down the basement stairs.

One of the men discharged both barrels of the shotgun into the stairwell. Unfortunately, the lead pellets penetrated the back of the staircase leading to the second floor, where another roomer in the house, a lady, was in the act of descending the stairs with her two small children. The children escaped being struck by the lead pellets, but the mother was hit in the left shoulder and chest. She was taken by ambulance to a nearby hospital, where ultimately she had to undergo several operations for removal of the lead shot. The two were charged with criminal negligence causing bodily harm, and were eventually convicted.

The most disturbing part of it was that even after viewing the results of this stupid and potentially fatal act, they insisted that there was nothing wrong with using a shotgun to awaken their friend: it had always worked before and it was "only a little accident" that had caused someone to be hurt.

IN JULY 1964, DETECTIVE George Thompson and I were partners on the homicide squad. One of the longest and most unrewarding investigations of our careers began that summer.

It had been brought to the chief coroner's attention that a young lady had died in an east-end Toronto hospital, and that a post-mortem examination of the body revealed that a surgical clamp had been left in the abdomen of the deceased, resulting in bowel strangulation, which was the cause of death. The chief coroner had received this information, not from the hospital or the medical people involved, but from an informant who wished to remain anonymous.

When the deputy chief of police assigned George and me to the investigation, he was unusually solemn, and gave us to understand that the case would be a difficult and very sensitive one, because the chief coroner was engaged in a running feud with the hospital involved and the directors of it.

In addition to this, the provincial government had had well-publicized and explosive verbal disagreements with the coroner on a number of issues.

These were the ingredients we had to deal with: a large, highly respected Metropolitan Toronto hospital; dozens of very talented medical people, surgeons, general practitioners, and nurses; a political party in power that was constantly at odds with a brilliant and headline-seeking coroner; and a mysterious death. George Thompson and I knew that our problems would be mountainous. We resolved that our investigation would be guided by the principle that our primary responsibility was to the woman who had died. We decided that any findings, no matter how unpleasant, no matter what possible effects they might have on anyone's career, would have to be brought to light, and publicly disclosed.

The operation that had been performed on the deceased, we soon learned, had been opposed by senior surgical staff at the hospital. The purpose of the procedure as proposed by the attending surgeon was to remove an obstruction between the esophagus and the stomach. The chief of surgery thought it was a risky procedure, with very little chance of success, but the attending surgeon, who had hospital and operating room privileges, prevailed upon senior hospital officials to allow him to try. He was certain the operation would give the young patient a chance of at least some improvement in the quality of her life. The chief agreed, but only on the condition that resident surgeons would be present and observe the entire procedure.

Shortly after the operation had begun, two of the young hospital surgeons verbally disagreed with the visiting surgeon and in fact said he was demonstrating an almost total lack of knowledge with regard to anatomy. The disagreement reached loud proportions, and one of the staff surgeons sent for the chief of surgery, who came at once. He agreed with the observers and directed that the visiting surgeon discontinue the operation immediately. He then left the room, not waiting to see the patient's closure.

For a few days after the operation the patient complained continually of abdominal pain. Then she went into a coma and died. The family of the deceased was asked for permission to perform a post-mortem examination. The permission was granted, and the autopsy was performed by a veteran medico-legal pathologist on the hospital's staff. When the steel clamp was found, the pathologist told the chief of surgery that he had better consult with the surgeon involved and decide on notifying the authorities as required by the Coroner's Act.

The officials in the hospital were in a state of shock, and could not quickly agree on how the situation should be handled. The body of the young woman was released to her family, but the direct cause of death was not revealed to them, and before the examining pathologist had reported any of these circumstances, the chief coroner received the damning anonymous information. The hospital and the medical personnel, including the pathologist, were now in serious trouble.

The story was front-page news for a number of weeks. At the conclusion of our investigation, several of the involved doctors were charged under the Coroner's Act for failing to notify the coroner when they were required to do so by law. I am sorry to say that this unfortunate occurrence destroyed the reputation and careers of some first-class surgeons and dedicated medical people. If any good came of the coroner's inquest and trial, it was that a new and more accurate way of counting clamps and other surgical implements began to be used during surgical procedures.

As this story shows, not all deaths investigated by homicide officers are crimes of passion and violence. Yet every death, as John Donne pointed out, diminishes all of us.

SOME OF THE MOST DEPRESSING investigations that I've been involved in were cases in which innocent people lost their lives just because they happened to be in the right place at the wrong time. One day, for example, three employees from Toronto's City Hall ran across the street to a bank at the corner of Bay and Queen to cash their pay cheques on their lunch hour. While they were standing in line for a teller, an armed man entered the bank and announced in a loud voice, "This is a hold-up." Even though he did not receive any opposition, he promptly shot the three customers. They died almost instantly.

In another case a bank in the North York area of Metropolitan Toronto was held up by one masked and disguised man, shortly after it opened one sunny July morning in 1964. To demonstrate that he meant business, the robber fired several shots at the walls in the bank. After scooping up several thousand dollars, he ordered everyone to remain still, and raced from the bank. One of the customers was a fifty-five-year-old man, a war veteran who had served in the Palestine Army with distinction. As the bandit cleared the front door of the building, this heroic, unarmed man gave chase. When he was about fifty yards from the bank, the gunman turned and fired one shot at his pursuer, killing him instantly.

On October 6, 1969, a twenty-six-year-old police constable was assigned the not too exciting job of guarding an area of land to prevent unauthorized dumping of garbage and other waste material. Some time after midnight, the officer had occasion to question a man in the area. The man pulled a revolver and shot the officer twice in the upper body. There this courageous young married man lay, dying in a cold, desolate field, while the gunman calmly removed the service revolver from his police holster and took off. In the darkness, with death slowly enveloping him, the constable made certain marks in his memorandum book, which eventually became crucial evidence at a subsequent trial.

Although I have sketched these occurrences in only a few brief words, they entailed days, weeks and months of diligent investigation on the part of me and my associates, before all three brutal murderers were eventually arrested, convicted of their crimes, and sentenced to long terms in the penitentiary. But it took only a matter of minutes for five families to be deprived of their loving husbands and fathers. In my long experience, I have found that families of murder victims are in some ways the real victims of the crime. They are the ones who have to live with the memories 365 days a year, and the initial tragedy often creates a chain reaction that disrupts and, in some instances, separates families when one sorrowing member of a family blames the tragedy on another.

Yes, the investigation of murder is a hard way to make a living, but as a former veteran jurist once said, "A homicide detective should feel proud, because he is the only one standing in the shoes of the victim to ensure that justice will eventually triumph."

As a homicide detective, I was called in on another grisly case of being in the right place at the wrong time late in the summer of 1965. A man by the name of Phillip Young, who had recently passed his sixty-fourth birthday, had an argument with his wife. During the argument, he struck her with his fists and an electric steam iron. Mrs. Young was treated at St. Joseph's Hospital for her injuries, and the following day she went to City Hall and had a warrant issued for the arrest of her husband, on a charge of wounding. Three days later, he was arrested at his home on Dufferin Street. After being photographed and fingerprinted at police headquarters, he was lodged in police cells.

Although the arrested man had a lengthy criminal record, none of the offences that he had been convicted of had involved acts of violence. Shortly after being placed in the police cell, he complained of shortness of breath and chest pains. He informed the police personnel that he had a long history of heart disease. He was immediately transported to Toronto Western Hospital. The doctors at the hospital couldn't find anything wrong with the prisoner, but because of his previous medical history, they decided to admit him for further tests.

At the request of the police, a justice of the peace held proceedings at the hospital and remanded Phillip Young, on his own recognizance, to appear in court one week later. This remand removed the necessity of placing a twenty-four-hour police guard at the bedside of the accused. One day after the remand, Young signed himself out of the hospital. When he failed to appear at City Hall courts on the date stated in the remand papers, a bench warrant was issued for his immediate arrest.

Although an intensive search was conducted to locate the wanted man, he seemed to have disappeared completely. But during the first week of September, a field worker for the Department of Public Welfare received a letter from Phillip Young. In the letter, he had a few nasty things to say about his wife, and he also said that he was going to take the "coward's way out." The welfare worker took this to mean that the wanted man was going to commit suicide. If only it had been as simple as that! It would have prevented a lifetime of sorrow for the families of two beautiful young girls murdered at the very threshold of life.

The two girls, both nineteen years of age, were students at a data-processing school on Bloor Street West, near Avenue Road. It was the usual routine for one of the girls to drive her car from her home in the western suburbs of the city to a parking lot on the south side of Lakeshore Boulevard, next to the Palais Royal Ballroom. Leaving the car there, she would walk across the footbridge to the intersection of Roncesvalles and Queen, and take public transportation to the school on Bloor.

The two victims met on September 8, 1965, and discovering that they both lived in the west end, the girl with the car offered to drive her new friend home if the other girl was willing to take the streetcar to the parking lot on Lakeshore. She agreed, and at four-thirty that afternoon, they were seen leaving the school together. Neither made it home.

About eight o'clock that evening, both sets of parents, unaware that their daughters knew each other, reported the girls missing. It was only after information was received from the school that it was learned that the girls had been seen together.

The following day, September 9, 1965, at about noon, a man was disposing of some tree cuttings in a municipal dump in Vaughan Township, which is just outside the boundary of Metropolitan Toronto. To his dismay, this citizen came upon the dead bodies of the wanted man and the two missing girls. Both girls were in the front seat of a car, and Phillip Young's body was lying on the ground seven feet away.

Both of these innocent teenagers had been shot several times. The murderer, Phillip Young, had shot himself once through the mouth, the bullet lodging in his brain. Subsequent investigation by our squad with the assistance of Vaughan Township officers located two witnesses who had seen a man of Phillip Young's description approach a woman in a small automobile in the Lakeshore Boulevard parking lot. She had appeared frightened, and had driven away quickly. The witnesses then observed the same man approach an automobile containing two girls who matched the description of the two victims. The man got into the front seat with the girls, and the car drove away.

Our investigation led us to conclude that Young had pointed his firearm at the girls, thus forcing the driver to go where he directed. When he got to the garbage dump, he not only took the coward's way out, he took two innocents out with him. It is probably of some consolation, though small, that neither girl was sexually assaulted and each died almost instantly.

When police officers are assigned to murder and other violent death investigations, we many times ask ourselves "Why?"

Why, indeed?

Of all the murders that I have investigated, one in particular fills me with sadness whenever I recall the pitiful statement of the seventeen-year-old youth whom we arrested and charged with murder. In November 1965, my partner was Sergeant Bob Bamlett, and although it was our day off, we were notified that we were wanted at a police station in Etobicoke. When we arrived we were met by several detectives from our own squad and the local division. Also in attendance was the chief of detectives. Sergeant Bamlett and I were immediately subjected to some good-natured ribbing by our fellow officers, such as, "Everything's okay now, here come the two brains. They'll have it solved within the hour."

Neither Bamlett nor I were in a laughing mood. After all, we were on our own time, and the group of joking detectives had already been working on the case for several hours without success. We were told that a fifty-year-old woman, who lived alone, had been found stabbed to death in a hallway on the ground floor of her Etobicoke home. She had been stabbed five times, twice in the chest and three times in the stomach. Her purse was missing, which certainly pointed toward robbery as the motive.

The victim had been separated from her husband for about eight years, and he of course had been thoroughly investigated, and cleared of involvement, by the detectives who had arrived on the scene earlier. A second suspect was a seventeen-year-old former roomer in the victim's home, and although this man was still being held in the police station, he had been thoroughly questioned, had an alibi for his time and recent activities, and was about to be released from the station. My partner and I asked the officers to delay his release until we had questioned him. They agreed, but only after having another laugh, and suggesting we were wasting our time.

In reading over the many supplementary reports, we noted that an expert for the forensic laboratory who had attended at the scene was of the opinion that the murderer was left-handed. He had formed this opinion by viewing the angle of entrance of the stab wounds.

Bamlett and I entered the room where the youth was being held, and it was a shock to us to see a good-looking, well-dressed young man, who stood up as we entered, held out his hand, and introduced himself. We introduced ourselves in turn and told him we wanted to ask him some questions about his former landlady. Very quickly, the young man said, "I already told the other detectives everything I know about the lady. I wish I could help you, because she was very good to me."

I gave the youth a piece of paper and a pencil and asked him to write down his full name and address. He did so, writing with his left hand. Sergeant Bamlett and I then sat very quietly for a few moments and just stared at the youth. He became restless, stood up, walked around the room, and then sat down again.

At this point Bamlett, who always had a very genuine concern for young people in trouble, said, "You know, son, I have three boys at home, just about your age, and it really distresses me to think that you, for some reason, took this lady's life."

There were a few moments of silence before the young man bowed his head and said, "Yes, I killed her. I have a terrible temper. I went to her house to borrow some money. She had always loaned me money in the past, but this time she refused. I had an argument with her, then picked up the knife and stabbed her."

We took a formal signed statement from this quiet, polite young man and when we re-entered the main detective office, we were greeted with shouts of "Well, how did you make out?" When we informed our incredulous associates that the murder was solved, and we were now going with the young murderer to recover the knife and his bloodstained clothing, silence fell over the room.

We later learned that the young man's father had been a police officer on our force, with an excellent reputation. He had resigned to start a small business, to try and make a better life for his wife and six children.

Sadness overcame Sergeant Bamlett and me when, after the killer was placed in the police cells, he asked us if his photograph would be in the newspapers. When we said that it probably would, he reverted to the young boy he really was and asked, "Could you fellows get me a couple of copies, so I can see how I look?"

ONE OF THE CASES BOB BAMLETT and I were assigned to in 1968 was the investigation of a magistrate in the provincial court system in Metropolitan Toronto. It was a sensitive situation, because our intelligence unit, which was under the very capable leadership of Inspector Roy Soplet at this time,

Detective Sergeant Jack Webster, Elgin Brown of the Forensic Crime Lab, and Detective Sergeant Bamlett examine a blood-stained wall in the room where Eileen Conium was murdered.

had had a telephone wiretap on the line of a well-known criminal, and the constant monitoring of the calls made and received by this convicted man picked up several calls from the magistrate we were now investigating. It was obvious from the content of the conversations that the magistrate was using his influence as a member of the judiciary to affect the verdicts of guilt or innocence of persons charged with criminal offences. It was also quite evident that he was receiving benefits for these favours.

It must be remembered that the telephone wiretap was on the criminal's phone, not the magistrate's, and the less than honest activities of the magistrate came to the attention of the authorities as a secondary result of the investigation of a known, convicted lawbreaker.

After the attorney general's department was apprised of these incriminating facts, they suspended the magistrate and ordered him to face a judicial inquiry. Of course, the media responded by making the investigation into front-page news, and the establishment of Old City Hall, which housed the provincial courts, was rocked to its foundations.

There were other magistrates whose names surfaced from time to time in the taped conversations, but we firmly believed that they were unsuspecting participants in shady activity, who were simply friends of the subject magistrate. However, in order to complete our investigation, Sergeant Bamlett and I had to attend at Old City Hall courts to question them.

We decided that the best place to speak to them, where they would be at ease and not feel themselves to be under suspicion, would be in the magistrates' lounge. This was a place for the presiding magistrates to relax and have a cup of coffee before court and during recesses. Bamlett and I had been guests in the lounge on many occasions. It was generally a quiet place, a club-like room out of the eye of the many court gossips and hangers-on, where we could talk to the people that we needed to in order to clear their positions in the investigation.

We telephoned the first magistrate we intended to question, and he agreed to meet us in the lounge at 9:00 a.m., on a particular day. This was about an hour before court sitting began and we figured it would give us ample time, in a relaxed atmosphere, to complete our inquiries.

When we arrived at the lounge, we were welcomed by several members of the judiciary, whom we had known professionally for many years. They insisted that we have coffee and Sergeant Bamlett and I were soon at ease in the company of old friends. However, within minutes, another magistrate entered the lounge and, seeing Bamlett and me, said, "What are these two rotten bastards doing here? Trying to find out our telephone numbers so they can tap our phones, too? Get out of here, you two pricks, and stay out."

The others were very embarrassed at this outburst from an associate, and asked us to ignore it. But the atmosphere was now extremely tense, and we felt like intruders. We left, and made other arrangements for our interviews. The irony of it was that the magistrate who insulted us by his obscenities was a first-class drunk and womanizer, whom Bamlett and I, as well as dozens of other police officers, had picked up and driven home many times. We had cleaned up vomit and excrement from him in our police cars on more than one occasion, when he was drunk and incapable, and we had provided transportation for him at all hours of the day and night.

I would say that more than 90 percent of the criminal lawyers I have known during my career have been first-class gentlemen. Of course, they

Webster (right) and Bamlett escort the seventeen-year-old who was accused of murdering his fifty-year-old former landlady, Eileen Conium.

have cross-examined me on many hundreds of occasions with such vigour that it has bordered on torture, but that is only to be expected. A police officer learns very early in his career that when he is in the witness box, he is on his own. Occasionally the presiding justice will intervene on his behalf if the cross-examination becomes totally unfair, or insulting, but in general you are put in a possibly uncomfortable and sometimes terrifying position. The only way to protect yourself is to be as well prepared as is humanly possible. If you come with badly prepared Crown briefs and make badly thought-out replies, a bright and dedicated defence counsel will make mincemeat of you.

My associates and I on the hold-up and homicide squads have found that when these terrors in the courtroom have discharged their responsibilities to their clients, they take on a different personality entirely and can laugh and socialize and party with the best of them. Many become valued life-long friends, despite their elevation to the most senior appointments in the judicial system in Canada.

And so I suppose Sergeant Bamlett and I were really more hurt than insulted, or disappointed, at the unwarranted outburst of abuse we received from a person we thought was an old friend, who held a position we had come to respect and whom we were, in this instance, trying to shield from harm.

CHAPTER EIGHT

The
Human Element

AN INCIDENT THAT OCCURRED IN *the mid-sixties was, for Webster, a bench-mark in his conviction that fairness was the norm in dealings of the Toronto force with ethnic minorities.*

He was a detective sergeant on the homicide squad when the call came. Arriving at an apartment at Parliament and Dundas, Webster and other members of the unit were horrified to find a seventeen-year-old girl shot to death. They knew at once that there would be no hot pursuit of the killers, for two distraught teens were already in the custody of the first uniformed officers on the scene. The weapon was also at hand – a rifle that had been in the possession of one of the boys, a seventeen-year-old black youth.

With the help of co-operative neighbours, it didn't take long to piece together a simple but tragic story. The deceased girl was pregnant at the time of her death. She had no husband and worked toward supporting her-self by babysitting for another young woman, who had rented the apartment where the killing took place.

Then, as now, there were arcades on Yonge Street where young people, often from out of town, met to play games and socialize. It's easy to assume that such mingling has a criminal intent, but that's not always so. Early in the week prior to her death, the young woman and her employer had stopped by one of the arcades and struck up a conversation with two, lively, cute, pleasant young black men from Buffalo. Against the rush and racket of the crowds at the arcade machines, the four had managed to get to know each other a little – enough, anyway, for the girls to invite the American boys up to the apartment. The boys were happy to accept.

Making their way east, the four arrived at Parliament, went to the apartment, drank a few cups of coffee, and called it a night. The boys headed back to the States. The girls went to bed. Nothing unusual – or improper – happened.

But these four young people were smitten with each other. The boys promised they'd come back the next night, which was Saturday, and true to their word, they did, driving straight through from Buffalo right to the apartment, where they planned to stay until Monday morning.

No witness could fault the four. According to all accounts, they did nothing but listen to records, play the guitar – and eat pizza.

There was, however, one interruption of their innocent pleasure. On the Sunday afternoon, without warning, the former boyfriend of the girl who rented the apartment walked in. His unexpected presence and his arrogant, warning gestures frightened his ex-girlfriend, though no one later recalled him making any verbal threats except for muttering, "I'll be back," as he left.

This act of intrusion left the girls visibly shaken. It also left open the door to the mistaken sense of heroism that caused one of them to die. As the door closed behind the ex-boyfriend, the seventeen-year-old guest sprang up. "Don't worry," he told his hostesses and his nineteen-year-old companion, "I can protect you." He, too, promised to be back. When he returned shortly, he was carrying the weapon.

The girls were impressed with the sight of the gun. Modestly, the young man explained that it wasn't meant for any sort of combat, but just for hunting. When they asked him how he'd got it, their attention made him proud. With bravado, he off-handedly mentioned that he'd bought it against his parents' wishes six months before. Because they couldn't understand his wanting a rifle, they made it hard for him to keep it in the house, which was why he had it stowed in his car. The girls thought this defiance rather daring.

Once more, the four settled into the relaxed rhythm of the weekend, though now that they were aware of an imminent confrontation there was a little edge of nervousness to their pleasure.

But the ex-boyfriend never came back. On Monday morning, the two young men got ready to head back to Buffalo.

Just as they were about to go, they decided to show the young women how to clean the rifle. The owner lifted the weapon, adjusted one of the mechanisms. To his immense surprise, the rifle discharged, blasting a bullet right into the chest of the watching girl, who died instantly.

As Webster questioned the two young men, he and his partner had to admire how hard they were trying to co-operate. Fear, remorse and shame choked them. More than once, Webster was sure the owner of the gun was going to keel over any second.

Webster and his partner, however, had no choice but to detain the two at the homicide office while they headed to City Hall to consult with the Crown attorney on whether charges would have to be laid. Carefully, they laid the results of their investigation before the official. For a moment, he pondered the case, his manner grave and unrevealing. Then he threw it back to the partners. "What do you think?" he asked. "Do you want to bring charges?"

Both Webster and his partner swore that they were convinced they were dealing not with a murder, but with a sad accident. They argued that the case should go before the coroner for an inquest, not the criminal courts for a trial. Again the Crown pondered. Then, he let them know that he agreed. But there was a major technical problem. The detainees were American citizens. Even if they had been Canadian, they couldn't be held without charge. It normally took months before coroner's inquests into accidental or suspicious deaths were held. How did Webster propose to legally keep these young men in Toronto?

Webster gave it a few moments' thought. He well knew how slow the workings of justice can be. He ventured a question. "Is there," he asked, "any legal reason for delaying the start of an inquest?"

"No," the official admitted, "the delay is just for the preparation of the case. How much time do you think you'd need? You'd have to have everything ready at once if you wanted to move faster than usual . . ."

"Give us forty-eight hours," Webster bargained. "We'll do it."

If his partner winced, Webster didn't see. What he did see was that the Crown was thinking it over. "All right," he said finally, "if you can guarantee that the young men will show up, we'll hold the inquest the day after tomorrow."

Webster and his partner barely waited to hear which coroner would be appointed before rushing out of City Hall and back to homicide to get to work. They knew they could count on the assistance of others in the homicide squad to help out with the mound of paperwork necessary to meet their pressing deadline. Webster was also sure he could count on the youths. On a calculated gamble, he and his partner let the boys go on the strength of a promise to return to Toronto in two days' time – Thursday. The boys left for Buffalo at once.

Of course, there were plenty of people, including members of the media, who condemned this release as an act of grave irresponsibility on the part of the police. A pregnant seventeen-year-old girl lay dead, as her killer and his accomplice headed out of the country with the blessing of the cops, as some saw it.

There was also quite a bit of controversy surrounding the speed with which the inquest was called and scheduled. Some wondered whether the judicial system usually dragged its heels – seeing it could move pretty damn fast when it wanted to. Others thought the system was treating American citizens better than it treated the average Canadian – neither a new idea nor a unique one. Still others felt justice could best be served by the speediest possible inquest into the innocent girl's death.

On Thursday morning, Webster and his partner were ready at police headquarters. If either of them had had the slightest doubt about their decision to release the boys, it didn't show. There was no hint of surprise, relief or even triumph as Webster looked up and saw the youths walk in. In a touching show of support, their parents had come with them. Webster and his partner took over, ready to transport the boys to the hearing.

Today, on any given morning, it's still possible for the observant passerby to catch sight of a little clutch of reporters huddled in front of the coroner's office, their bodies tense with waiting and their pens poised in anticipation. The coroner's office today, however, is in a sleek modern building near Yonge, and the reporter is very likely accompanied by someone with a video camera perched on his or her shoulder, its lens trained on the door from which a coroner or a pathologist serving as a witness, or even a young person under investigation, might spring. In the old days, the coroner's office was a much-used building on narrow Lombard Street. The day Webster arrived there, the two youths in tow, reporters crawled over each other scrambling to get close to the action. Webster could almost hear them settling the bets they'd made as to whether the boys from Buffalo would show. He didn't have to think hard to guess what would have happened to his rapidly rising career if they hadn't!

In accordance with the provisions of the Coroner's Act of Ontario, a jury was selected on the spot by conscripting ordinary citizens walking by on Lombard Street.

The hearing took all day. Painstakingly, Webster and his partner laid their case before the inquest. Each known detail was precisely presented. Each question was carefully and fully answered. In the end, the citizens of the coroner's jury brought in a verdict of accidental death.

Once more, regardless of what he felt in his heart, Webster revealed no sense of relief. To have done so would have implied that he had doubted that his case was strong enough to win.

But it was an emotional moment despite his stoicism. The parents and their sons were crying and hugging the two cops they felt had saved them. Both parents told Webster that had the situation occurred in their home country – two black suspects accused of shooting dead a white girl – the day would have ended on an entirely different note. Ecstatic, the American families headed home again.

Of course, Webster tells this story now from a distance of twenty-five years. Though the details remain clear and correct, he points out that the racial element in Toronto has changed – for better and for worse – time and time again in the intervening years.

He still remembers, though, that his office received many letters from black organizations in the United States, commending the Toronto force for the compassion and integrity with which they proved the innocence of a young man in a foreign country.

For Webster, this was certainly one of the more dramatic examples of dedication to fairness. But it was far from the only one. Experience taught him that fairness was the norm. Over the years he saw it exercised without fanfare or publicity. It was part of the job.

W HEN I WAS A YOUNG DETECTIVE, my first-hand experience of people's reaction to personal tragedy was quite limited. I believed people suffered their grief forever, as my parents had when they lost my brother through drowning. As I became more experienced, I was to find that this was not always true.

Once, early in my career, I was working with a veteran detective sergeant on the day relief when we were notified to attend at an address in central Toronto. When we got there a uniformed officer informed us that a young lady had returned to her rented flat, which was on the second floor of the house, to find her six-month-old baby hanging from a coat hook on a bedroom door, on the other side of which she found her husband hanging from a similar coat hook.

She ran downstairs to her neighbours, who called the police. The wife was now being comforted by the downstairs residents, and the uniformed officer had determined that both victims had been dead for some hours. When my partner and I attended upstairs, we agreed with his findings, and we cut the ligatures from the bodies and lowered them to the floor.

After his examination of the scene and the bodies, the coroner declared an obvious case of murder and suicide. We investigated, questioning friends and associates of the deceased man, as well as his sorrowing wife. We learned that the couple had immigrated from Europe where, in his homeland, the man had been a highly educated member of a profession; but in Canada, because of his lack of English and the requirement for further education in the Canadian system, he was unable to work at his profession. He became depressed at his low level of employment, and with his mind so disturbed, he took his own life and the life of their baby.

I was deeply moved by the plight of this young mother. When our reports were done and we were about to book off, I said to my veteran partner, "This poor woman, what will she do now? For all intents and purposes, her life is over. It wouldn't surprise me if she took her own life."

My partner took what I thought at the time was a callous view of the situation. "Don't worry, Jack," he said, "two weeks from now she'll have a boyfriend and all this will be forgotten." I was shocked at his insensitivity.

Six weeks later, we received a letter from a relative of the deceased man, requesting that we contact his wife and ask her to write home with details of her husband's death. As the original investigators, we were given the letter for delivery to the wife. We soon learned that she'd moved from her former Toronto address and was living in an apartment downtown. That didn't surprise me – who would want to remain where such a tragedy had occurred?

When we attended at the new address, we were greeted by a middle-aged man, who quizzed us as to why we wanted to speak to the lady. When we refused to discuss the matter with him, he called into the apartment for her to come to the door. She appeared, and we asked to speak to her in private. She and he both became incensed at this and began swearing at us. We were told in no uncertain terms that she was starting a new life that was none of our business. She demanded that we not bother her again.

We left the premises in silence. As we were driving away, my partner did not say, "I told you so," but he did say, "Jack, none of us will really understand human nature."

Murder has a way of teaching about strange human behaviour, and this was not the only time we were reminded of that fact. For example, there was the case of the operator of a butcher shop in the east end of Toronto who lived off the premises, in another neighbourhood. There had been a rash of break-ins at the store after closing hours, so he gave permission to a local drifter to sleep in a small loft above the store as a sort of security guard. The loft was connected to the store proper by an eight-step staircase. One bright summer's morning, the proprietor opened the front door of his business to discover the nude body of his lodger, lying face up on the short flight of stairs. One of the butcher's large knives had been plunged into the victim's heart and was still sticking out of the body. The eyes of the dead man were wide open. The owner telephoned the police and after viewing the scene, the uniformed officer notified us at the homicide squad.

When my partner and I arrived at the store, we found the murder victim still in the same position and condition as I have described. The almost unbelievable part of this situation was that the owner of the shop was busily making sausages, not two feet from the staring eyes of the corpse. When I suggested to the butcher that this was an incongruous situation, he replied that a man had to make a living and that his customers would be arriving shortly.

An interesting sidelight to this murder is that the person or persons responsible removed a television set from the premises on leaving. The serial number of the television was forwarded to all pawn shops and second-hand dealers in the Toronto area. Nearly three years after the murder, two men were arrested while attempting to pawn the television. They were charged and subsequently convicted of the killing.

Another murder case I vividly remember was one in which a family was at the dinner table when the abusive and alcoholic husband started a fight. The wife stabbed him to death. When my partner and I arrived at the scene, we were amazed and shocked to find the woman and her three small children finishing their meal, while the dead husband and father was lying nearby on the kitchen floor. Human nature is truly remarkable.

IN THE MANY YEARS THAT I was a homicide investigator, I found that the murder of an organized-crime figure was the most difficult to even attempt to solve, because there was always a total lack of co-operation, even from the victim's family, and sudden loss of memory on the part of close friends and associates.

After I had questioned dozens of friends and family members of gangland murder victims, a repetitive theme in their replies began to emerge. The dead man, they always insisted, was a good family man who always took care of his family and loved his children, a hard-working man who never took any time off from his work, and a very active church-attending man who gave liberal amounts of money to support religious charities. He also had no enemies, and his killing was a mistake; it was probably meant for someone else. Nobody had any other theories as to possible motives for his murder.

In the early seventies, when I was inspector in command of the homicide squad, a businessman with reputed organized-crime connections was shot to death. During the intense and time-consuming investigation immediately after this murder, detectives assigned to my squad searched a house that was the residence of a prime suspect in the killing. In the basement, they found a quantity of counterfeit money. Needless to say, this came as a complete surprise to everyone who lived in the house. No one knew anything about it!

The whole family was taken to a nearby police station for further questioning. I attended at this station and confronted the lot of them, holding the counterfeit money in my hand. I warned the suspect, "If you don't admit knowledge of this counterfeit currency, I'm going to charge your mother, your father, your brother, and your sister-in-law with the possession of it, and of course I'll charge you too!"

He looked at me with unblinking eyes, and replied, "That's your fucking privilege."

In another mob slaying in the same era, the victim was shot, in typical gangland fashion, very close to his home. The day after the murder, I attended at the residence with Staff Superintendent Adolphus Payne. The purpose of the visit was for me to explain to the widow and her brood of small children the financial assistance that was available to her, via the crime-victim compensation fund of the Province of Ontario.

The eldest child, who was a boy in his early teens, interpreted our conversation for the mother, who did not speak any English. After I had explained, he answered without a moment's hesitation, and I am sure without a full explanation to his mother, "We don't want any of your money. My father's friends will look after us, and my mother says please go now."

It has always been a police practice to attend the funeral of organized-crime victims, in order to observe those in attendance, identify them if possible, and (using information from our intelligence files) try to determine if they were friends or enemies of the dead man. These massive funerals, with thousands of dollars' worth of floral tributes, were usually held in the small local parish church of which the victim was a member.

What never failed to amaze me and other organized-crime investigators was the distance some of these well-known mob figures would travel, from all over Canada and the United States, in order to publicly offer their sympathy and condolences to the widow and her family. The ironic part of this charade was that the intelligence information possessed by the police often indicated that many of those who appeared to be the most sympathetic were sworn enemies of the dead man! There would be no socializing after the funeral, and all of these mysterious people would depart for their home territory as quickly as they had arrived.

In 1972, while I was inspector of the homicide squad, I had to send two of my detectives to southern Italy to continue an investigation of a case of murder and arson, which we suspected was linked to organized crime. John Leybourne and Bill Kerr were both fine investigators (both have gone on to high ranks in law enforcement, Kerr being the present deputy chief of police in charge of criminal investigation on the Metropolitan Toronto Police Force), and I personally felt great anxiety about their safety. I remembered, only too clearly, the fate of the New York City detective James Petrosino, who went to Sicily in the early 1900s on a similar mission, and was gunned down by persons who wanted to put an end to his investigation.

I was most relieved when detectives Leybourn and Kerr returned safely to Toronto, and I'm happy to say their investigations both here and in Italy resulted in the arrest and conviction of several men.

MY DUTIES AT THIS TIME were not always directly concerned with homicide and unrelentingly grim. In fact, they sometimes had an almost humorous aspect. For example, in the spring of 1962, Sergeant Bob Bamlett and I were summoned to the office of Chief Mackey. When we got there, we were met by the chief of detectives, George Elliott, who informed us that the chairman of the police commission had received a complaint from a medical doctor who had recently arrived in Toronto. He and his wife were living in a townhouse in the Don Mills area, and his wife, a highly attractive woman, frequently drove into the city along the road commonly referred to as the Bayview Extension.

On one recent occasion, she had been stopped by a uniformed traffic officer, who suggested that she had been speeding. Although the lady didn't think she had been travelling above the limit, she didn't argue. She resigned herself to the prospect of receiving a ticket, but much to her surprise, the young officer suggested that in lieu of a ticket, she might consider getting together with him some time.

Never having experienced such a proposition, she was frightened. In order to get away gracefully, she agreed to give the officer her phone number. The minute she got home, she called her husband and told him what had happened. The husband confided in a medical associate, who suggested that he call Judge Charles Bick, the police commission chairman. He did, and Sergeant Bamlett, Sergeant Bassett and I were assigned to investigate.

The doctor's wife was unable to give us any clues to the identity of this amorous police officer, so we instructed her to wait until she received a telephone call from him, then invite him to her home, but to make sure she gave us plenty of lead time to get there before he did.

The lady called us the following afternoon. She said the officer had phoned her and suggested that they get together at her place after he finished work that day. She had agreed. The man was expected at 4:30 p.m. This gave us ample time to get to the house and hide in various closets in proximity to where the lady would be sitting.

We had no idea what type of individual we would be dealing with, and we certainly couldn't take even the slightest chance of the lady being harmed.

A little before four-thirty, the doorbell rang. When the doctor's wife answered, we heard a male voice say, "How are you today? You're just as pretty as ever. Can I come in?"

After being admitted to the living room, the fully uniformed policeman lost no time in getting to the point. At his request for intimacy, Bamlett, Bassett and I jumped out of our hiding place, confronted the officer, identified ourselves, and took possession of his fully loaded firearm, just in case (although that was not the weapon we thought he planned to use!).

We transported him and his personal automobile to police headquarters for questioning. The car was examined, and we found that it had been painted and altered in such a way that almost anyone would assume it to be an official unmarked police vehicle.

We also discovered a sophisticated code in the back of his official memo book. It was deciphered, and it proved to be the telephone numbers of dozens of ladies he had encountered, using the same ploy he had used on the doctor's wife. He admitted that when he was off duty and in his own car, he had used this approach to meet countless attractive female drivers. This was the first time anyone had complained!

Neither the doctor nor his wife wanted any charges proceeded with. They said they would be satisfied if he resigned or was dismissed from the force. The officer did not seem repentant in the slightest, only sorry to be caught; but he agreed to sign his resignation papers, and we had him do so immediately. He changed into sports clothing, which he had in his automobile, and turned in his uniform. We took possession of all other articles of police clothing and equipment. As we escorted him to the front door of police headquarters, he turned to the very big Sergeant of Detectives Bamlett and said: "It's okay for the likes of you, because you don't know what it's like to be born good looking."

Sergeant Bamlett took one step towards him and said, "If you don't get out of my sight, you asshole, I'll break your goddamned neck!"

The last we saw of him, he was doing the one-hundred-yard dash north on Church Street.

THE WORK OF A CRIMINAL investigator is occasionally made a lot easier by the stupidity of the offenders. For example, I have already mentioned the bank robber who left his hat at the scene of the crime, with his full name, including his middle initial, on the inside band. In another case, during a large warehouse break-and-enter in which $175,000 worth of television sets were stolen, one of the burglars was caught short, had a bowel movement, then wiped himself with his parole release form, which contained his name and address. I believe that the identification personnel on this occasion went above and beyond the call of duty when they delicately retrieved this important document and examined it.

There have been many similar *faux pas* committed by criminals of all kinds. Housebreakers have dropped their wallets at the scene of their crimes, and on more than one occasion, the culprits have made long distance telephone calls while on the premises of their entry. Even during authorized wiretaps of telephones of known and very experienced organized-crime syndicate members, the criminals have occasionally given themselves away by foolish errors. Sharp-thinking criminals, always assuming that their telephones are being monitored, often talk in a sophisticated code. Sometimes at the end of such conversations, both the caller and the receiver will sign off with a laugh and a gibe, such as "Figure that out, copper." But there are many documented occasions when an emergency has arisen and the criminals have got on the phone, completely forgetting the possibility of a wiretap, and have blurted out damaging statements. When they realize their mistake, there is no laughter at the end of their conversation.

I touched earlier in these pages on the subject of informants, noting how important it is for a police informer to be treated fairly, and for his or her identity to be kept confidential – known only to your unit or squad. My partner and I once received information from a trusted informer about a gang that was planning a major break-and-enter operation in a municipality outside Toronto. We attended at the police office in the target community and informed a detective of what we had learned. Somehow, during our conversation with the officer, we accidentally mentioned the name of our informer. Two days later, my partner and I received a telephone call from a Toronto hospital, telling us that an unnamed patient had asked to see us.

When we arrived we were given the room number of the person in question. It was our informer. He was swathed in bandages on the upper part of his body and had a broken leg in a cast. The instant he saw us he began swearing at us for double-crossing him. We emphatically denied leaking his name to anyone. He asked us if we had given his name to any member of the police force where the break-in was to occur. We admitted that we had discussed it with one particular detective, and on hearing the detective's name our informant resumed his profanities. When he calmed down, he told us that this particular officer was a constant house guest of the gang leader who had him beaten.

It was a bitter lesson for my partner and me, and a painful, life-threatening experience for our informer. He never again provided us with any information; in fact, he never spoke to us again. The only good part of this experience was that the less than honest suburban detective was dismissed from his force a few weeks later, for an unrelated reason.

In this same vein, we stupidly included the name of an informer in a police report that was supposed to be confidential. Shortly after we had submitted it, our informer had three shots fired at him while he was leaving his place of business. This so unnerved him that he sold up and took his family to another country. I still have the letter he sent me, in which he called me every obscene name he could think of!

The very nature of criminal investigator's work is dangerous. A slight error in judgement can have serious consequences for him, or for someone else. Yet that very danger adds to the interest and attraction of a detective's life. For me, it was certainly never a nine-to-five job, with the boredom that accompanies that sort of routine.

DURING MY SERVICE IN THE Criminal Investigation Branch, I worked very closely with a man who has been described, correctly, as the finest detective Canada has ever produced. Adolphus J. Payne was born on a farm in southeastern Ontario, and he had enough patience, skill, dedication, integrity and absolute fearlessness to make the legendary Sherlock Holmes look like a bumbling oaf.

It would take ten books of this size to describe the many successes this man achieved in major criminal investigations, and I was extremely fortunate to have had the chance, early in my career, to work with this man and learn from him. By "working with him," I mean that I was one of the many young detectives who toiled under his direction. It has been said by former chiefs of police that Staff Superintendent Dolph Payne was the father of the present-day Criminal Investigation Branch in Toronto. These sentiments

Personnel in charge of the successful investigation into of the murder of Police Constable Goldsworthy, who was killed in November 1969. Standing, left to right: Detectives Wally Harkness, Wally Tyrrell; Centre of Forensic Sciences firearms expert Mr. Bob Nichol; Detective Sergeant Jim Crawford; Detective Ron Byron; Detective Sergeant Jack Evans; and Detective Bill Bishop. Seated, left to right: *Staff Superintendent Adolphus Payne (chief of detectives), Mr. James Crossland, Q.C. (assistant Crown attorney), and Inspector Jack Webster (chlef of the homicide squad).*

have been echoed by dozens of senior members of the criminal bar and presiding justices at all levels of the court system. Adolphus Payne was not only a teacher to me, he represented everything that was good in a man, and I am proud to say that I was a friend of his.

Unfortunately, chronic ill health spoiled his retirement years, which should have been a pleasant time of well-earned rest. When he died at the early age of seventy-two, I was deeply honoured to be selected as one of the uniformed pall bearers at his large funeral. Some day, I hope, someone will write a book about the exploits of this great Toronto detective – I am positive it would be a best-seller.

Besides his admirable crime-fighting abilities, there was another side to Adolphus Payne. I would be derelict in my duty if I failed to say something about the practical jokes he played on fellow officers during sometimes-trying situations. On one occasion, I was on the receiving end. It was in a shambles of a west-end Toronto home, where a very elderly man was found bludgeoned to death. The victim was well past ninety years old, lived alone and never threw anything away. As a result, the rooms were piled high with garbage and enormous mounds of newspapers. I was the inspector in command of the homicide squad at the time and I had several members of my squad searching through the rooms looking for clues. Our big boss, Staff Superintendent Payne, joined us at the murder scene (as he usually did). In a hall cupboard of the house, there were several coats hanging from a coat rack. Staff Payne, without looking at anyone, said, "Jack, did someone search through the pockets of those coats in the closet?" I replied that I was sure someone had.

This reply did not appear to satisfy the master detective, because he looked directly at me and said, "Well, Inspector, why don't you be sure, and do it yourself?" His voice had an unaccustomed sharpness to it, so I agreed.

When I plunged my hand into the first coat pocket, there was a loud bang, and I felt a severe pain. I quickly withdrew my hand to find a rat trap pinching my fingers. The roars of laughter from my men, as well as Staff Superintendent Payne, did nothing to alleviate the sharp stinging in my fingers. He had set the trap with the full knowledge of my men, and I of course was the designated patsy.

The following day, I had the police doctor at headquarters make phoney splints for my fingers and a sling for my arm. I pretended to all and sundry that I was going off on workmen's compensation, because they were going to operate on my fingers. This tale was soon carried back to the staff superintendent and he promptly appeared at my office, walked up to me and said, "Look, you malingering son of a bitch, if there is any operating to be done on you, I'll do it. Now take off that sling and get back to work." Once again, this brought howls of laughter from my hard-working detectives.

A second practical joke that this famous man played on an unsuspecting comrade was at the scene of a murder. Once again, the victim had lived alone, and the body had been lying undiscovered for over a week. Decomposition had set in and neither the sight nor the smell of the scene was very appealing. On the unlit stove in the kitchen, there was a rusty frying pan, with the mouldy, foul-smelling remains of some type of food.

Of course, we were joined at the scene by Staff Superintendent Payne. After looking around, he decided that we needed help to make a proper search of the less than tidy premises. Staff Payne left orders with the uniformed officers on guard at the front door to send the two new detectives directly into the kitchen to see him.

In the meantime, Payne took a dirty plate, piled some of this awful-looking, mouldy, insect-infested food, put the frying pan on the table beside him, got a knife and fork, and sat down. As the two detective reinforcements came into the kitchen, Staff Payne put his tongue in his cheek to extend it, to give the appearance that he had a mouthful of food. He then waved the fork at the detectives and said in a garbled voice, "I'm just having my supper, won't you sit down and join me?" The officers looked at the food, got a whiff of the awful smell, and promptly threw up. They had to be assisted outside to the fresh air, and absolutely refused to re-enter the premises. The staff superintendent and the rest of us laughed for ten minutes straight, and Payne said, "They don't make detectives like they used to."

Some people reading this may feel that this was a poor demonstration of humour for a senior officer to make during a serious investigation. To these people, I can only say that if you have never been present at an investigation of this type, you wouldn't understand how much you need a good laugh from time to time!

WHEN AN ADULT PERSON, HEALTHY in mind and body, suddenly disappears from sight without any indication of his or her intentions, it leaves the missing person's family in a state of shock and mystification, from which they seldom recover. During my career, I have investigated many such disappearances.

One very enigmatic case occurred about twenty years ago, when I was the inspector in command of both the homicide and the missing persons squad. A South African millionaire, by the name of Abraham Wolfson, dropped out of sight, and despite offers of a large reward by his family and an intensive and lengthy investigation by police forces in Canada, the United States and Europe, he has never been seen or heard from since.

Mr. Wolfson had many business interests, including department stores in South Africa and a large apartment complex in Metropolitan Toronto. He was in Toronto negotiating the sale of this building, which, even in 1970, involved several millions of dollars. The day before his disappearance, he had made a deposit of $5,000 in a bank near his apartment building, although he was not staying there, but in a downtown apartment hotel.

Although comparatively new to business circles in Toronto, he was well respected as a quiet, family-loving person, and a shrewd businessman. He had substantial deposit accounts in the United States as well as Canada, and constant monitoring of each and every account indicated no movement

– no transactions whatsoever after his disappearance. To all intents and purposes, Mr. Abraham Wolfson, at the age of sixty-four, disappeared from the face of the earth for no known reason. It was another frustrating unsolved case.

A HOMICIDE INVESTIGATOR works within a wide net of other professionals. I am fortunate to have established friendships over the many years with people in the practice of medicine and law. Although most of my contacts with persons of these professions have been excellent, I still recall, with some anger, incidents involving both professions that were less than gratifying to me.

One dates back more than forty years. It was about nine o'clock on a late fall evening. I was driving my police motorcycle south on St. George Street when I observed a man, obviously under the influence of alcohol, on the northwest corner of the Bloor Street intersection. I parked my motorcycle and took physical control of the person, placing him under arrest. He struggled violently. Even though he had been drinking to excess, it was all I could do to wrestle him into the front lobby of the Medical Arts Building, which was closed at that hour. In a room at the side of the lobby was a sole female switchboard operator, talking to a middle-aged man, who stood nearby.

Still struggling with my prisoner, I asked the telephone operator to call the police for assistance. Before she could respond, the man she had been talking to said to me, "Who the hell do you think you are, coming in here and giving orders? We are not here to do your work or the work of the police department, so go and make your own phone call some place else."

When I again asked the operator to make the call, he told me he was a doctor and ordered me out of the building.

I then ordered the switchboard operator, in the name of the law, to telephone for assistance, or I would arrest her for obstructing me in the execution of my duty. She began to cry, but placed the call to the police as requested. At this point, the doctor walked out the door, and I was left to struggle with my prisoner until back-up arrived.

After turning over my prisoner, I took the operator's name and thanked her for her assistance. She begged me not to make any trouble for the doctor, as it would go hard with her in the future. With my uniform torn and more than a few bruises on my body, I reluctantly agreed. The operator informed me that this particular doctor hated traffic officers, because he had received a summons for speeding.

Metropolitan Toronto Police Force Homicide Squad, 1972. Homicide Chief Jack Webster (front row, second from left) is seated to the left of Staff Superintendent Adolphus Payne. Back row, from left to right: *Bill McCormack, Bill Kerr, Frank Barbetta, Mark Dodson, Wally Harkness, Bernie Nadeau, Jim Read and Jack McBride.* Centre row: *George Thompson, Winston Weatherbie, stenographer Sandra Morgan, John Mitchell, Jim Majury and Wally Tyrrell.* Front row: *Jack Evans, Jack Webster, Adolphus Payne, Jim Noble and Jim Crawford.*

MOST EXPERIENCED INVESTIGATORS WOULD agree that one of the most important professional allies a police officer has at his disposal is the "crime lab" or, to give it its more formal name, the Centre of Forensic Sciences, which is an arm of the Ministry of the Solicitor General of Ontario.

The ballistic examinations necessary in most offences involving firearms, the hair and fibre identification in murder and rape cases, the typing of blood, post-mortem examinations to determine the sometimes less than obvious causes of death – all of these are the responsibility of the highly educated and trained professionals on call at the crime lab, and their dedicated efforts are often the deciding factor in bringing a criminal investigation to a successful conclusion. I have enormous respect for the numerous pathologists that I have had the pleasure of knowing during my time as an active homicide investigator.

It has been my experience that, during post-mortems, there is always an atmosphere of quiet in the room, with conversation only when absolutely necessary between police officers and the pathologist. There is none of the wise-cracking and disrespect that one sometimes sees in morgue scenes on television or in films.

About the only occasion I can think of when my associates on the homicide squad and I ever let humour creep into our professional demeanour at the morgue was a number of years ago, when an out-of-town known criminal had been shot to death in a violent gunfight with police. The fatal wound was entirely in the area of the face, which gave the victim's remains a decidedly grotesque appearance.

I was the inspector in command of the homicide squad, and about 10:00 a.m. on the day following the shooting, one of my sergeants came into my office to inform me that a man was in our main office, demanding to view the body. He claimed that he was a friend of the dead man's family, and that he only wanted to make sure it was in fact his friend who had been killed. My sergeant had assured him that a positive identification had already been made by means of personal papers, clothing and so on, and that further identification was quite unnecessary. It was also explained to him that the deceased man had suffered wounds that had rendered him unattractive to view.

I went out to the main office to talk to the man, but I too found that he would not take no for an answer. He now became loud and somewhat abusive. He threatened to go to the attorney general and somehow force us to allow him to see the body. At the same time, he intimated that the police might be hiding something.

After this outburst, I asked him for some identification, reviewed it, and returning it to him, I went to my office and called the head of the detective department of the large Canadian city he and the dead man both came from. I learned that our insistent visitor had a long criminal record and was in fact a member of a violent gang of bank robbers, who were sworn enemies of our dead criminal. Our police associate on the telephone thought, and we agreed, that he probably wanted to see the body for two reasons: first, to make sure that his enemy was in fact dead, and second, so that when he returned to his home turf he could brag about seeing the son of a bitch on a slab in the morgue.

I returned to the main office, and while feigning fear that he would complain to the attorney general, I told him my sergeant and I would take him to the morgue and allow him to see the body. At the storage area of the morgue, I had the attendant point out the drawer containing the remains of our robber. Then, with our obnoxious visitor standing at the head of the sliding drawer, my sergeant suddenly pulled the sheet off the top of the body.

After one quick look at this terrifying sight, the man turned pale and his knees buckled; he collapsed to the floor and vomited. It was with some delight that we assisted him outside, where my mischievous sergeant whispered in his ear, "Does this mean you are not going to the attorney general?"

We heard some time later that this so-called big shot gangster reformed and became involved in a somewhat less violent occupation. It may even be true.

The importance to our work of the pathologist and the forensic experts at the crime lab became a matter of jokes among us. We would say that in a twenty-four-hour day, we would spend eight hours at a crime scene, eight hours in court, two hours at the morgue, two hours at the crime lab and four hours at home with our families.

IN RECENT YEARS, AND CERTAINLY in 1991, it seems it is no longer possible to pick up a daily paper in Toronto without reading about alleged racism by members of the Metropolitan Toronto Police Force and other large police agencies in Canada. In my nearly forty-three years of active police services, I cannot recall one incident of intentional racial discrimination. I swear this statement to be true!

In many instances, I have found the very opposite to be the case: members of a visible minority are treated with more care and attention than persons who are classed as the majority. It has always been my view and the view of my associates that persons who violate the laws of this country, no matter what their creed or colour, should face the consequences and let their guilt or innocence be decided in a court of law.

It is obvious to me, and to many other members of the community, that the so-called leaders (they are usually self-appointed) of the various visible minority groups are not satisfied to let the legislated system of investigation and trial take its course. Instead they hold press conferences to scream and shout that certain tragic, fatal occurrences are racially motivated. I am fully convinced, as a veteran investigator with many years of experience, that not one – and I repeat *not one* – of these high-profile occurrences in recent years has resulted from racial insensitivity.

It is a tremendous responsibility for a young police officer to face, but today, in our drug-oriented society, there may be times when he (or she) will be called upon to make a split-second decision as to who will die: he himself or the violent criminal confronting him. I defy anyone, no matter what their status in society, to honestly tell me that the colour of one's skin can have any effect on the decision the police officer makes, in the brief seconds that he has at his disposal.

There is no doubt in my mind or in the minds of other high-ranking police commanders and administrators that serious errors in judgement have from time to time been made, and they have resulted in grief and a sense of terrible loss, not only to victims' families but also to the police officers involved and their families. It has been my experience that a police officer does not easily recover from the shock of having caused the death of another human being. In occurrences where errors in judgement have been made, it is usually attributable to a lack of experience and training.

Let us all strive to have the brightest and most highly qualified of our young men and women think of policing as a valuable, honourable and respected profession, as it once was. In that way we will be able to fill the ranks with young, dedicated Canadians of all colours and ethnic backgrounds. The constant negative reporting of police forces and police actions by some of the media does nothing but deter the recruitment of first-class people from all segments of our community.

This is not to say that the media should not report on the negative or illegal actions of any member or group within a police force. Of course, they must; but they should not give a platform to persons who, for personal gain or notoriety, will spout lies, half-truths, and innuendo.

It is my belief that the inflammatory rhetoric spewed out by a few highly vocal individuals does not reflect the beliefs of the huge majority of all colours and races in our multicultural metropolis. I believe that most of them know that their police force is scrupulously professional and fair in its approach to all matters of public concern. The story that opens this chapter is just one of the many I could cite in evidence.

There will always be people in this world who believe that the lives and property of others are theirs for the taking, and this type of person comes in all colours: white, black, red and yellow. The only defence is the police force. It has often been said that the police force is a thin blue line between the good and the bad. That is the only colour barrier I recognize.

CHAPTER NINE

A Dangerous Profession

THE MOST HIGHLY PUBLICIZED *hostage-taking Jack Webster was ever in-volved in took place – on the air – on Monday, March 21, 1977.*

At the time, the well-known journalist Barbara Frum was host of a coast-to-coast noon-hour news and information show on CBC radio. Across the country, millions, including Webster's daughter (who was hav-ing her hair done in Winnipeg), eavesdropped on one of the most unusual negotiations in hostage-taking history.

Jack, on duty, had not been listening when the broadcast began. Had he snapped the radio on, he would have heard for himself the calm, as-sured, staccato voice of Frum as she made contact with a man holed up in a Yonge Street bank forcibly confining eighteen bank employees by means of a sawed-off shotgun.

His demand was uncomplicated. All he wanted was a Hercules aircraft to fly him to Uganda to visit the dictator Idi Amin, who, he told Frum, was his "pal." Under the careful, controlled questioning of the interviewer, the hostage-taker admitted that he had never met the African tyrant, but that he was "a fan of his."

After a few moments of conversation, Frum got the captor to let her speak to one of the hostages, a chipper, intelligent woman who seemed very together. After determining that none of the hostages was seriously hurt or ill, Frum told the spokeswoman that she had the police on the other line. In a conversational tone, polite as a tea party, Frum and the hostage extended an invitation to the man with the gun to speak to the police.

Several blocks away, at 590 Jarvis, Webster was at work at his desk in the deputy chief's office, where he was acting deputy in charge of field operations. At 11:55 a.m., he looked up to see his executive receptionist run into the office, in a highly agitated state that was completely at odds with the tranquil atmosphere of the executive floor at headquarters. "Barbara Frum is on the phone," she blurted. "Someone's holding people hostage in a bank. They want to speak to the chief. Everybody's out but you."

Webster immediately ran out of the private office into the reception area in the main corridor, grabbed the phone, and leaning awkwardly over the reception desk, commenced a conversation that he had no idea was being broadcast live across Canada. Later that day, it was repeated on "As It Happens":

"Mr. Webster?" Barbara Frum inquired.

"Yes."

"We have one of the hostages on the line. Do you want to talk to her?"

"Yes."

"She's prepared to get the gunman for you."

"All right. Okay."

"Go ahead."

"Hello," came the bright voice of the hostage.

"Hello. It's Staff Superintendent Webster speaking."

"Yes, sir."

"And you are . . . ?"

"My name is Lois . . . "

" . . . and does this chap want to speak to a police officer?"

"Yes, he does."

"All right, I'll speak to him."

Obligingly, the hostage brought the gunman to the phone. "Hello . . . " he ventured, in a voice that was tentative, hard to hear.

Webster's voice was strong but in no way threatening, "Hello. It's Staff Superintendent Webster, Metro Police, speaking . . . Who's this?"

"It's Bob . . . "

"Bob?"

"Yeah," the voice answered softly, "That's right. I'm the fellow with the gun."

"Yes, all right. What can I do for you now – to ease this situation?"

Like a child reciting his Christmas list, Bob answered, "I want a C-130 Hercules . . . and I want to fly down to Uganda."

"To Uganda . . . ," Webster repeated.

"Right."

"And where do you want this aircraft, Bob?"

"It doesn't matter to me."

"That's a military-type plane, isn't it?" Webster asked, as casually as if the conversation were taking place between two strangers in a bar.

"There's a couple of civilian airlines that have them," Bob answered, "but . . . it makes no difference, really, but it's got to be a C-130."

"C-130," Webster said thoughtfully. "Are you familiar with Hercules aircraft?"

"Well, I . . . I don't fly in them."

"Oh," Webster answered, his voice dipping almost imperceptibly, as if he'd realized Bob was perhaps a little more distraught than had originally appeared. The man did not sound like a pilot or like anyone who had any legitimate connection with the type of aircraft he was requesting. Immediately, Webster moved to a different topic. "All right now, how many people do you have there, Bob?"

"Eighteen."

"Eighteen. Are they all well?"

"Oh, yeah, sure."

"Now, this aircraft will have to be at some air force base nearby, won't it. Like Downsview?"

"Sure. Downsview sounds great."

"Well, how do you propose, now, to get from there to Downsview?'

The gunman was well aware that the Emergency Task Force was surrounding the building. He may have been able to see snipers on the roof across from the room where he was enacting his little drama. As if remembering that he was the star of it all, his voice was suddenly less flat, a little eager. "Well, we'll get one of your little tactical squad vans and have him back up to the door, and we'll just . . . about half a dozen of us'll just step inside."

"Half a dozen?" Webster asked cautiously.

Suddenly the voice on the other end was rushed, hoarse – either angry or scared. It was a dangerous moment. "I don't want to step in there by myself and have you guys – "

"Do you need all those people, Bob, with you there?" Webster queried without seeming to note the panic evident in the gunman's voice. "Those are innocent people there . . . We'll co-operate in every way we can with you. We want to keep the situation calm and cool. And I think, probably to show good faith, if you have eighteen people there, it would be certainly to your credit if you were to release them. I don't think you need them. We'll co-operate with you."

"Un-huh," Bob answered, as though thinking things over.

"Without any tricks," Webster added, *"and I can assure you of that. But I think that you should release some of those people there . . . who may have illnesses that we're not aware of. Would you agree with that?"*

Without hesitation, Bob responded, "Well, I'll check out any of them that might have illnesses, and if they seem to be all right, I think we'll just keep things the way they are for now. I'll maybe release them a bit later, you know, as things progress. But I see your boys out here are getting a little bit psyched up, and uh, the front door's unlocked – "

"Un-huh," Webster replied, his voice rising.

"They've managed that so far. I don't think they've managed to get anybody in the lower level. And I've got a damned good vantage point where I can see the door, and I can see the stairwell."

"Un-huh."

"Outside of a gung-ho charge or anything, there's not really a hell of a lot you can do . . . "

"Well," Webster answered, his voice still strong – almost, one could say, friendly, *"we certainly don't want anyone to get hurt, and that includes you. And we'll do what we can to bring this situation as back to normal as can be, as quickly as possible. Now what is the next thing you want . . . and what is the time-frame you want me to operate in here?"*

Bob repeated his demand for the plane, and Webster carried on the conversation with him a few minutes longer before promising to check things out with the chief.

By this time, the chief was on the scene. Webster had bought enough time for a skilled police hostage negotiator – Detective Sergeant Bill Donaldson – to move in.

In the meantime, the chief instructed Webster to get hold of the provincial solicitor general's office to set things in motion in case they did have to get the requested aircraft from the Department of National Defence.

In a very short time, Webster was able to report that the chief of the Canadian Armed Forces was actually prepared to supply the aircraft, the crew, and all the necessary support for the plane to be landed at Downsview to await police orders.

But it never came to that. By about 5:30 p.m., when the piece concluded on "As It Happens," fifteen hostages had been released, but three men, plus Bill Donaldson, were still inside, the gunman claiming he needed to bring them aboard the plane – possibly as far as Uganda.

Finally, though, through the work of Donaldson, Sergeant Brian Peel, and radio personality Charlie Doering, all of whom risked their lives coaxing the man to surrender, he gave himself up.

It was a long, strange, tense day, but it ended without a shot being fired or a person being injured.

Years later, Webster would sometimes listen to the CBC tape of "As It Happens," from which the excerpts of the conversation here are taken. To this day, he marvels at how good an acting job he did on the radio. For, though he sounds as calm as the radio professionals, he says his heart was pounding so hard he was sure the sound must have carried over the airwaves to Winnipeg.

———————

W HEN I WAS A DETECTIVE sergeant on the homicide squad, I investigated some eighty-five murder occurrences, and I am pleased to say that there were convictions in 95 percent of the cases.

In November of 1969 my promotion to the rank of inspector put me in command of the homicide squad, and my day-to-day duties took on an ever-increasing amount of administrative detail, but I still found the time, night or day, to attend at murder scenes and try to assist my investigators. I'm sure that on many occasions, upon my uninvited arrival at a scene, my detectives would whisper to one another, "Here comes the old bastard again. I wish he would stay home in bed." But then again, I personally felt that the commanding officer's presence at a trying and difficult situation was appreciated if for no other reason than that you were there.

When you are the "inspector of the homicide squad," you are given the authority to direct and work with the cream of the crop of detectives on the Metropolitan Toronto Police Force. Not only are you envied by other senior officers, but you are treated with the respect befitting your position by members of the media, the legal profession, politicians, the public at large, and – last but not least – police officers of all ranks. I was proud to have been thought worthy of this important position, and proud of the men I worked with. Most of the detectives who were on the squad at that time eventually rose to the highest levels of the force. To name a few of these fine investigators and the ranks they attained: Chief of Police William McCormack, Deputy Chief of Police Jim Noble, Deputy Chief Bill Kerr, Deputy Chief of Police Wally Tyrrell, Staff Superintendent Bernie Nadeau, Staff Superintendent Frank Barbetta, Staff Superintendent George Thompson and many staff inspectors, too numerous to mention. I like to believe that my direction during this period on the homicide squad had a positive effect on their upward-spiralling careers.

Then, in January of 1973, Chief of Police Harold Adamson called me into his office and informed me that I was being transferred to the uniformed branch, as an inspector in charge of a field division. After spending some twenty-three years as a plainclothes criminal investigator, I was less than enthralled about this transfer. I did everything but beg Chief Adamson to allow me to remain on the homicide squad, or at least in the detective department in some capacity.

Chief Adamson was a fine chief of police, admired by members of the force for his many sterling attributes, one of which was that he did not mince words. You could count on his statements to be truthful, sincere and direct. This would apply whether he was tearing a strip off you or commending you. The chief was firm in his response to my request. He reminded me that everything we talked about in his office was to be kept confidential, that I was not to repeat anything to anyone. I agreed, of course. He then told me that I had been selected for advancement in the ranks of the police force and in order to achieve these forthcoming promotions, I must have uniform command experience. He further told me in confidence that both Staff Superintendent Adolphus Payne and Deputy Bernard Simmonds would be retiring in the next couple of years and that I was in direct line to succeed them. Of course I was flattered by these comments and would honour the confidentiality of them.

Toward the end of the month, I was transferred from the prestigious command of the homicide squad to become a divisional uniformed inspector, in charge of Number 55 Station. This station was the original Number 10 Station of the old City of Toronto Police and was located at the easternmost edge of Toronto. It was slated for closing in six months' time, when a new 55 Division building would be completed on Coxwell Avenue. This new station would encompass two police divisions, Numbers 55 and 56.

I had a total of 124 officers of all ranks in my new command and I soon realized that I would have to change my former somewhat parochial views of policing to accommodate the multitudinous and varied responsibilities of day-to-day uniformed policing activities.

Veteran criminal investigators are prone to believe that all there is to police work is the investigation of serious crimes, such as murders, armed hold-ups, kidnappings and break-and-enters, but on returning to divisional uniformed police duties, one finds that malicious damage to property, dog bites, lost children, fender benders, shoplifting, common assaults, and other such "minor" occurrences are every bit as important to the citizens involved as the headline-grabbing, so-called major league crime.

It did not take me long to learn – or to remember – that the ordinary, everyday, much maligned uniformed police officer is the backbone of the police force. If it were not for these front-line men and women, the high-profile criminal investigation department would not exist.

I WAS THREE WEEKS INTO my new job, and it had become my habit to leave for lunch around 12:15 p.m. One day, as I was on my way to lunch, a veteran divisional detective I had known for years, Louis Thain, stopped me and introduced me to a young Scottish-born police constable. This fine-looking young man was Leslie Maitland, and Detective Thain said to me, "Keep your eye on this fellow, Inspector, because he will be a senior officer some day."

We all laughed about this future projection, and I said, "I hope I'm around to shake your hand." One hour later, this young policeman was shot dead by a bank robber on Danforth Avenue. And so, very early in my new career as a uniformed police commander, I had to accompany the chief of police to the officer's home and notify his wife, who was pregnant with their third child. It was a sad experience that I was to repeat on two other occasions in the near future. (The murderer of the police officer was arrested after a violent gunfight and was subsequently sentenced to life imprisonment, and at the time of this writing is still in prison.)

I was instructed by my deputy chief to arrange a complete ceremonial police funeral, and I found to my dismay that our force had no written procedures to follow for such a funeral. I gathered together a group of police officers to assist me in this large undertaking, and, by trial and error, we were able to arrange and stage a public funeral that demonstrated, to the family and friends of the murdered police officer as well as to the general public, how much we in the force honoured and loved our dead comrade.

Over the next five years, some other officers and I produced an official police funeral plan, which was accepted by the Board of Police Commissioners, and is now part of the rules and directives of the Metropolitan Toronto Police Force. The Ontario Police Commission also approved the step-by-step arrangements, and recommended the plan to all police forces in Ontario.

In the over forty years that I was a serving police officer, twelve officers of my force lost their lives in the line of duty – shot to death by persons committing offences. Three of these officers were directly under my command and, along with the chief of police at the time, I had the unpleasant duty of notifying the wives and in one case the parents of the murdered officers. When a police officer has been killed on duty, a pall is cast over the entire police force. One no longer hears the usual good-natured banter between associates that is natural among a large group of healthy young men and women, who many times depend on each other for their very lives. This serious, quiet mood lasts until the massive police funeral is over.

When I describe a police funeral as massive, I am not exaggerating. Thousands of police officers from all over Canada and the United States attend the solemn military-style ceremony. In the regulations and procedures of the police force, the funeral logistics are the responsibility of the district commander. I have had direct responsibility for overseeing such arrangements on four occasions. When the public sees such a demonstration of police solidarity, with thousands of uniformed officers and detectives marching shoulder to shoulder behind the pipe bands with their mournful music, they have no way of knowing how many days and nights of planning were needed before such a tribute could become a reality.

We had to arrange, for example, accommodation for out-of-town officers, parking for hundreds of motor vehicles, church or chapel seating arrangements, sophisticated loudspeaker equipment, open areas large enough to accommodate the marshalling of the thousands of attending police officers, the borrowing of bands from other police forces for evenly spaced placement in the line of march, many portable toilets for different assembly areas, pallbearers, hat bearer, honour guard, duty uniformed officers for the church or funeral chapel during visiting hours, rental of buses for transportation to the sometimes distant cemetery, and of course, a caterer or caterers to provide food and drink for the attending thousands, at the conclusion of the funeral. In my experience, the locating of a hall or area that is both available and large enough to accommodate such numbers has always been a problem. But all the agonizing work seemed well worth it when one marched with the others in tribute.

Two further tragedies befell my immediate area of command within one week of Officer Maitland's funeral. A twenty-one-year-old recruit constable dropped dead on parade in the station guard room, as a result of a cerebral hemorrhage. Three days later one of my elderly school crossing guards was struck down and killed by a drunk driver.

All of this happening in such a short time certainly brought home to me the responsibilities of my new position.

IN MAY OF THAT SAME year, 1973, shortly before the closing of the old police station, I was telephoned at home around eight o'clock one evening. It was

Funeral procession, led by Staff Superintendent Jack Webster, for the late police constable Henry Snedden, September 1978.

my desk sergeant, who informed me that we had a hostage situation in a house in my division. The call was for my information only; it was not necessary for me to attend, but because I was a new uniformed commander, I thought I should be there, and I informed the sergeant that I would go directly to the scene. I put on my brand-new inspector's uniform and set off.

When I got there, I could see a dozen uniformed officers with their firearms drawn, in position behind vehicles and on neighbouring front porches. The sergeant in charge told me the armed man in the house had fired several random gunshots in the house and on the street, and was now holding his estranged wife as a hostage. I was further informed that the man's firearm was an automatic rifle, and that he had an extensive criminal record for acts of violence, including firearms offences.

My officers at the scene had established telephone contact with the house from a nearby store. The most recent telephone conversation indicated that the wanted man was demanding to talk to the chief of police. I instructed the sergeant to take me to the store and attempt to make telephone connection again. After several rings, the suspect finally answered the phone. I said, "This is the chief speaking."

"Is that you, Adamson?" he asked.

I replied, "No, this is Webster, and I am acting chief while Chief Adamson is on holidays."

He replied that he would only talk to Adamson, because he had been arrested by Adamson several years earlier and trusted him. I again told him that Chief Adamson was not available, but that I would help if I could.

He said he was sure the cops waiting would shoot and kill him the minute he showed his face outside. He wanted the chief to come into the house so that they could walk out together. I told him that as the acting chief of police, I would guarantee his safety, and that I would come into the house and walk out with him. After some hesitation he agreed to this, making me promise that I would not be armed.

When I informed my officers of the plan, they were unanimous in their opposition. They reminded me of the dangerous background of the gunman and suggested that he only wanted to lure me inside, then take me hostage in order to effect his escape from the house. I appreciated their concern, but my instinct told me he was serious about wanting someone he trusted. Any police officer would have served his purpose if all he wanted was a hostage. He could have lured someone before my arrival if that had been his intention. I was the highest-ranking officer at a scene of violence. I knew my responsibility and I accepted it.

A person placed in this situation has a duty to bring the situation under control as quickly as possible, without injury to anyone – police officers, members of the public, or the hostage-takers themselves.

With a vision of my new gold-braided uniform being blown to shreds, and with a very dry mouth and trembling knees, I mounted the veranda steps, knocked on the door and heard a voice say, "Come in, Chief." I slowly entered the house and walked to the kitchen, where I found the suspect and his wife drinking beer together. He pointed to his rifle, which lay on a table by the kitchen sink, told me to take it, and said he had no more ammunition.

The wife told me that they had settled their differences and were going to get back together again. The three of us walked out of the house in single file, with me in front, and that ended an action-and-suspense-filled two hours in an otherwise quiet neighbourhood.

In retrospect, I think I wanted to prove that this new uniformed inspector wasn't just another hotshot detective from headquarters.

Hostage-taking situations can be terrifying for a senior officer. There are certain decisions that he or she is required to make, in addition to the many rules and directives that he or she is expected to follow. I have had the unfortunate experience of being the senior officer in charge of several volatile situations of this type. Two of these in particular were high profile and made headlines in the daily newspapers.

I had just recently been promoted to district staff superintendent and was placed in command of Number Four District, which is the entire City of Scarborough. It was a snowy Sunday morning in January 1976. Uniformed police were involved in the chase of an armed man, who was suspected of robbing and shooting a taxi driver. The wanted man had fired several shots at the pursuing officers before forcing his way into a house and holding the occupants hostage. After a few hours of non-negotiations, everything appeared to be at a stalemate. In the meantime, I had arrived on the scene and was encouraged to see the efficient Emergency Task Force unit was on site, under the direct command of their very capable commander, Inspector David Cowan.

This highly specialized unit could be compared to the commandos of the Second World War. Every member is hand-picked for his coolness under pressure, above-average intelligence, first-class physical condition, and expert knowledge of the wide variety of high-powered firearms that are issued to this crack unit (and to them alone). I believe it was in the mid-1960s that the Emergency Task Force was first formed, but by the mid-1970s it had become so finely tuned and had developed such expertise that its reputation was – and is – respected in police circles throughout Canada and the United States.

In addition to the Emergency Task Force members, there were many dozens of police officers in the immediate vicinity, including detectives from the hold-up squad, who would of course take custody of the wanted armed robber when he had been flushed from the house by the task force officers. With the assistance of Inspector Cowan and his men, we established an inner and outer perimeter around the house and nearby streets. This was accomplished by placing the many uniformed officers and their marked police vehicles at the entrances and exits of the surrounding streets, as barricades. As the names would imply, the inner perimeter was reserved for police officers who had specific duties to perform in attempting to free the hostages and arrest the wanted man. The outer perimeter was an area reasonably clear of danger, where non-assigned police officers waited, ready to be assigned tasks when needed, and where members of the press and other news media and of course curious onlookers were gathered. The residents of the immediate neighbourhood were ordered to remain indoors, and the representatives of the news media were assigned a sergeant who kept them continuously informed of developments in the inner perimeter.

After one hour of this stand-off, the gunman was observed leaving the house, holding a gun to the head of a male hostage. They entered an automobile that was parked in the driveway, the hostage in the driver's seat and the armed man in the rear, still with his firearm pointed at the driver's head.

As the vehicle backed out and then pulled ahead, Inspector Cowan, who was considered to be one of the most expert marksmen on the force, saw an opportunity when the hostage-taker's attention was momentarily diverted, and fired one shot into the suspect's head, causing instantaneous death. I was standing only about three feet away from Inspector Cowan, and I could appreciate the dangerous and momentous decision that he had made. The wanted man was only a foot away from the innocent abducted citizen and the inspector had about three seconds to take action. His aim was accurate, his decision to fire correct, and I will always have tremendous admiration for this police inspector, who retired from the force as deputy chief of police in January of 1991.

A second serious hostage situation occurred on Sunday, November 14, 1982. I was the staff superintendent in charge of Number Two District, which is the City of Etobicoke. At approximately 8:00 a.m., I received a telephone call at my home, informing me of a multiple shooting and a possible hostage being held in a house in central Etobicoke. At the scene, I once again was pleased to see that our Emergency Task Force was on site and that other uniformed and plainclothes officers had a protective perimeter in place around the house. I was informed by the task force commander that the neighbours had heard several loud gunshots from inside the house; since then there had been complete silence. Officers at the scene had telephoned but there had been no response.

From time to time, one could see a slight movement of the curtains and drapes. This would occur first at the front window and then at different windows at the side and rear of the house. Some officers who had seen these movements thought that they had momentarily observed a face, and a long object, which could have been a rifle barrel.

After a very lengthy stand-off, the inspector in charge of the heavily armed and efficient task force asked me, as the senior officer in charge, to give the order for them to fire tear gas into the premises and then mount a full armed attack on the house.

I gave this some deep thought, and just before I gave the order, I asked the communications sergeant to try and telephone the occupant or occupants once more. He did this, and after several rings, the phone was answered by a faint female voice, asking for help. They were able to determine from her that her son-in-law had killed her daughter and her two grandsons, and he had now gone away. She was given instructions about unlocking the doors and told to then move back into the house proper. When she had informed them on the phone that she had done as instructed, the task force officers gave her time to move away from the doors and then they hit the front and back at the same time.

After securing the premises, they emerged with a badly shaken lady in her mid-eighties. A search of the house revealed the dead bodies of a woman in the hallway on the ground floor, the dead body of a youth in the basement bedroom, and another dead young man in the backyard. All had suffered gunshot wounds from what appeared to have been a heavy calibre weapon. Investigations revealed that the gunman, who had lived in the house with his second wife, her two sons, and the elderly mother-in-law, had for some unknown reason taken the lives of his wife and her two sons in a violent manner. After departing from the house he drove to an out-of-town cemetery, where, at the graveside of his first wife, he shot himself and died instantly.

The poor, fragile mother-in-law was left in this slaughterhouse with the badly mutilated bodies of her daughter and grandsons. No wonder she was almost out of her mind when she was finally rescued by the task force officers.

The site commander, in a situation like this, has a heavy responsibility. The wrong decision may have grave consequences. In this case, had an all-out attack with tear gas and other weapons been authorized, it would have resulted in an innocent woman suffering serious injury or death. It still makes me shudder to think of what might have been. During the early years of my police career, the fear of violence or death did not enter my mind. It was only after I had been promoted to senior command positions that I began to be concerned about such possibilities. I was not concerned for myself; I was haunted by the fear that, some day, someone might suffer death as a direct result of an error in judgement on my part.

I HAVE OFTEN BEEN ASKED whether I myself have ever experienced a close brush with death. My answer is yes, on two occasions. I can vividly remember feeling my number had just about come up. Strangely enough, both times were at the hands of fellow officers.

The first occasion was in 1946, when I was attached to the Traffic Division. I was on the four-to-twelve relief, and I was assigned as the driver for the patrol sergeant. (A patrol sergeant is what is referred to as the first line supervisor, and it is his job to tour the many areas where officers from his division are on duty; he usually makes his rounds on a motorcycle, but if the weather is less than favourable, he will assign himself a car and a driver.)

That night, we had just completed what was called the "brewers' escort." This was an armed escort for a truck that drove to all the various brewers' retail stores, just prior to closing time, to collect the day's receipts. The Traffic Division had been assigned this duty by headquarters because the large amounts of money taken in by the beer stores made them very attractive to robbers. Each unit on this money escort duty would be assigned a single-barrelled shotgun, so that we would be at least equal in firepower to the shotgun-toting bandits.

The sergeant and I were on our way back to the police garage to return our issued shotgun when our radio notified all cars in the vicinity to attend at a break-in in progress at a tire warehouse on Jarvis Street. Being reasonably close to the scene, we attended, and in a matter of minutes we joined about six or seven other detectives and uniformed officers at the site.

Our now retired chief of police, James P. Mackey, was a detective sergeant at this time, and he was in charge of the action. He instructed my sergeant and me to go to the rear of the premises along with some other uniformed officers. Detective Sergeant Mackey told us there were two or three men inside the tire warehouse and they were believed to be armed.

In the darkness of late evening, I didn't notice that my sergeant had brought along the shotgun from our vehicle. When we arrived at the back of the building we encountered a high brick wall. I clambered up onto an adjoining roof, with the sergeant behind me. Suddenly I heard a shot very close behind me – and answering gunfire from inside the warehouse. At the same time, I felt a blast of heat at the left side of my face. Before I could figure out what was going on, I heard my sergeant saying, "Sorry, Jack, the goddamned safety was left off. Are you all right?"

"Yes," I replied, "but no thanks to you!"

Detective Sergeant Mackey and his associates arrested the burglars, but in the ensuing gunfight one of the bandits was shot and killed.

My second brush with death was in the basement firing range at old Number 12 Station. It was our annual departmental shoot, when all members of the force have to fire a certain number of rounds at specified targets, in order to qualify as armed police officers.

The range officers at these shoots were better-than-average marksmen and were usually very active in firearm competitions. (I think this is still the case today.) When you compare the safety features of the inside departmental firing ranges of 1947 with the state-of-the-art design and equipment that are in place now at the C.O. Bick Police College or the modern Number 52 Division, one can readily see that conditions then left a lot to be desired.

I was on the extreme left of four officers ready to shoot. When the range officer said, "Ready on the left, ready on the right, commence firing," I fired one shot. But the officer on my immediate right had a misfire. Contrary to all instructions, he brought his revolver back up to his chest, and as he tried to determine the cause of the misfire, he pulled the trigger. The bullet passed so close to my face that it left a visible powder burn. Once again, I heard that "Sorry, Jack, but the goddamned thing just went off."

I HAVE NEVER REALLY BELIEVED in fate, but I must say that after a tragic event in 1963, I came close.

My steady partner on the homicide squad at that time was Detective Sergeant John Bassett, a fine man and a brilliant investigator. (Readers will recall that he and I conducted the Arthur Lucas investigation.) In September of 1963, Bassett and I had arrested a man at the request of the Montreal City Police Force. The arrested man was wanted for the robbery of a store in downtown Montreal and was a possible accomplice in the murder of the storekeeper. He was taken back to that city by Montreal officers.

Shortly after the arrest I was sent on a ten-week course to the RCMP College in Ottawa, Ontario. At the time, it was a prestigious course to be selected for and I felt honoured. As I recall, it was a very tough and demanding schedule they set for us, with five and a half days of intense instruction, and examinations every Saturday morning.

Early in November Sergeant Bassett telephoned me at the police college to inform me we were both required to appear in Montreal to give evidence in the case of our arrested man.

I told Bassett that it was getting close to our final examinations and I couldn't afford to miss too much. Sergeant Bassett told me not to worry, that he and his temporary partner, Detective Kenneth Evans, would appear, and if I was needed the RCMP could quickly drive me to Montreal from Ottawa. I was pleased about the arrangements and settled down for the final stretch of my course.

Bassett and Evans were in Montreal, accompanied by a witness from Toronto. It was a Friday and the presiding judge decided to remand the case over until Monday morning, when Sergeant Bassett might be required to testify. Our officers could have stayed over until Monday at the expense of the attorney general's office, but they both had tickets for the rodeo at Maple Leaf Gardens that Friday, and they had promised their young sons that they would be back in Toronto in time to take them to the show. They managed to book seats on a supper flight and their Montreal hosts rushed them to the airport over ice-covered roads, getting them there just in time to board the aircraft while it was on the tarmac. They were the last passengers to make it on to the flight.

The aircraft had been airborne for only ten minutes when it crashed near the town of Ste. Thérèse, Quebec. There were no survivors of the some 250 passengers and crew. I do not know why, but for me fate seemed to have intervened – if I had not been sent on that RCMP course, I would have been with Sergeant Bassett, on that ill-fated aircraft in the autumn of 1963.

CHAPTER TEN

Public Security

ONE OF THE MOST DIFFICULT – and famous – cases Jack Webster worked on is well remembered by millions of Canadians.

Shortly before midnight on Thursday, October 14, 1982, Webster was at home asleep. Abruptly, he was awakened by the telephone, and the desk sergeant at 23 Division tersely informed him that there had been a major bombing incident in Etobicoke. Litton Systems on City View Drive had sustained extensive damage. Several people had suffered injuries. Three of them, the sergeant said, were cops.

After nearly forty years on the force, Webster could dress faster than an actor in a one-man play. In half an hour, he was on the scene.

What he saw when he got to Litton threw him into flashback. For a minute, it was as if he were back at war. The scene was one of absolute devastation. A huge hole gaped in the front of the main building, exposing several rooms, as though the wall had just peeled away. In front of the building lay a heap of sheared, tangled metal, with what looked like an axle protruding from the twisted mass. Nearby, a car that was recognizably a cruiser sat on four flat tires, its windshield shattered, its windows smashed, its flanks riddled as if by shrapnel.

As he surveyed the destruction, Webster was joined by the mayor of Etobicoke. Both were quickly briefed on what was known about the blast.

An observant Litton employee had seen a van drive up onto a grassy area in front of the building. Mysteriously, the driver had backed the van up to a wall in an obvious effort to partially conceal it in shrubs; then he *jumped from the van, ran from the area, and disappeared into the darkness.*

A dutiful plant security guard moved toward the vehicle to check it out. Within seconds he came on a cardboard box, painted fluorescent orange, on the grass in front of the van. On top of the box was a stick of dynamite. The intrepid guard saw that a note was stuck on the box. He read,

> **DANGER EXPLOSIVES** – *Inside this van are 550 pounds of commercial dynamite, which will explode anytime, from within fifteen minutes to twenty-five minutes after the van was parked here. The dynamite will be set off by two completely separate detonating systems. Do not enter or move the van – it will explode. Phone the police immediately and have them block off Highway 27, City View Drive, Dixon Road and other roads surrounding the Litton plants and have the workers inside the plants moved to protected areas. Nearby hotels and factories should also be notified so that no one will be hurt by the blast. On top of this box is an authentic sample stick of the dynamite contained in the van. This is to confirm that this is a real bomb.*

About the same time as the van had driven up, the security office had received a telephone message. The guard, realizing the importance of the message of the female caller, put the telephone on "record." The taped message said, "And it will explode in fifteen to twenty-five minutes. Do not enter or move the van because it will explode. This is no prank. We have left for you on the lawn beside the van a box which is not dangerous. Taped to the box are further instructions and a stick of the same dynamite that we have used in the bomb. This should be ample evidence in confirming to you the severity of our attack. Act immediately to phone the police and have them block off the surrounding streets. Move all workers to protected areas, and notify nearby hotels to tell their guests to stay away from windows. I want to be sure that you understand what I have just said. Could you repeat the crucial information to me?"

The guard said he did not understand. The female caller hung up.

The police had been called, and two cars arrived shortly after, reaching the scene at 11:25 p.m.

The four officers quickly located the van, moved toward it, and began to inspect it. When they reached the orange box, they were warned by Sergeant Harry Dungey to stand back. Obeying, they headed for one of the cruisers. The instant they got in, there was a shattering explosion, and the car was heavily pelted by flying metal and broken glass. They had been on the scene only six minutes. They had missed certain death by a few seconds.

The sounds of the blast were heard for miles around. Damage was estimated at five to six million dollars. Besides the mess made of the building closest to the van, two other Litton buildings were damaged. A hotel a kilometre away lost two plate glass windows; frightened guests didn't know what was going on. Other hotels and industrial buildings in the area also got a good shaking.

Of the ten people injured, three were police officers, five were Litton employees, and two were innocent citizens minding their own business who just happened to be driving along Highway 27 at the wrong time.

It wasn't really hard to guess why Litton had been chosen as the target of this vicious attack. In 1979, $1.2 billion worth of work had been handed to the firm in a contract to make 5,500 guidance systems for cruise missiles. This was common knowledge. Demonstrations had been staged at the site, and picketers were a familiar occurrence. It had all been going on for some time. No one was surprised at this "resistance." But no one at the firm had imagined that the efforts of so-called "peace activists" could reach so high a level of violence as to render three Litton employees unable to return to work for years – if ever.

On the cold, rainy morning of Friday, October 15, after Webster had assured himself that an adequate number of police specialists were on site to continue the investigation, he headed over to Etobicoke General Hospital to visit the injured.

As he surveyed the emergency treatment area of the hospital, he was again struck by its similarity to a wartime casualty clearing station. Years later, he swore that at that moment, he formed an opinion of peace activists that was "neither complicated nor supportive." Subsequent terrorist activities around the world have never altered Webster's view.

Yet he hastens to point out that he himself remains a staunch advocate of peace. A person who has spent five years in active war service, then more than forty years in police work, comes to feel he has witnessed every conceivable way that violence can be committed by one human being against another. When he says he supports peace, he speaks from experience.

On Saturday, October 16, Webster arrived early at his office to hold a conference with his divisional commanders. They selected thirty-five top-notch investigators to start on the case immediately, intensively, and full time. Over the next few months they would lose a lot of sleep, holidays and time spent with family. No effort was too great to expend on catching the Litton bombers.

Predictably, a few days later, communiqués began to come by mail to various organizations. These lengthy messages claimed that responsibility for the bombing lay with a group of activists known as Direct Action. This was only one of thousands of clues that the investigative squad had to wrestle with. They had the twisted wreckage of the van – along with its description and its markings. They had the dynamite, which, like all dynamite, had been marked during manufacture so that it could be traced if stolen. They had trace evidence to submit to extensive forensic testing. And of course, they had eyewitnesses, including the recovering victims.

The news media across Canada headlined the Litton bombing as the first major terrorist attack committed in this country – a dubious distinction that perhaps discounted events in 1970 in Quebec, but which was otherwise close enough to the truth. At least the RCMP, CSIS, the FBI and the CIA thought it was a major terrorist attack. They were all in on catching the perpetrators.

Eventually, the pieces began to fit together. Similar but less extensive explosions had occurred in British Columbia, where, during the previous July, a Department of Highways explosives magazine had been entered by thieves who'd made off with thirty-eight and a half cases of dynamite. This magazine was located on the northern edge of the town of Squamish, B.C.

For seven weeks, the various members of the vast team working on the case carried out unrelenting surveillance in Ontario and British Columbia. This vigilance finally paid off when, through a brilliant piece of work on the part of a select group of Mounties and Vancouver City Police, five suspects were arrested, in part by an innocent-looking road crew hard at work repairing a patch of pavement outside Vancouver, and looking nothing like what they really were: a police tactical squad!

What made the arrests possible was a network of investigators linking people, incidents, and far-flung locations. One of the most important links was achieved through the careful work of Webster's people as they carried out an authorized, legal wiretap.

The arrests took place in January of 1983. Five people, who came to be known as the Squamish Five, were found to have been involved in several terrorist bombings, including three of video stores that they accused of distributing pornography.

Webster, though he never doubted there would be a successful conclusion to the massive investigation, was pleased at the relative speed with which the Squamish Five were brought to justice. They were not amateurs. Their tactics were brutal and their arsenal of weapons proved to be extensive. Immediately after the Litton bombing, they had included regrets and apologies as well as explanations in their communiqués, but their excuses for committing violence in the name of peace seemed lame to Webster, especially since he had seen first-hand the fruits of their labour. He was

*gratified to think they would not be able to continue what they considered
to be peace work at any time in the near future.*

*He was glad of success for another reason as well. In the beginning, he
had been bombarded with letters and calls from sympathizers of the bombers. These came from individuals and groups who identified themselves as
peace advocates and activists in a variety of causes as well as anti-missile
activists. Some messages were threats. Some were bold taunts, claiming
that Webster and the investigators were no match for the Litton "heroes"
and would never catch them.*

Wrong.

*After the arrests, Webster did not receive a single negative comment.
But the RCMP and the Toronto Police received many commendations from
ordinary citizens thanking them for a job well done.*

*As for the Litton bombers, the Squamish Five, they pleaded guilty to a
long list of criminal charges, and were sentenced to lengthy prison terms.*

O NE OF THE MOST ILLUMINATING aspects of my life on the force was the
wide view of all levels of policing the years gave me. Sometimes I reflect
back on my days as a beat constable and think about what a long road I
have travelled, from the boy that I was to the man I became, at the top of
my profession.

When I was selected as one of the very few foreign police officers in
the world to attend the FBI Academy in April of 1975, I had already
reached my fiftieth birthday. Although I knew I would probably be the old-
est and most senior police officer in service to attend my particular session,
I was determined to do well. I always had reasonably good study habits, a
better than average memory and good work practices, which had been perfected in my long and varied police career. These assets and a lot of diligence enabled me to graduate from the world-famous law enforcement
academy with an enviable standing.

Halfway through the eleven-week course, I was given the honour of being selected as the first Canadian class president. Some of my associates
have told me that the only reason I was given this high appointment was
that – being the longest in the tooth – I could out-talk even the instructors!

As any graduate of the FBI Academy can tell you, there never seemed
to be enough hours in the day to accomplish the intense study necessary for

examinations that were continually thrust upon the student. The variety of subjects taught ranged from forensic science, psychology, sociology, criminal law, personnel management and a multitude of special lectures on sky-jacking, barricaded criminals, hostage-taking, etc. The written examinations that flowed from the lectures and presentations were unrelenting. It was not at all uncommon for us veteran and many times high-ranking police officers to be up studying until three o'clock in the morning, burning the midnight oil like the most junior of cadets. The competition was fierce among the students, each one wanting to do his own force proud, not to mention how each harboured the fear of an adverse report being sent to his chief of police, which would certainly have an effect on his career path.

One of the most enjoyable activities at the academy was firearm instructions. This course had a mandatory accomplishment percentage, which necessitated each student firing a minimum of 2,500 rounds of ammunition during the term of instruction. The ammunition was from a variety of weapons – rapid-fire automatic rifles, shotguns and last but not least, the standard .38 calibre handgun, which was the type of firearm usually carried by the North American police officer at the time.

Although I had carried a firearm of one sort or another since the age of sixteen, I never developed a great interest in them, and I could fairly have been classed as a less than proficient marksman. However, after eleven weeks of instruction by world-class firearms experts, in a state-of-the-art facility, I was proud to graduate as an "expert" marksman and was presented with a certificate to prove it.

It was a great pleasure for me to work closely with some fine and dedicated police officers during my stay at the FBI Academy, ranging from members from two- and three-man forces to officers from the gigantic New York Police Department. The tremendous respect that I have for these hardworking brother police officers only grows as the years pass.

Having had the privilege of holding two of the most prestigious and sought-after positions on the Metropolitan Toronto Police Force, first that of inspector in command of the homicide squad and then that of superintendent of investigative services – or as the news media said, "chief of detectives" – I feel most fortunate and grateful for this period of my career. I suppose my promotion to "chief of detectives," in January of 1973, was a little like a dream. The position gave me personal command of all investigative personnel in the homicide squad, hold-up squad, fraud squad, auto theft squad, general assignment squad, morality squad and the Intelligence Bureau. It was a tremendous responsibility, but I relished it.

But the years I was to spend as a high-ranking uniformed commander gave me some of my greatest satisfaction. As staff superintendent in charge

Staff Superintendent Jack Webster (chief of detectives), Metropolitan Toronto Police Force.

of one of Metropolitan Toronto's five police districts, you are responsible for the safety and well-being of thousands of citizens in addition to the several hundred police officers under your direct command. My application of the discipline code of the police force and of the many hundreds of rules and regulations was firm, but I believe it was fair.

I have never forgotten some of the less than intelligent moves I had made as a young police constable and I tried continually to live by my father's old saying: "You can't put an old head on young shoulders." Sometimes I found, as other senior supervisors have found, that when you are kind and considerate some people take it as a sign of weakness, and rather than take advice, they continue to demonstrate serious discipline lapses. At such times I admit I would lose patience and fall on the erring individual from great heights with deadly accuracy.

It was a great honour to have served with the vast majority of police officers, both male and female, while I was a senior commander. As I have repeatedly stated in this writing, it is a tough and dangerous and many times thankless job being a police officer out on the street in today's society. But there have been occasions when a police officer has made a serious error in judgement that would by his actions bring himself and the reputation of the force into disrepute. One of these occasions happened in December of 1986.

It was 7:15 a.m. and I had just arrived at my office. My district detective inspector, David Boothby, and his second-in-command, Staff Sergeant John Jackson, came into my office and related the following circumstances to me.

They had just received a telephone call from a very distraught woman who resided in the Lakeshore area of Etobicoke, with her husband and two children. Her husband was well known to officers in the local division. I had never met him (nor have I met him to this day), but I was aware that there seemed to be a constant battle going on between him and some officers of Number 21 Division, who had identified him as a trouble-maker and constant complainer about police actions in the Lakeshore area.

His wife had told Boothby and Jackson that her husband had gone to the local police station around one-thirty that morning to lodge a complaint against a police sergeant. The alleged complaint concerned a real or imagined wrong committed by the sergeant against her husband. The man was not satisfied with his reception at the station and began to shout at everybody within earshot. Reports from the immediate investigators left me in no doubt that the man had acted in a totally objectionable manner.

My information was that when he left the police station at around 2:00 a.m., the complainer was immediately followed by an experienced police constable, who in his haste to tail the man did not wait for his own partner, but conscripted a nearby recruit constable to accompany him. The two officers followed the citizen's car south on Islington Avenue. When he had gone about five hundred yards from the police station, the two officers stopped him.

When the senior of the two constables made a radio check with the police dispatcher, he was informed that the subject was not wanted but that, as a result of information on file, he was identified as a potential suicide. Even after receiving this information, the experienced officer still issued three traffic offence violation summonses to the man. One summons was for crossing over a marked highway lane. One must remember that this was two o'clock in the morning, with no cars on the road but the police car and the alleged offending automobile. These circumstances, it seemed to me, would invalidate any such summons.

The second summons was for not having his complete seat belt assembly in place, and the third was for failing to have signed his driving permit in ink. All three Toronto newspapers subsequently described these three traffic summonses as "tacky tickets."

When he got home the man was beside himself with outrage at this final police injustice, and threatened to kill himself. His wife became almost hysterical, and telephoned the station to tell them that she was afraid that he was serious, and she was terrified she would be left alone with two young children to care for.

After hearing this obvious harassment of a citizen by a police officer under my command, I directed Boothby and Jackson to make an immediate investigation into all the circumstances and report back to me. Within an hour they did report back and confirmed that the circumstances appeared to be true as recounted. I immediately ordered Inspector Boothby to remove the three summons applications from the Metropolitan Toronto Police system and in so doing to comply with all the procedures then in place in the regulations of our police force. The most important of these directives was to have a written supplementary report attached to the applications for withdrawal of summonses. This report was to contain, in full detail, the reasons why this withdrawal action was taking place. Upon completion the entire package was to be forwarded to the officer in charge of the summons issuing bureau. This procedure was completed in its entirety.

I then telephoned the inspector in charge of the police division concerned and ordered him to speak to the senior constable who had issued the summonses and relay to him the reasons why I felt the wisest course was to withdraw them. I made it clear that this information was to be given to the officer before he reported off duty that same morning.

During my normal morning telephone report to my deputy police chief, I told him the whole story of what had happened, and the action that I had taken to correct what seemed to me to be a serious injustice by the police against a citizen. My deputy chief fully agreed with what I had done and in fact he informed me that he had already received a telephone call from the wife of the citizen, bitterly complaining about the actions of the police.

The crucial and deciding factor for me in this matter was the fact that the motorist had not been encountered by a patrolling police unit and issued a summons as a response to traffic violations discovered in the normal course of their job. If this had been the case, the matter would have been handled in the normal way; that is, it would have gone to court. But I felt that what we had instead was an experienced police officer, not part of the original complaint by the citizen, who nevertheless took it upon himself to follow the man from the police building in some haste, for the sole purpose of stopping him, and him only, for some offence that had yet to occur. In my view this was then – and is now – totally unacceptable behaviour by an officer of the Metropolitan Toronto Police Force, especially one directly under my command.

Unknown to me at the time was the fact that the inspector in charge of the division did not speak to the police constable involved on that morning and when the officer left the station, he was on five days off. During this long absence from duty, incorrect and exaggerated information reached him concerning the cancellation of the traffic summonses.

When the officer returned to duty, I attempted to correct this neglect on the part of his unit commander by holding a meeting in my office at nine o'clock on the first morning of the constable's return. I invited all those I felt had a stake in the case, including senior personnel and the commander of the internal affairs unit. The meeting lasted an hour and the constable was given the opportunity to state his views, but at the end, I still had the feeling that this veteran police officer had not accepted management's view of the necessity of the action taken.

About six weeks after this meeting, the *Toronto Star* ran a front-page story about a "major ticket fix" involving senior police officers. This news was totally inaccurate as to the circumstances, and it even hinted that a "locked summons box" had been illegally opened and the applications for the summonses surreptitiously removed by a senior police officer. This absolute falsehood was credited to unnamed "informants" used as sources by the author.

When I saw this article, I immediately telephoned Acting Chief of Police William Kerr and suggested that he call a press conference at headquarters that very morning to rebut the contents of the piece. The acting chief agreed to this and the call went out to all the news agencies and press bureaus.

I was stunned at the response to our invitation. There must have been more than fifty representatives of the various television and news bureaus. I'm sure they thought they were about to hear a real-life true confession, or that someone was going to be fired – or both.

Kerr chaired the conference, flanked by me on the right and my criminal branch inspector, David Boothby, on the left. The chief drew the media's attention to the fact that totally false information had been published about the case. He stressed that the command officers had investigated and questioned the circumstances thoroughly and had collectively decided that an injustice had been done to a citizen. He made it clear that an injustice to a private citizen was not a matter to be condoned by the police. Therefore immediate measures to avert that injustice had been taken.

When it was my turn I explained, point by point, the true circumstances of how the summonses had been issued, and my reasons for deciding they were unjustified. I reminded the media that when a citizen attends at a police station to lodge a complaint against a member of the force, whether the complaint be real or imagined, he has rights that cannot be denied. That he should be followed from the station and issued three summonses of a doubtful nature was totally inacceptable to the force. At this point, over half of the media packed up and left the room. I heard one of the more prominent representatives say, "There's no story here, chief. In fact Staff Superintendent Webster should be commended for taking the action he did."

I was satisfied that the general public now had the correct version of what had happened and why. Unfortunately, though, the matter did not end there. The reporter who had done the original article continued to write about my so-called illegal withdrawal of summonses. The unrelenting media attention fuelled a venomous attack by the then president of the police association. This top union executive had the audacity to inform the chief of police that he wanted Webster charged with obstructing justice!

For a number of years, I had been constantly at war with this elected official, who often attempted to interfere in matters that I felt were structurally the prerogative of management. Perhaps he hoped that I might be fired over this incident. Personally, it baffled me. How could this man, who was of above-average intelligence, believe that I – a forty-one-year police veteran holding the third-highest rank on the force, with an enviable record of achievement – would be stupid enough to do something illegal, which would jeopardize my family, my reputation, and last but not least, my pension, as a favour to a person I had never even met?

In any event, after our news conference all three daily newspapers had lengthy editorials praising me for what I had done. There were dozens of letters to the editors supporting me, and some of Canada's top television and radio personalities produced special segments of their programs congratulating me and my senior officers for taking the quick action we did to correct an obvious injustice.

As a result of this positive attention from the media, the matter was dropped from the newspapers. At that point, some of my fellow senior officers began telephoning me again. I have never forgotten these few so-called friends, who until the massive support from the press and the public was clearly demonstrated, had felt there might be some stigma attached to Webster, the "ticket-fixer," and that their careers might be affected by even talking to me on the telephone. I was not too responsive to their late calls of support.

This was a trying time for my family and me, but my wife never once suggested that I should not have become involved. Other senior officers indicated to me that they would have let more junior officers handle such matters. This was *not* how I chose to exercise my command. This incident was but one in a long history of events in my career covered by the media. I have always had a first-class attitude toward most news-gathering agencies. I have always had a better than average working relationship with them, and in the spirit of my co-operation in most matters of mutual interest, the media have reciprocated.

THE METROPOLITAN TORONTO POLICE ASSOCIATION is the union to which all members of the force belong, both uniformed and civilian employees, with the exception of senior officers, who upon promotion to the rank of inspector resign from the association and become members of the Metropolitan Toronto Senior Officers' Organization. Civilian members achieve senior-officer status when they work in a supervisory capacity with responsibilities similar to those of a uniformed police inspector. I have always believed that this is a proper separation of rank and position, if for no other reason than that it would be an incongruous situation for a police constable, who is usually the elected head of the association, to bargain for salary increases and improved working conditions for inspectors, staff inspectors, superintendents, and staff superintendents.

We in the officers' organization have our own elected representatives, and even though we never had a formal written contract, we have always been treated fairly and responsibly by the Board of Police Commissioners, at least during my nearly twenty-five years of service as a senior officer.

One must remember that all senior officers, at one time in their service, were members of the police association. And although, as I have previously mentioned, I have had battles with one president and some of his elected officials regarding matters that they felt were breaches of the working agreement by management, I still hold the association in high regard. Officers who have served as long as I have remember only too well some of the horrific conditions that policemen were subjected to: for example, when I joined we got only one day off a week, a half-hour for lunch in the summer, and no compensation for overtime or court appearances (even if that appearance was on our day off). One of the most devastating conditions of our employment was the power of the commanding officer over scheduling: if he chose to, he could order an individual to work twelve weeks of straight nights on the midnight-to-eight o'clock relief.

It was only the continuous, energetic, and (in the early days) brave efforts of the elected officials of the police association that eventually established the right of all members to the first-class conditions that they enjoy today. They had to be brave because in those days an official could be fired just for demanding better working conditions. Imagine what it meant to a man who had a wife and family, in the deep economic depression of the thirties, to know he could be thrown out of work for speaking up for the betterment of his comrades! It would be less than fair and in fact not very intelligent for any member of the force from the chief of police down to the most junior constable, to show disrespect for these many elected representatives of years gone by, who made the improved working conditions possible.

Having explained the background, let me tell you of a series of events that left me, and many other veteran members of the force of all ranks, feeling more than a little ashamed of the actions of the police association.

In the early part of 1985, the executive officers and general membership of the Metropolitan Toronto Police Association became extremely dissatisfied with the negotiations, which were then in progress, for a new working agreement. The salary increase offered by the Board of Police Commissioners was, according to a vote taken at an emergency meeting, totally unacceptable to the rank and file members of the association.

To demonstrate their impatience with and disapproval of the most recent offer from the Board of Police Commissioners, the members voted overwhelmingly to institute an immediate work slowdown, which proved to be quite effective. The issuance of parking tags and traffic summonses ground to a halt. The management of the force, of which I was a part, was hard pressed just to keep a minuscule amount of traffic enforcement in place. But when it became apparent to the senior executives of the association that the slowdown was not bringing about the desired response from the board of commissioners, they decided to try a more highly visible means of demonstrating their anger.

On March 4, 1985, the majority of uniformed members of the Metropolitan Toronto Police Force discarded their officially issued, red-banded, badge-affixed hat, and in its place, they began to wear blue baseball caps. These were issued to the members of the association and many hundreds of them soon came into possession of the general public. The ball cap had a crest similar to the Metropolitan Toronto Police logo, except the wording identified the Metropolitan Toronto Police Association.

Thousands of police officers, all of them members of one of the most respected police forces in North America, reported for duty wearing the full issued uniform of the day, but minus their smart and readily identifiable headgear. To a veteran police officer like myself, with respect for the quasi-military discipline of the force instilled in him over many years, this was worse than embarrassment, it was a disgrace. I still feel that it was an affront and an insult to the many thousands of retired and deceased veterans of the police force, who for well over one hundred years had literally fought on the streets of Toronto in order that a police officer could wear his official uniform with pride and dignity.

It wasn't long before the association-issued ball caps were being worn by school children, taxi drivers and construction workers. I believe that this less than professional display of rebellion created a public feeling of disrespect for the members of the Metropolitan Toronto Police Force that still exists today.

ONE OF THE MOST SERIOUS threats to public safety that Toronto has ever experienced came when the uniformed members of the force were still on their work-to-rule slowdown, and it is to their everlasting credit that when they were notified of this emergency situation, they responded like the true professionals they can be, and worked diligently for long hours in what was a potentially dangerous environment.

An official federal government agency had received an anonymous letter demanding the release of several Armenian activists who had been arrested in Ottawa and were in custody, facing serious criminal charges for offences against members of the Turkish diplomatic corps. The letter also contained an ultimatum: if the release of these people were not effected within a certain time-frame, a bombing would occur somewhere within the transportation system in Metropolitan Toronto.

A copy of the letter was sent to all the police agencies in Toronto and an emergency meeting was held among the assistant commissioner of the RCMP stationed in Toronto, the commander of the Ontario Provincial Police, and Chief Jack Marks of the Metropolitan Toronto Police Force to plan the security response to this threat, which was treated very seriously. It was a well-established fact that certain Armenian activists were capable of violence and in fact had demonstrated their willingness to resort to such actions; and the Canadian government, of course, had no intention of releasing the persons under arrest.

It was decided by the commanders of the three major police agencies involved to notify the general public of this terrorist threat to the massive public transportation system in Metropolitan Toronto. Contrary to the opinions of some Monday-morning quarterbacks, I think that the decision was a correct one. The press release was sent out and it was headline news throughout North America.

Planning now began for the almost impossible task of policing the many miles of rail track, both on the surface and in the underground of the Metropolitan Toronto transit system. The approach decided on called for the deployment of every member of the force, as well as many hundreds of officers from the Ontario Provincial Police, the Royal Canadian Mounted Police and other regional police forces in the Toronto area.

The massive police presence in and around the public transit system continued for about eight days, but no bombs or bombers were found, and it was scaled down to periodic spot-check inspections. This was a week of public nervousness, but the volume of passengers carried on the transit system during this period did not appreciably decrease from the norm.

A terrorist threat to the public was unusual, but large-scale security operations are well known to the Toronto police. During my career, I have been involved in many such massive deployments, when dignitaries of all kinds have had the occasion to visit the city.

For twelve straight years, I was the staff superintendent in charge of all police personnel at the annual running of the Queen's Plate, at the New Woodbine Race Track in Etobicoke. The number of officers detailed to this assignment would vary from year to year, depending upon which member of the royal family was in attendance. When the Queen and Prince Philip were the attending royalty, we would begin setting up the security arrangements with representatives of the Royal Canadian Mounted Police and Britain's Scotland Yard immediately after confirmation was received from Buckingham Palace. This would usually be at least three months in advance of the race day and would necessitate the assignment of over three hundred uniformed and plainclothes police officers for duty within the race track proper. The same degree and level of security would apply for the heir to the throne, the Prince of Wales.

When lesser members of the royal family attended, arrangements would be scaled down to approximately ninety officers of all ranks. When I use the term lesser members of the royal family, I do not wish to leave the impression that they are any less loved and respected than the Queen or the Prince of Wales, but that the level of threat to their safety and well-being greatly diminishes. Over the years, I have had the honour of personally meeting most of these fine people and if I were asked who was my favourite, I would unhesitatingly name Elizabeth, the Queen Mother. This gentle, lovely lady never wanted to cause problems for those in charge of her security by altering her prescribed and protected route.

When you are charged with the responsibility of protecting royal personages from injury or embarrassment, you are, of necessity, constantly observing every move they make. Sometimes you cannot help noticing a certain boredom on their part, and a feeling, which they are attempting to conceal, that they wish they were anywhere but where they are.

A few years ago Her Majesty Queen Elizabeth presided at the official opening ceremonies of Ontario Place, on the shores of Lake Ontario, in Toronto. At the time, I was a uniformed inspector and assigned as part of the walkabout security. I was walking slightly to the right and about fifteen feet in front of the Queen as she strolled through the lines of flag-waving Girl Guides and Brownies. Periodically she would stop and speak to a startled, tongue-tied young girl, then move on. As Her Majesty was passing a particularly enthusiastic group of little Brownies, one of the girls called out, "How are you today, Queen?" The Queen replied, "I am very well, thank you, and how are you?"

The small girl said, "Just so-so."

The largest demonstration of police security arrangements that I have ever experienced was during the visit of Pope John Paul II to the Metropolitan Toronto area in 1984. In fact, the *Toronto Star* called the police presence for the papal visit the largest security operation in Canadian history.

The media had plenty of large numbers to toss around. Fourteen hundred buses were said to have come from the U.S., bringing the devout to see their hero. The cost of the tour was estimated to be $50,000,000, and later on it was reported that $1,000,000 of that remained as a debt the faithful still had to pay. Seven field hospitals and fourteen ambulances were at the ready in case disaster should befall His Holiness. Seven hundred million people around the world caught the event on radio and television. Three hundred thousand students got the day off. Seven thousand people volunteered to help the police during the visit. The ironic part of all this was the small number of hours the visit would actually take: Pope John Paul II was in Toronto a mere forty-four hours.

The Toronto security arrangements were being worked on full time a whole year ahead of the visit with hundreds of police diligently occupied at the task. The RCMP, as Canada's federal agency, was in command of all areas of planning. Dozens of high-ranking and specialized officers from city, regional and provincial police forces were permanently assigned to duty with the planning personnel. On the day itself, the primary responsibility for Toronto security remained with the RCMP, the OPP and Metro, with six local suburban forces assisting on the margins of the city, to handle the traffic expected with an anticipated crowd of more than a million. The Swiss Guard, the Pope's own security team, also guarded him, and overhead, helicopters kept an aerial watch (including two on loan from the Detroit Police Force).

As site commander for two proposed stops the Pope would make during his stay, I spent the year prior to the event attending meetings. I was impressed with the dedication and thoroughness demonstrated in the planning, and with the attention to detail required in an operation of this magnitude and complexity. The Pope stopped at two airports, two churches, a stadium, and Nathan Phillips Square. Each location presented security risks of great danger not only to the Pope, but to the crowd, whose safety was also the responsibility of the police agencies. At St. Michael's Cathedral at Shuter and Bond, for example, tall buildings on the west side of narrow Bond Street presented opportunities for snipers to target the Pope as he entered the cathedral on the east side of the street.

In order to anticipate – and prevent – any such occurrence, armed officers were stationed on all surrounding rooftops. When the Pope arrived, if you had happened to look up at the building kitty-corner from the cathedral, which is St. Mike's hospital, you would have seen doctors, nurses and patients leaning out the window cheering the Pope, while overhead, police kept binoculars trained on the crowd pressing forward toward the church, in case anyone tried anything unusual. At the same time, a wall of officers faced the street, forming a human fence between the people out there and the dignitaries, including the Pope, entering the cathedral through its front courtyard. These officers never took their eyes off the crowd, which meant that their backs had to be kept to the Pope. None of them even got a glimpse of him. Their duty prevented it!

At St. Paul's Anglican, another church stop at Bloor and Jarvis, not only office buildings, but also apartments flanked the stop-off. Some apartment dwellers actually sold tickets to stand at their windows and look down on the Pope. Residents, workers, maintenance staff and even some of the patients at St. Mike's had gone through police security checks as soon as it had become known what stops the Pope would make. These security measures on people in the surrounding buildings were continued scrupulously during the minutes the Pope was at each site.

In the end, it was a most impressive display of organization and effectiveness. The public was impressed that no one was injured and not even the slightest disturbance embarrassed the citizens of Toronto on their day as host to a man who was making history by being among them.

The fact that the officers of all ranks and from many different police forces could work so closely together, without any of the jealousies and ill-feeling you might expect, is a credit to the overall commander of the security operations, Chief Superintendent Donald Heaton of the RCMP. Don Heaton is an old friend of mine, and I was more than pleased when after the Pope's visit he was promoted to the rank of assistant commissioner.

It was a tremendous feeling of relief for the police forces involved when the Pope concluded a successful and incident-free visit to Metropolitan Toronto. It gave us a feeling of a job well done.

W ITH MY CAREER RAPIDLY APPROACHING its end, I had one more opportunity to be a street policeman again. This was in July of 1988, when the International Monetary Summit was held in Toronto. These meetings were held in different countries from time to time, and were attended by the ministers of finance of most countries of the free world.

At several previous summits, there had been demonstrations of extreme violence, and there was every reason to believe that a meeting in a peaceful country such as ours would give terrorists from many parts of the world the opportunity to try to enter illegally. It was feared that in some sophisticated manner, they might violently disrupt the meetings.

For many months in advance of the conference, the Royal Canadian Mounted Police assigned hundreds of their officers from divisions across the country, to head up the security arrangements. With Toronto being the host city, it became the responsibility of the Metropolitan Toronto Police Force to supply a similar contingent of hundreds of officers to work with and assist the RCMP.

The various locations where the attending ministers and their entourages would be residing and meeting with one another were subject to the heaviest security blanket that I have ever witnessed in over forty years of policing. One of the prime targets for demonstrations by groups opposing the conference was the United States Consulate, on University Avenue. The various groups of dissidents and organizations who for one reason or another opposed this high-level meeting publicly declared their intention to march to the consulate building, and perhaps commit mischief of some kind.

On the day of the proposed demonstration, Staff Superintendent David Cowan was the officer in charge of several hundred police officers, who were on duty in a six-block area surrounding the consulate. I was there to assist him. We had barricades set up to block off University Avenue to both vehicular and pedestrian traffic, from Dundas Street on the north to Queen Street on the south. This area was, in fact, designated a "no-go area."

I was stationed at the Dundas Street barricades, with about 150 uniformed officers placed at intervals behind the barriers from west to east across University Avenue. Around one o'clock in the afternoon, a mob of several hundred marching protesters came south on University Avenue. When they reached Dundas Street they were stopped by the barricades and the long line of police officers. They became incensed at this obstruction and began to jeer and hurl verbal abuse at the silent officers.

The quiet professionalism displayed by the police officers obviously disturbed the more militant members of the mob and a periodic rain of various objects fell on the police. As the size of the crowd increased, dozens of the more vociferous participants attempted to climb over the barriers. Most of these scaling attempts were defeated by the defending police officers, but several were successful in reaching the no-go area, and they were promptly arrested.

It was during this period of the demonstration that I, Staff Superintendent Jack Webster, sixty-five years old and in full uniform, with over forty years of police service behind me, personally arrested two of the people who had successfully defied the barricades. These were the final arrests of my career, and by chance they were captured by some enterprising photographers, and subsequently shown on world-wide television.

I felt that this was a fitting finale to the career of an active old cop

Top: *Jack and Marion Webster at the senior officers' ball, where Jack received recognition for long and meritorious service, November 1988.*
Above: *Jack and Marion Webster with their three grandsons.*

POSTSCRIPT

W HEN I JOINED THE Toronto Police Department on June 12, 1945, the total strength of the force was approximately one thousand of all ranks. It is interesting to note that the department had just about as many bicycles as motor cars.

My salary at that time was $1,750 per year.

On September 1, 1988, some forty-three years later, on the date of my retirement, the Metropolitan Toronto Police Force had in excess of one thousand motor vehicles, not including about 150 motorcycles.

The mounted unit has some fifty horses, and the marine division operates a fleet of about fifteen power boats of all sizes.

My salary upon retirement, with the rank of staff superintendent, was $88,000 per year.

I had an exciting, interesting and action-packed career. It was by diligence, dedication and long hours of hard work that I was able to attain the third-highest rank on the force.

Some years ago, it is a matter of record that I was approached by several people in authority, asking me if I would be interested in becoming a deputy chief, with the possibility of becoming chief of police in the near future. I thanked them for considering me as a front-line candidate for these important and prestigious positions, but declined without hesitation.

It was my feeling then, as it is now, that I did not possess the ability, the tact or the finesse to deal with politicians of every stripe on a daily basis. I felt that I would very quickly have confrontations that would destroy my career completely. I have no regrets about my decision, and I'd like, in this connection, to mention something a very good friend of mine once said. When Dennis Flynn was my mayor in Etobicoke, prior to his holding the position of chairman of Metropolitan Toronto Council, he told me in exasperation, "Staff Superintendent Webster, you are a first-class police officer, but you are a piss-poor politician, and what's more, you're the world's worst." That, I think, was one of the finest compliments I ever received.

On September 9, 1988, my fellow officers, civilian friends and supporters from the business community held a retirement dinner for my wife and me at the Constellation Hotel in Etobicoke.

It was attended by over 750 people. When I think back to that magical evening, I feel proud that a man such as I, from a humble beginning and with a minimum of education, could be so honoured by friends and associates from within and outside the police force. That power-house executives of the corporate world, high-ranking members of the judiciary and the legal profession, and some of the top specialists in the medical profession would take the time, on a Friday evening, to honour a "cop" and his family, is something I will always treasure.

In closing this biographical account of my life, I suppose I should answer the question that has been asked of me a hundred times, and that is – would you recommend a career in the police service for a young man or woman?

My answer – of course! – would be yes . . . Especially with one of the finest police organizations anywhere in the world, the Metropolitan Toronto Police Force.

Printed in Canada